THE COMPLETE GUIDE TO

QUILTING
TECHNIQUES

THE COMPLETE GUIDE TO
QUILTING TECHNIQUES

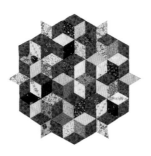

*Essential techniques and step-by-step
projects for making beautiful quilts*

PAULINE BROWN

Ivy Press

This edition published in Great Britain in 2014 by

Ivy Press

210 High Street, Lewes,
East Sussex BN7 2NS, UK
www.ivypress.co.uk

British Library Cataloguing-in-Publication Data
A CIP catalogue record for this book is available
from the British Library.

Printed and bound in China

This book was conceived, designed and produced by

Ivy Press

Creative Director: Peter Bridgewater
Publisher: Sophie Collins
Editorial Director: Jason Hook
Art Director: Karl Shanahan
Project Editor: Caroline Earle
Designer: Jane Lanaway
Illustrations: Kate Simunek
Additional Illustrations: John Woodcock
Photography: John Hamel, Andrew Perris, Calvey Taylor-Haw

10 9 8 7 6 5 4 3 2 1

Distributed worldwide (except North America) by
Thames & Hudson Ltd., 181A High Holborn,
London WC1V 7QX, United Kingdom

Contents

Introduction

PATCHWORK, QUILTING, AND APPLIQUÉ ARE OFTEN LINKED UNDER THE SAME GENERIC TERM OF QUILTING. EACH IS, HOWEVER, QUITE DIFFERENT FROM THE OTHERS AND ALL THREE DESERVE INDIVIDUAL ATTENTION.

Patchwork

The craft of patchwork developed among pioneer women in early America, who found it both a necessary and an economical way of keeping themselves and their families warm during the cold winter weather. Its history in Europe began in poor rural areas and gradually developed into widespread areas. Some of the earliest patchwork patterns were named after the areas where they originated, such as Texas Flower, Kentucky Chain, or Idaho Beauty. Other block names reflect the daily lives and surroundings of early pioneers, including Autumn Leaves or Bear's Paw.

Since its earliest days, patchwork has grown to include a wide array of both traditional and contemporary patterns, as well as both new and tried-and-true techniques. If you are interested in learning how to make a quilt, you will enjoy making the easy patchwork projects in this book. In addition to quilts, wall hangings, and throws, you will also find a number of small soft-furnishing items, such as pillows, that are sure to add touches of individuality to your home décor. You can practice several quiltmaking techniques with each project you make, and enjoy seeing your skills grow and develop into a personal repertoire of favorites.

TOP The Rail Fence pattern (*see page 42*) is a traditional block that is both attractive and quick to piece.

ABOVE AND RIGHT The intricate folds of the Secret Garden Glen quilt (*see page 94*) give it a beautiful three-dimensional quality.

Quilting

A quilt consists of two layers of fabric with a layer of batting between them. The three layers are stitched together, either by hand or machine, in decorative patterns to form a padded textile. Originally, quilting was done on clothing to provide warmth and protection. Later, quilting

developed as a decorative way to pad bedcovers, even in areas of America where pioneers experienced considerable poverty. In the north of England and Wales, village women created beautiful wholecloth quilts that were delicately hand-quilted with central medallion designs surrounded by several borders of quilted feathers, cables, or braids.

Quilting can serve many different functions within a quilt. Sometimes, quilting stitches serve merely to anchor the three layers of a quilt together, while in other cases, quilted designs enhance patchwork patterns by accentuating or contrasting with the fabrics in the patches. In both Italian and trapunto quilting, raised quilting patterns stand out in relief against a flat background fabric. Designs for Italian quilting are linear in character, while trapunto quilting designs consist of more decorative motifs padded from the reverse side of a quilt. Quilting does not necessarily have to be confined to quilts either. It is a great way to accent smaller projects, like pillows, jackets, and vests. In the following pages, you will be able to explore the beauty of both hand- and machine-quilting techniques for these and many other projects.

ABOVE The heart and leaves in this pillow feature trapunto quilting against a cross-hatched background fabric, with piping around the edges.

RIGHT The traditional Churn Dash pattern becomes a colorful bed topper for a young child when the blocks are reduced in size, and sashing strips and corner squares are added to frame the blocks. Triangles in the border echo the ones in the blocks, helping to give a feeling of continuity throughout the quilt design.

8

Appliqué

In the simplest terms, appliqué is the process of stitching fabric patches

to a background fabric to create decorative block or quilt designs.

A versatile craft, appliqué is relatively quick to do by either hand or machine.

It can be used on both quilts and wall hangings, as well as on garments

and accessories. The most famous type of traditional appliqué is found

in the Baltimore album quilts of the nineteenth century. These exquisite

ABOVE This pillow features
Hawaiian appliqué motifs
surrounded by echo quilting that
repeats each shape at evenly
spaced intervals.

quilts were usually made to commemorate special occasions, such as weddings or housewarmings. The intricate appliqué blocks in these quilts featured delicate flowers, wreaths, and landscapes, and were often stitched by a group of friends or relatives.

Since the mid-nineteenth century, there have been many new developments in the art of appliqué. These include such things as the symmetrical designs of Hawaiian appliqué and the linear patterns of Celtic appliqué. Stained-glass appliqué, usually constructed with bright jewel-colored fabrics, is also an attractive technique, especially for wall quilts. You can enjoy all the beauty of these and the other appliqué techniques in this book to make projects that will delight you and your loved ones for generations to come.

BELOW Explore the many beautiful fabric options available in today's marketplace, such as these jewel-toned fabrics.

Adventures in Quiltmaking

While traditional designs and techniques continue to have broad appeal, quiltmaking is a craft that is constantly changing, since new techniques, ideas, and equipment continue to be developed. It is my hope that as you try the many different techniques in this book and make projects for yourself and others, you will enjoy the exciting quiltmaking adventures that await you.

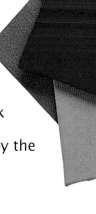

Pauline Brown

Equipment and Materials

EMBARKING ON AN ADVENTURE IN QUILTMAKING REQUIRES SOME BASIC SEWING EQUIPMENT, FABRICS, AND QUILTING SUPPLIES. YOU PROBABLY ALREADY OWN MANY OF THE ITEMS LISTED BELOW, AND YOU CAN PURCHASE ADDITIONAL THINGS AS YOUR SKILLS AND NEEDS INCREASE. ONE OF THE MOST FUN HABITS QUILTMAKERS TEND TO DEVELOP IS SCOPING OUT ALL OF THE NEW PRODUCTS ON THE MARKET EVERY TIME THEY VISIT THEIR FAVORITE QUILT SHOP.

12 Sewing Equipment

Sewing Machine

Although many sewing machines today are extremely sophisticated pieces of equipment that feature automatic and computerized stitches and various attachments, a simple electric zigzag sewing machine is all that you need for making quilts. Choose a machine that has the capability to alter the position of the needle, so that you can control the width of the seam allowance accurately. A size 80/12 machine needle is best for machine quilting.

Additional attachments, such as a walking or even-feed foot, a free-motion or darning foot, and a transparent embroidery or appliqué foot are all useful accessories for machine piecing and machine quilting. A double needle and an accompanying presser foot are useful for stitching the parallel lines in Italian quilting. A braiding foot is invaluable for machine couching. For free-motion quilting, you will need a darning foot and a machine that allows you to lower the feed dogs.

Machine needles

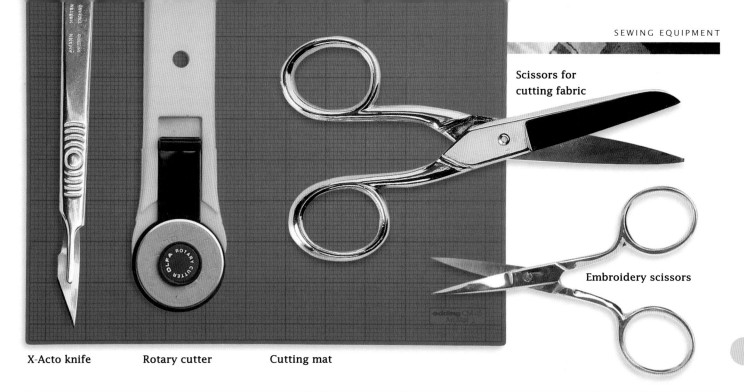

Scissors for cutting fabric

Embroidery scissors

X-Acto knife   Rotary cutter   Cutting mat

Cutting Tools

Using the right tools makes any task easier. The following cutting equipment will enable you to cut accurate strips and patches for patchwork quilts.

Rotary Cutter

Probably the single most useful cutting tool in quiltmaking history is the rotary cutter, which has a round blade that will cut easily through four layers of fabric at a time. This will speed up the cutting process and give you consistently accurate strips or patches for machine piecing. Rotary cutters are available in three sizes, for either left- or right-handed use. To keep your rotary cutter in top condition, replace the blade as soon as it shows any sign of becoming dull or developing a burr. Choose one that has a retractable blade, and remember to engage the safety guard between each operation.

Cutting Mat

To use a rotary cutter, you will need a self-healing cutting mat. These have measurements in inches or centimeters clearly marked on them, so it is easy to cut fabrics with precision. Unless you intend to transport your equipment regularly to classes or workshops, it is advisable to choose the largest cutting mat you can afford. Store your cutting mat flat, in a cool, dry place that will not allow it to warp.

Acrylic Rulers

For general use, start with an acrylic ruler that is long enough to cover the full width of your cutting mat. As you progress, you can add other rulers to your collection.

Scissors and X-Acto Knives

In addition to rotary cutting equipment, you will need several pairs of scissors, including a sharp pair that you use only for cutting fabric, and a different pair that you use only for cutting paper. A small pair of embroidery scissors is also helpful for clipping threads and appliqué seam allowances. An X-Acto knife is useful for cutting your own templates or stencils from template plastic.

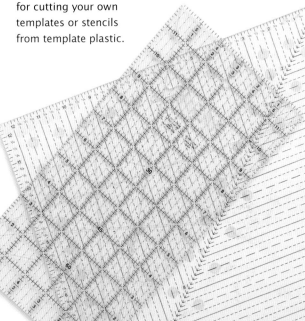

Acrylic rulers

Threads

Sewing threads come in cotton, silk, and polyester, in various thicknesses, and in a wide range of colors. For patchwork or appliqué, match the fiber content of your thread to that of the fabric you use. Choose a thread color that blends with or matches the predominant fabric in your design. For machine piecing, a beige or gray thread usually blends successfully with almost all fabric colors. Machine appliqué motifs can be stitched with a neutral, matching, or contrast thread color, depending on the effect you want to create. For hand appliqué, match the thread color to the appliqué shape.

For most hand quilting, you will want to use 100 percent cotton quilting thread, which is thicker and more durable than ordinary sewing thread. You can also use specialty threads, such as metallic threads, crochet threads, embroidery threads, or pearl cotton, for interesting effects.

Match the Dark Fabric

For sewing strongly contrasting fabrics together by hand, using the English method, select a thread that matches the darker fabric.

Use Wool Yarn

For creating the raised channels of Italian quilting, you will need a soft, thick, wool yarn, which comes in hanks or skeins. An alternative is to use chunky double-knitting or tapestry yarn. Look for this type of fiber in a needlework or knitting shop.

Needles and Pins

Use the following hints to help you select the best hand or machine needles and pins for the type of task you wish to accomplish.

Machine Piecing

Use a size 80/12 machine needle. For machine quilting, consider the size of the thread you wish to use on top of your machine, and choose a larger needle than you would normally use for piecing.

Hand Appliqué and Hand Piecing

Use needles called sharps for hand appliqué. These needles have short, round eyes and come in several sizes. A size 8 or 9 is suitable for most hand-sewing purposes.

Hand Quilting

The traditional needles for hand quilting are called betweens. These needles are short, which gives them the strength to move repeatedly through the three layers of a quilt sandwich. Betweens have round eyes that accommodate thicker quilting thread. The most popular sizes for hand quilting are 9, 10, and 12.

Italian Quilting

Choose a large-eyed tapestry needle for threading the thick yarn used in Italian quilting.

Pinning

Use thin, rustproof straight pins for pinning together patches or appliqué motifs. To pin the layers of a quilt sandwich together for machine quilting, use rustproof safety pins.

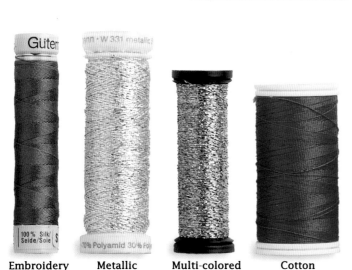

Embroidery thread   Metallic thread   Multi-colored metallic thread   Cotton quilting thread

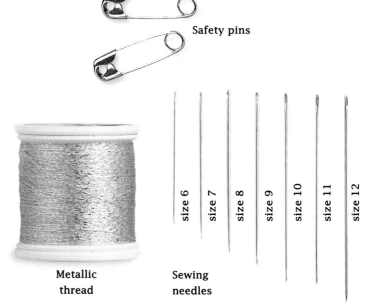

Safety pins

Metallic thread   Sewing needles

size 6   size 7   size 8   size 9   size 10   size 11   size 12

Hoops and Frames

Today we have many types of hoops or frames available for holding a quilt sandwich in position for hand quilting.

Hoops
Plastic and wood hoops are available in a range of sizes and shapes, including round, oval, and square. They are suitable for small-to-medium projects and have the advantage of being portable, enabling you to work on the move.

Tubular Frames
Made from PVC pipe, the rectangular shape of these frames prevents a quilt sandwich from distorting along the bias, which can occur in circular or oval hoops. They are available in a range of sizes, the largest of which will be big enough to accommodate a large quilting space.

Floor Frames
Although it can sometimes be a time-consuming task to mount a quilt on this type of frame, and it takes up a lot of room, the smooth results of the quilting make it a worthwhile choice.

Quilting hoops and frames

Accessories
The following accessories are likely to find their way to the top of your "must-have" list.

Thimbles Using a thimble for sewing is often a matter of choice, but if you wish to quilt by hand, you will need some protection for the finger that pushes the needle through the layers. Protection is also advisable for the finger underneath, which is likely to be pricked repeatedly by the needle tip. Metal, plastic, and leather thimbles in many styles are readily available in quilt shops.

Beeswax For strengthening thread and preventing it from twisting and tangling, natural beeswax is unbeatable.

Tweezers For Italian quilting, you will find a pair of small tweezers an invaluable aid for pulling through threaded yarns.

Quarter Seamer A quarter seamer is very useful for marking 1/4-in. (6-mm) seam lines.

Press Bars Bias press bars, which come in several widths, are great for making bias strips for Celtic or stained-glass appliqué.

Basting Guns To speed up the process of preparing a quilt sandwich for quilting, try using a basting gun to insert small, plastic tacks through all three layers at regular intervals.

Masking Tape For quilting grids of straight lines, masking tape is available in several widths. To avoid getting a residue of adhesive on your quilt, purchase masking tape at quilt shops or look for low-tack painter's tape at paint stores.

15

Beeswax

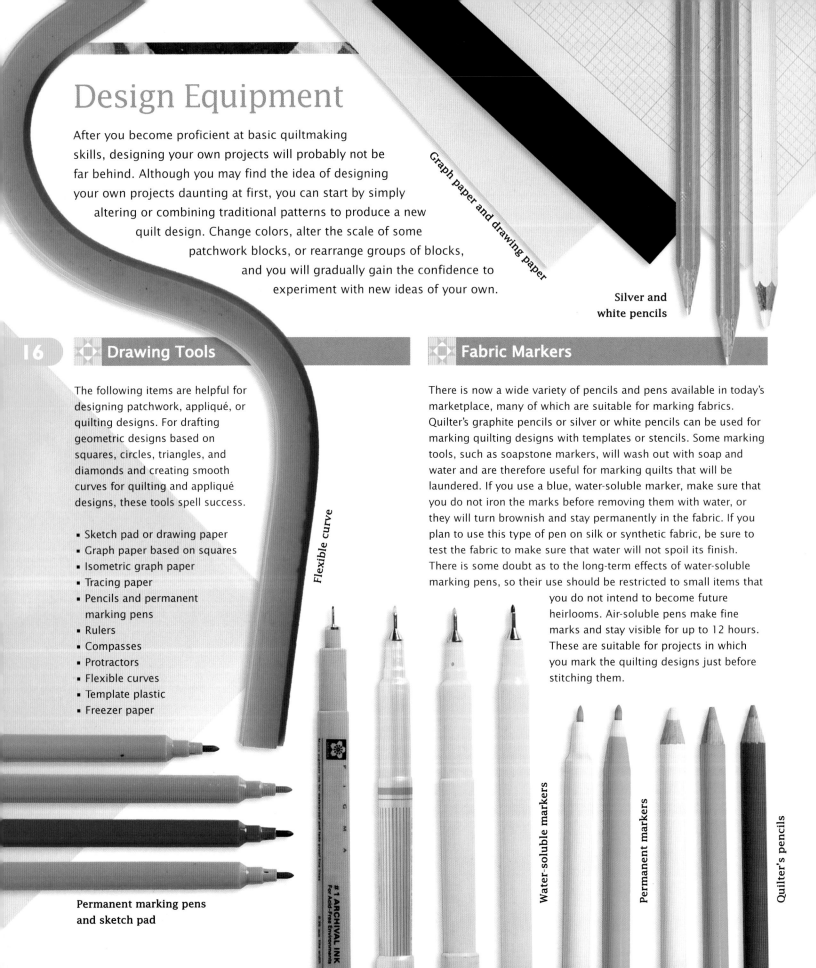

Design Equipment

After you become proficient at basic quiltmaking skills, designing your own projects will probably not be far behind. Although you may find the idea of designing your own projects daunting at first, you can start by simply altering or combining traditional patterns to produce a new quilt design. Change colors, alter the scale of some patchwork blocks, or rearrange groups of blocks, and you will gradually gain the confidence to experiment with new ideas of your own.

Graph paper and drawing paper

Silver and white pencils

Drawing Tools

The following items are helpful for designing patchwork, appliqué, or quilting designs. For drafting geometric designs based on squares, circles, triangles, and diamonds and creating smooth curves for quilting and appliqué designs, these tools spell success.

- Sketch pad or drawing paper
- Graph paper based on squares
- Isometric graph paper
- Tracing paper
- Pencils and permanent marking pens
- Rulers
- Compasses
- Protractors
- Flexible curves
- Template plastic
- Freezer paper

Flexible curve

Permanent marking pens and sketch pad

Fabric Markers

There is now a wide variety of pencils and pens available in today's marketplace, many of which are suitable for marking fabrics. Quilter's graphite pencils or silver or white pencils can be used for marking quilting designs with templates or stencils. Some marking tools, such as soapstone markers, will wash out with soap and water and are therefore useful for marking quilts that will be laundered. If you use a blue, water-soluble marker, make sure that you do not iron the marks before removing them with water, or they will turn brownish and stay permanently in the fabric. If you plan to use this type of pen on silk or synthetic fabric, be sure to test the fabric to make sure that water will not spoil its finish. There is some doubt as to the long-term effects of water-soluble marking pens, so their use should be restricted to small items that you do not intend to become future heirlooms. Air-soluble pens make fine marks and stay visible for up to 12 hours. These are suitable for projects in which you mark the quilting designs just before stitching them.

Water-soluble markers

Permanent markers

Quilter's pencils

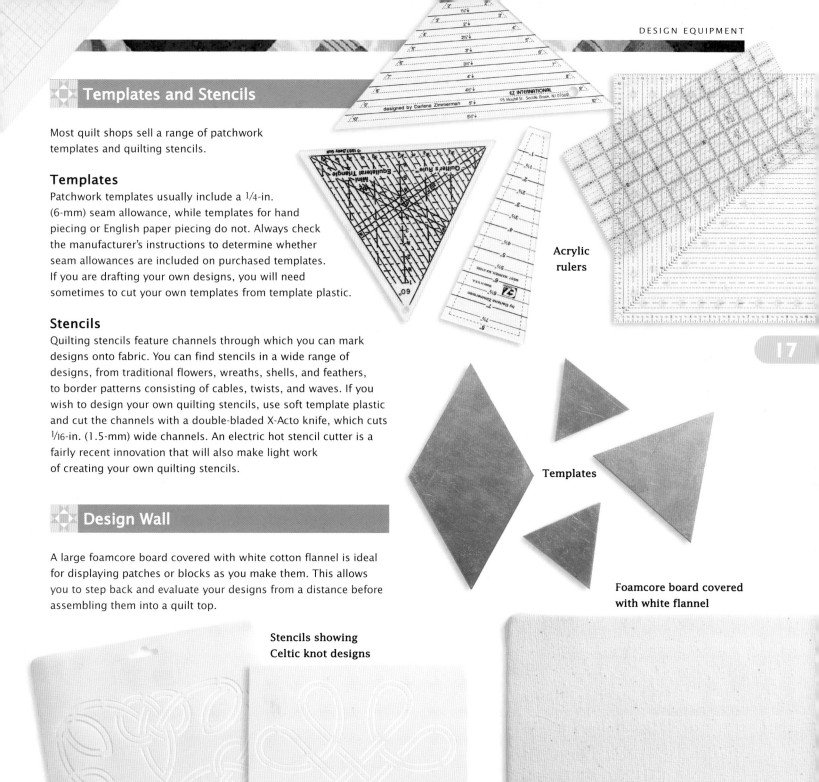

Templates and Stencils

Most quilt shops sell a range of patchwork templates and quilting stencils.

Templates

Patchwork templates usually include a 1/4-in. (6-mm) seam allowance, while templates for hand piecing or English paper piecing do not. Always check the manufacturer's instructions to determine whether seam allowances are included on purchased templates. If you are drafting your own designs, you will need sometimes to cut your own templates from template plastic.

Stencils

Quilting stencils feature channels through which you can mark designs onto fabric. You can find stencils in a wide range of designs, from traditional flowers, wreaths, shells, and feathers, to border patterns consisting of cables, twists, and waves. If you wish to design your own quilting stencils, use soft template plastic and cut the channels with a double-bladed X-Acto knife, which cuts 1/16-in. (1.5-mm) wide channels. An electric hot stencil cutter is a fairly recent innovation that will also make light work of creating your own quilting stencils.

Design Wall

A large foamcore board covered with white cotton flannel is ideal for displaying patches or blocks as you make them. This allows you to step back and evaluate your designs from a distance before assembling them into a quilt top.

Acrylic rulers

Templates

Foamcore board covered with white flannel

Stencils showing Celtic knot designs

17

Fabric Savvy

The structure of a quilt sandwich consists of two layers of fabric and a middle layer of batting. Making the best fabric choices in regard to fiber content, color, pattern, and texture will ensure that your quilts are visually effective, and selecting the best batting will give your quilt the perfect amount of dimensionality.

Pretreating

Today's cotton quilt fabrics are easier to handle and less springy than synthetics, so cottons are the ideal choice for most quilts. It is best to wash, dry, and iron any cotton fabric before using it, in order to avoid shrinkage in your finished quilt. Although most of today's cotton fabrics are colorfast, dark colors like navy blue, deep reds, and greens can still bleed. Make it a habit to test any dark fabric for colorfastness by soaking it in hot water to see if any dye seeps into the water. You may be able to remove excess dye from the fabric by soaking it in Retayne, following the manufacturer's instructions. If that does not work, you may wish to discard that fabric and replace it with another.

Color

A good sense of color can be an intuitive talent—we all express our personalities in the colors we choose to decorate our homes and the clothes we wear. But if color choices do not come intuitively to you, some knowledge of color theory can help you choose fabrics successfully for your quilts. The color wheel on the right shows the colors of the rainbow arranged in a circle. Equidistant on the wheel are the three primary colors: red, yellow, and blue, from which all other colors come. Between the three primary colors are the secondary colors, which are made by mixing equal quantities of two adjacent primaries together. Thus, blue and red make purple, red and yellow make orange, and yellow and blue make green. The remaining colors—red-orange, yellow-orange, yellow-green, blue-green, blue-violet, and red-violet—are called tertiary colors.

A standard color wheel shows the three primary colors (red, yellow, and blue), the secondary colors created by mixing two primaries together as shown at far right (green, purple, and orange), and the tertiary colors that lie between them on the color wheel (red-purple, red-orange, yellow-orange, yellow-green, blue-green, and blue-purple).

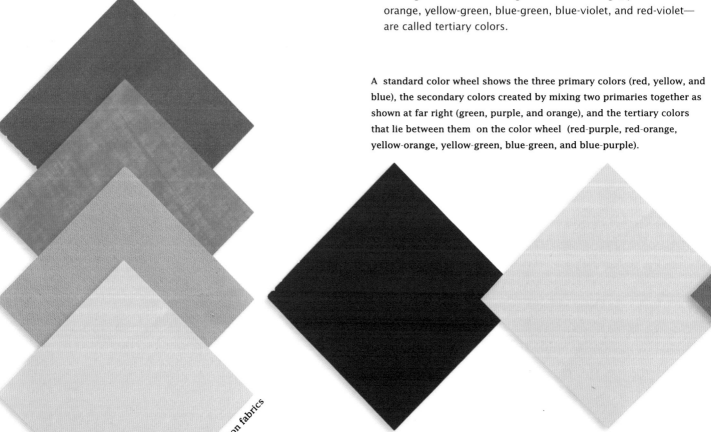

Cotton fabrics

18

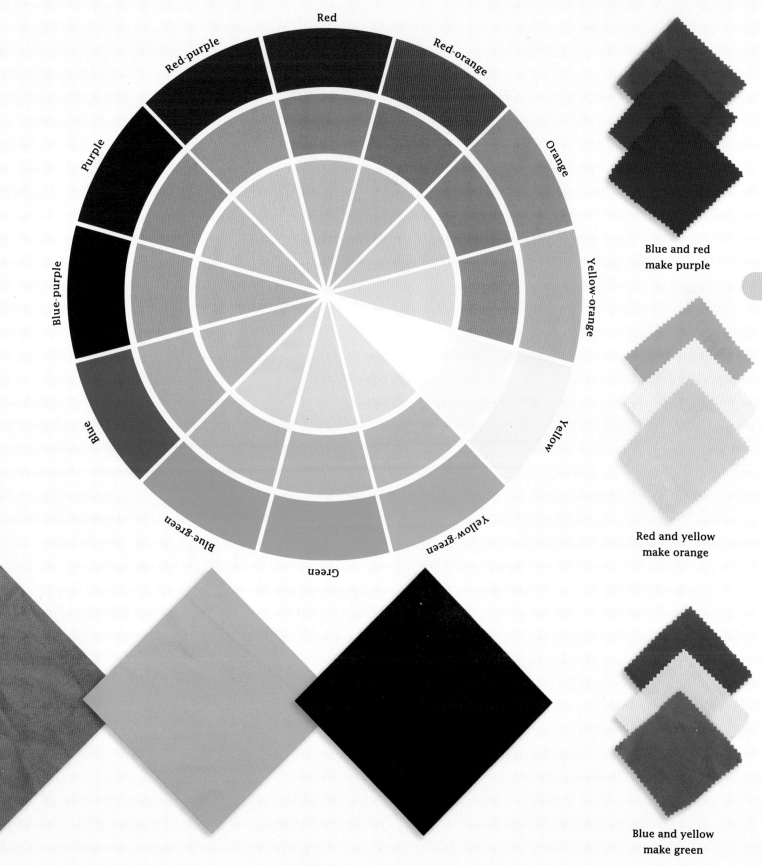

Red

Red-purple

Red-orange

Purple

Orange

Blue-purple

Yellow-orange

Blue

Yellow

Blue-green

Yellow-green

Green

Blue and red
make purple

19

Red and yellow
make orange

Blue and yellow
make green

Light and dark colors

Color Effects

The word "value" means the lightness or darkness of a color. On the color wheel, the values of each color are shown inside the circle. Closest to the center are the "tints," or the paler versions of each hue. Moving outward from the center are the "shades," which are the darker versions of the colors. Darker colors absorb light, which make them recede, while lighter colors reflect light, making them advance. This means that warm, bright colors, such as the red and white in the landscape on page 21, stand out visually in the design, while the cool, dark greens fade into the distance.

When you select fabrics for a quilt, analyze the relative values of the fabrics you are considering. Place them together on a flat surface, and squint at them through nearly closed eyelids. The darks and lights will be immediately apparent to you, and you can use that knowledge to create an effective mix of various values for your quilt.

BELOW A harmonious color scheme is one that features colors that appear near one another on the color wheel. These colors, along with their corresponding tints and shades, will blend together well and create a visually restful design.

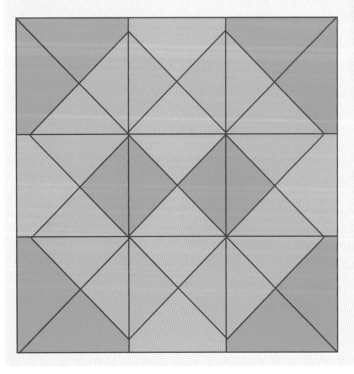

ABOVE Contrasting colors, known as complementary colors, are those placed on opposite sides of the wheel. Red is complementary to green, yellow to purple, and blue to orange. (Black and white are also highly contrasting.) Designs that feature strongly contrasting colors will be more visually exciting than harmonious color schemes. You can also use just a little bit of a contrasting color as an accent that will liven up a quilt design that would otherwise be uninteresting.

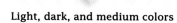

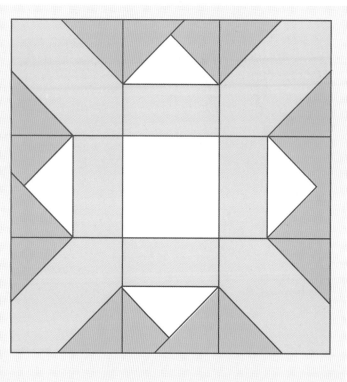

Light, dark, and medium colors

Changing Color Emphasis

When designing a patchwork project, it is a good idea to experiment with different colorways and also to try out the same colors in different positions within a block. You can also use the colors in different proportions to change the visual emphasis within a block. These kinds of experiments often lead to unexpected and exciting results.

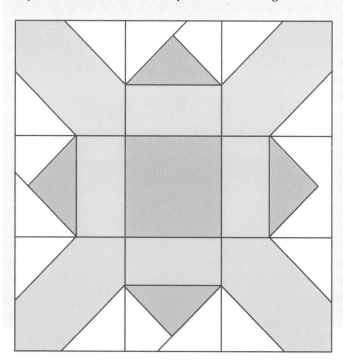

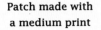
Patch made with
a medium print

Patch made with a
directional print

Velvet and cotton fabrics

Pattern

There is a wide range of beautiful print fabrics on the market today. When choosing patterned fabrics, it is not only the colors they contain that are important but also the value, density, and scale. One way to create an effective color scheme is to choose a multicolored theme print and add fabrics in colors that occur in the print. In many quilt shops, you can often purchase packets of coordinated prints in varying scales and colorways.

Squint at the fabrics to assess their values; then take time to stand back and look at them from a distance to consider the visual effect they create. Some allover designs, such as those with a scattering of tiny flowers, will appear as a muted blur with the actual pattern indistinguishable. A larger-scale print with a lot of contrast, particularly one containing white, will look visually dominant. This type of fabric can be difficult to use, as it will stand out in a way that may affect a quilt design negatively.

Nearly solid fabrics, such as tie-dyed or space-dyed cottons, make interesting alternatives to plain fabrics. You can buy these commercially or dye your own, following the instructions on the package of dye. If you dye a group of different print fabrics together, the colors will blend together for a harmonious effect.

Medium-scale prints can sometimes look busier than small prints and often have an allover pattern. Those with strongly contrasting colors are likely to be more challenging to work with, but those with motifs, such as flowers, leaves, animals, or toys, can often be isolated and used in the center of a patch, as in the Grandmother's Flower Garden patch (above far left). Large-scale prints can also be used for designs with large patches.

Directional prints include stripes or fabrics that have a one-way design. These offer plenty of scope for creating chevroned borders and three-dimensional effects, such as in the block shown above (near left).

Texture

Although many quilters do not view texture as an important consideration when planning a project, the use of textured fabrics can add an interesting dimension to a quilt. Traditional crazy quilts were made with a variety of different types of fabrics, from napped velvets or corduroys to satins, taffetas, and moirés. If you include specialty fabrics like these, make sure that you will be able to launder them in the same way as the other fabrics in your quilt.

Backing and Foundation Fabrics

Batting

The fabric you choose for the backing of your quilt should be of similar weight and fiber content as those in your quilt top. A solid-colored backing fabric will showcase quilting stitches, while a printed fabric tends to hide them. In today's marketplace, you can purchase fabrics from 44 in. (112 cm) long up to 108 in. (274 cm) wide, which are great for hand quilting because the backing may not need to have any seam allowances in it.

The range of batting choices today is better than ever before. To select the batting that is right for your project, consider the type and purpose of the quilt you are making, the manner in which you plan to quilt it, and the characteristics of various battings. If you like making wall hangings and plan to hand-quilt them, polyester is a good choice. If you are making a baby quilt, you may want to choose 100 percent cotton batting over polyester, which has a higher flammability quotient. If you are machine quilting, choose cotton over polyester batting, which is more slippery than cotton and harder to manipulate through a sewing machine. To re-create the look of a nineteenth-century heirloom appliqué quilt, choose a cotton batting with low loft and graceful drapability. For a crazy quilt, you may wish to use either a cotton sheet or a layer of flannel fabric as the batting. Visit your local quilt shop and check out the many batting options now available. Read the information on the packaging and compare several battings to determine which characteristics are most suitable for your project. And make it a point to ask other quilters which battings they like and why.

Backing fabrics

If you are new to quilting, you may enjoy stitching on prints for both the top and the backing of your first quilt, because they tend to disguise quilting stitches.

23

Designing Patchwork

PIECING TOGETHER GEOMETRIC SHAPES ALLOWS YOU TO CREATE AN UNLIMITED ARRAY OF DIFFERENT PATTERNS. CHOOSING THE FABRIC AND ARRANGING AND CUTTING PATCHWORK SHAPES ARE ALL PART OF THE DESIGN PROCESS, AND ALTHOUGH SOME PEOPLE MAY BE HESITANT TO TRY DESIGNING THEIR OWN QUILTS, SIMPLE PATCHWORK PROJECTS ARE AN EASY AND EXCITING WAY TO BEGIN.

Start by looking at traditional designs and change and adapt them to coincide with your particular preferences. You can alter the scale, change the emphasis of the colors, and develop the original into something new and interesting.

Commercially produced templates are available for many popular patterns. These include simple geometric shapes for blocks, which can be repeated, reversed, or rotated to create dozens of different designs. Templates for the more complex Dresden Plate and Double Wedding Ring designs, which have curved patches, are also produced commercially.

Some patterns, such as crazy patchwork, folded patchwork, and yo-yos, can be designed in a more random way, without the use of any templates.

Simple squares and triangles in dark and light colors combine to create this beautiful quilt.

Drafting Block Designs

Graph paper is suitable for drafting traditional patchwork patterns based on squares, triangles, and rectangles, such as the one shown below. Isometric paper, made up of isosceles triangles, is used for hexagons, triangles, six-point stars, trapezoids, parallelograms, and diamonds, such as the design at right.

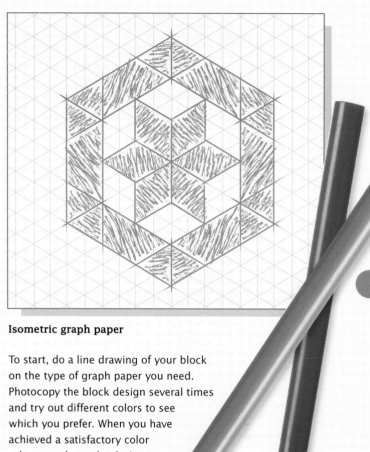

Isometric graph paper

To start, do a line drawing of your block on the type of graph paper you need. Photocopy the block design several times and try out different colors to see which you prefer. When you have achieved a satisfactory color scheme, enlarge the design to full size. Next, make the templates, adding $\frac{1}{4}$-in. (6-mm) seam allowances to all sides.

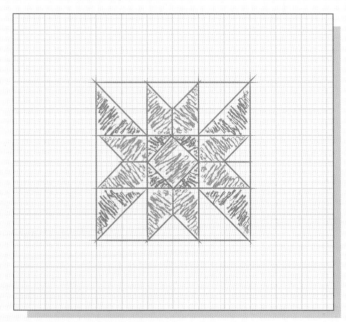

Graph paper based on squares

Computer Design for Patchwork

With the advent of specialized computer programs, the patchwork design process has become much easier, particularly for large-scale projects with repeat blocks. Having designed a single block, you can alter the colors at will, as well as rotate, mirror, and reverse the blocks for an unlimited number of variations. You can even place blocks on-point and add sashing and decorative borders on your computer and print them out for comparison.

Most programs have a built-in library of traditional blocks and borders that can be re-colored, adapted, or rearranged. They are sometimes capable of showing not only colors but also different fabric patterns. Some programs also allow you to superimpose quilting designs that may either be built-in or drawn freehand. One of the most useful features is the ability to print out templates and estimate the yardage for each fabric.

25

Enlarging and Cutting Templates

The essence of all good patchwork is the precision with which the fabric patches fit together. Thus, the most important aspect of cutting your own templates is accuracy, as even small discrepancies will cause problems. Although you can use a photocopier for enlarging quilting designs, this method should not be relied upon for making templates, since some distortion may occur.

◈ Transparent Templates

1 For cutting templates for geometric shapes, use either transparent template plastic or the type with a printed ¼-in. (6-mm) grid on it. Count the number of squares or triangles per inch or centimeter on the paper design, and mark the lines of the design in the desired finished size.

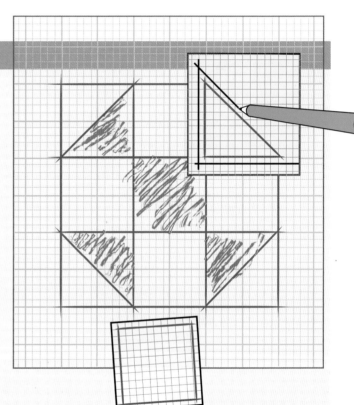

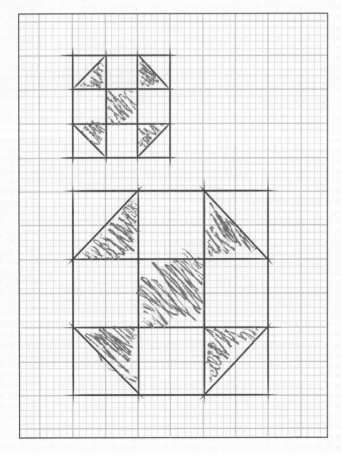

2 Count the number of individual shapes in your block design. Here, only a triangle and a square are required. Trace each shape onto template plastic, and add a ¼-in. (6-mm) seam allowance around the edge of each piece, as shown above.

3 Cut out each shape accurately, using a craft knife, or a rotary cutter with a blade saved only for this type of cutting, and ruler on your cutting mat.

Using Templates

The old-fashioned way to cut out patches for a project is to mark around a template and cut the fabric with scissors. If this is your chosen method, accuracy is still the main concern, as discrepancies can result from the patches not fitting together precisely.

27

Straight and Bias Grain

Grain is the direction of the thread weave. The edges of the fabric are *selvages*. The lengthwise grain runs parallel to the selvage—and the crosswise grain is perpendicular to it—the true bias runs at a 45-degree angle to it and is much stretchier than the other grain.

The Fabric Grain

1 You will need to consider the grain of the fabric in relation to the shape of each patch. Squares, rectangles, parallelograms, hexagons, pentagons, and triangles should be positioned with one edge aligned with the selvage (edge) of the fabric, as shown below. Some, such as Clamshell and Dresden Plate templates, are usually placed with the straight grain running vertically through the center of the template.

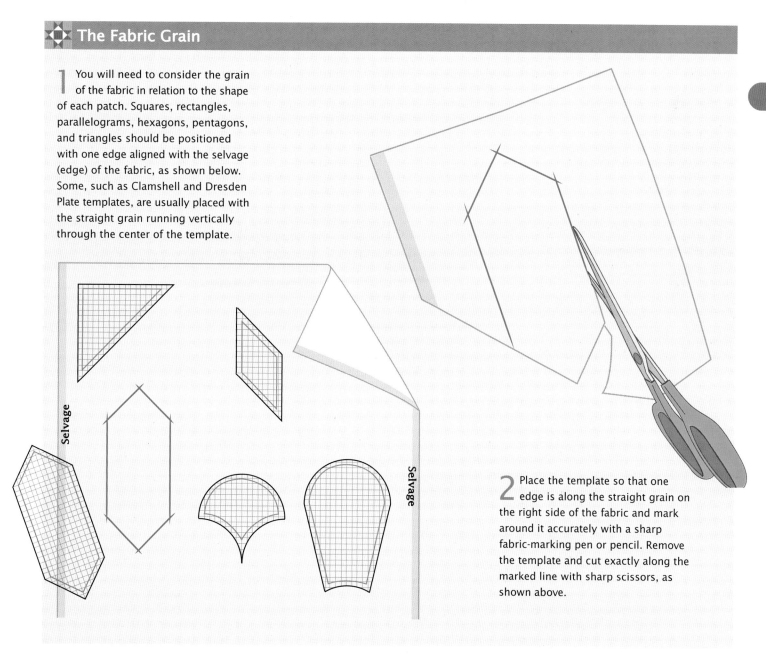

Selvage

Selvage

2 Place the template so that one edge is along the straight grain on the right side of the fabric and mark around it accurately with a sharp fabric-marking pen or pencil. Remove the template and cut exactly along the marked line with sharp scissors, as shown above.

Using a Rotary Cutter

This twentieth-century innovation has revolutionized the process of cutting strips and allows you to cut up to four layers of geometric patches at a time. With care, you can also cut around templates made from template plastic. Rotary cutters are normally used in conjunction with a quilter's acrylic ruler and a cutting mat.

Cut strips to measure, by using the marks on the quilter's ruler or the cutting mat, but not both at the same time. Always press your fabric before beginning. To make a cut, release the safety lock on the cutter and, keeping the handle at a 45-degree angle to the mat, start rolling the cutter away from you, alongside the ruler. Always remember to engage the safety guard between each cut.

Safety Rules When Using Rotary Cutters

- Always cut away from yourself.
- Hold the ruler steady, with your fingers away from the edge.
- Work standing up, to control the cutter and put more pressure on the ruler.
- For long cuts, "walk" your hand along the ruler as you cut.
- Close the safety lock between each cut you make.
- Change the rotary cutter's blade regularly to avoid inaccurate cuts from burrs on the blade.

◈ Cutting the Fabric

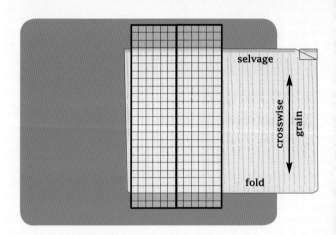

1 To square up the folded fabric, smooth it on the mat with the crosswise grain running vertically. If you wish to cut through four layers, refold the fabric on the straight grain. Place two acrylic rulers on top of the fabric, with their horizontal lines along the fold, as shown above.

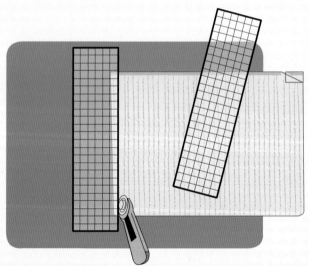

2 Move both rulers left, until the left ruler creates a perfect right angle at the very left-hand edge of the fabric. Remove the right-hand ruler, keeping the left one precisely in position. Rotary-cut along the right edge of the left-hand ruler to establish a perfectly straight edge at a right angle to the fold.

Cutting Fabric Strips with Ruler and Scissors

For the Log Cabin pattern and other designs that require strips of fabric, you can use a long template or measure and cut out the strips with scissors, though this is a slower method than using a rotary cutter. A quarter seamer is used to add the seam allowances.

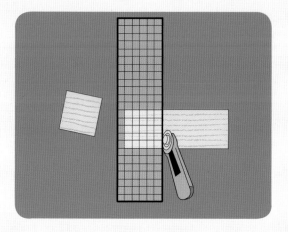

3 Align a vertical line on the ruler with the cut edge of the fabric, with the ruler's right edge measuring the desired width of the strip. Cut, as shown above.

4 To cut the strips into squares or rectangles, align a vertical line on the ruler with the short cut edge of the strip and line up the horizontal lines on the ruler with the top and bottom edges of the strip. Cut, as shown above.

◆ Fabric Strips

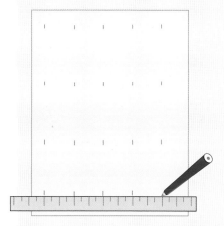

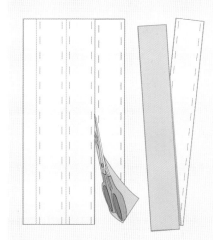

1 Lay the fabric out smoothly on a flat work surface with the straight (lengthwise or crosswise) grain running vertically. Calculate the finished width, adding a ¼-in. (6-mm) seam allowance on both long edges. Using a sharp pencil or fabric marker, and a ruler aligned with the straight grain of the fabric, measure and mark the strip lengths in several places.

2 Place the ruler alongside the marks and draw lines to indicate the finished width. Place the ¼-in. (6-mm) seamer along the lines and mark the seam allowances with dotted lines to differentiate between the cutting lines and the seam lines.

3 Repeat, drawing more lines the correct width, and then cut out with sharp scissors.

Hand Piecing

Accurate piecing is essential for the success of any project. This means that you must sew a consistent 1/4-in. (6-mm) seam allowance. This can be marked on the fabric using a 1/4-in. (6-mm) seamer. Choose a thread that matches or blends with the darker of the two fabrics. If in doubt, use a neutral gray or beige. Use a size 10 or 11 sharp needle and 100 percent cotton thread in 50 or 60 denier for hand piecing.

◇ **The Running Stitch**

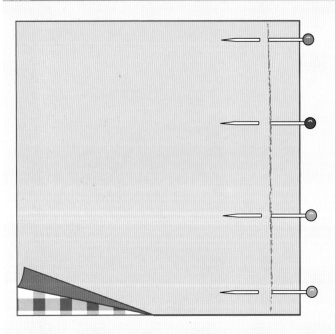

1 Pin the right sides of the first two patches together, making sure that the corners are aligned. After you have marked the seam allowance, insert the pins through the line on both patches.

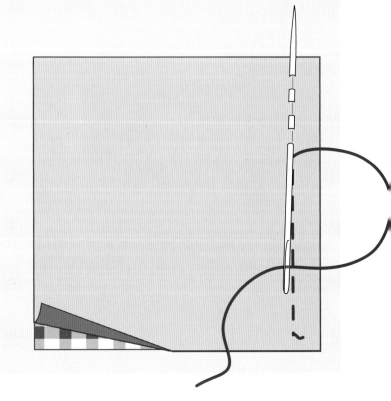

2 Starting with a tiny knot or a double backstitch 1/4 in. (6 mm) in from the edge of the fabric, work small, even running stitches along the seam line, bringing the needle in and out of the layers of fabric at regular intervals and checking the seam allowance on both sides. You may be able to pick up two or three stitches before pulling the needle through. Finish with a backstitch 1/4 in. (6 mm) in from the edge of the fabric.

Pressing

Press Gently

It is generally accepted that pressing seams open weakens the stitching. Special care should be taken not to distort the fabric when pressing bias seams on triangles or diamonds, especially in hand-pieced blocks.

Pressing is essential for a professional finish. Whichever way you choose to press your work—using a non-steam iron or by finger pressing—it should be done carefully, so as not to damage or distort the fabrics.

Press each seam as you go—for a large-scale project, set up your iron and ironing board close to your sewing area so that you can move easily between them.

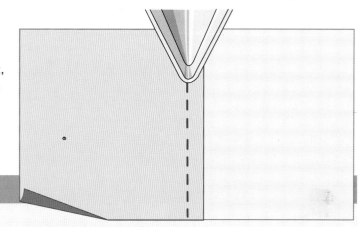

◆ Pressing Seam Allowances

1 Set the iron to the correct setting for your fabric and place the patchwork right side down on the ironing board. Apply slight pressure along the seam, as shown at right above.

2 Turn the fabric to the right side and press again, as shown at right.

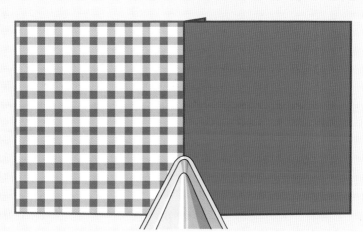

◆ Finger-Pressing Seam Allowances

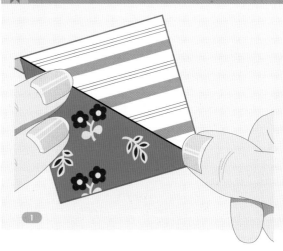

1 This is most successful for small patches and for careful manipulation of bias seams. Place the patchwork right side up on a hard surface, with the seam allowance folded toward the darker fabric. Run your thumbnail along the seam. If necessary, repeat on the wrong side.

2 If you prefer, you can use a wooden or plastic finger-pressing tool, as shown at right. These are sold in quilt shops.

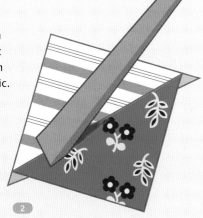

Machine Piecing

ALTHOUGH MANY PEOPLE ENJOY THE RELAXATION OF SEWING BY HAND, MACHINE PIECING IS OFTEN MORE COMPATIBLE WITH TODAY'S BUSY LIFESTYLES. MODERN SEWING MACHINES ARE EXTREMELY SOPHISTICATED, BUT YOU CAN STILL CREATE SUCCESSFUL PIECED PROJECTS WITH AN ORDINARY STRAIGHT-STITCH MACHINE.

For machine piecing, set the stitch width on your machine to 0 and the stitch length for approximately 10–12 stitches per inch (2.5 cm). The machine can be used for patchwork, for machine appliqué (*see page 166*), and machine quilting (*see page 110*).

The Rail Fence pattern is one of the easiest designs for novice quilters to piece, and its classic simplicity makes it a good choice for accessories like this pillow.

Maintaining a Correct Seam Allowance

For machine piecing, it is essential to maintain a consistent ¼-in. (6-mm) seam allowance. Although some people may be able to judge this by eye, it is better to use a more foolproof method. Some machines have ¼-in. (6-mm) markings engraved on the throat plate; you can also sometimes use the width of the presser foot as a guide, or add masking tape to the throat plate, and adjust the needle position, if necessary.

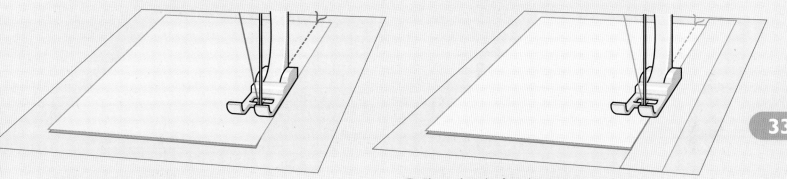

1 Place the patches to be joined under the presser foot so that the raw edge and the right edge of the presser foot are aligned.

2 Place a length of masking tape across the needle plate ¼ in. (6 mm) from the needle. Align the raw edge of the patches with the masking tape as you stitch.

Chain Piecing

If you are making a project with a number of identical blocks, the quickest and most efficient way to work is chain piecing in assembly-line fashion.

1 Pin pairs of patches with right sides facing. Stitch the first pair together and feed the second pair under the presser foot, doing a few stitches between, without cutting the threads. Continue joining more pairs of patches in the same manner. Then clip the pairs of patches apart, as shown right.

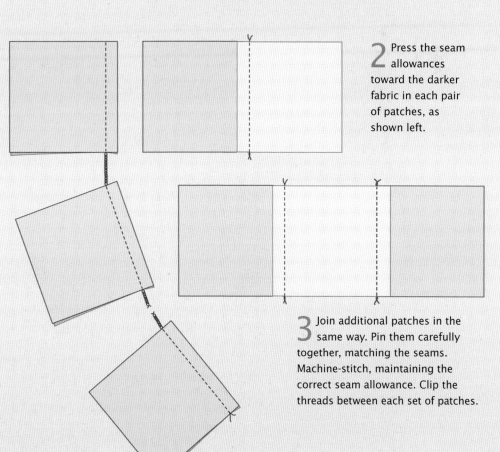

2 Press the seam allowances toward the darker fabric in each pair of patches, as shown left.

3 Join additional patches in the same way. Pin them carefully together, matching the seams. Machine-stitch, maintaining the correct seam allowance. Clip the threads between each set of patches.

Strip Piecing

Many patchwork blocks are made up of strips that are assembled in different ways. For simple designs, such as this Rail Fence, the strips are assembled and then recut, before rearranging them in the block pattern. Log Cabin (*see page 38*) and its many variations involve stitching strips of fabric around a center square.

Rail Fence

This design would be slow to piece from small individual patches but strip piecing speeds up the process. The contrast between the pink and blue strips and the lively mix of patterns adds to the overall vibrancy of the finished project.

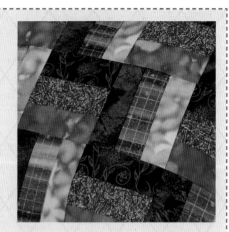

34 ◇ Strip-Piecing Basics

1 Rotary-cut the required number of strips accurately, including 1/4-in. (6-mm) seam allowances on both sides. Pin and stitch two strips with raw edges aligned, maintaining the correct seam allowance. Press the seam allowance to one side.

2 Add subsequent strips in the same way, working in the same direction. If the strips start to curve or warp, try stitching alternate rows in the opposite direction.

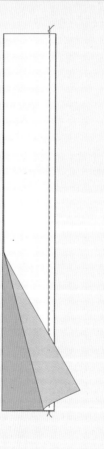

Nine-Patch Blocks

Simple nine-patch blocks can be used alone or in combination with other blocks.
For this, you will need two strip sets containing three strips each, in alternating
colors. These strip sets are then cut and reassembled to create a nine-patch block.

◆ Constructing Nine-Patch Blocks

1 Sew one strip set of three 3 1/2- x 42-in. (8- x 107-cm) strips, with a light color between two dark ones. Sew another strip set with the colors reversed, as shown at right and below.

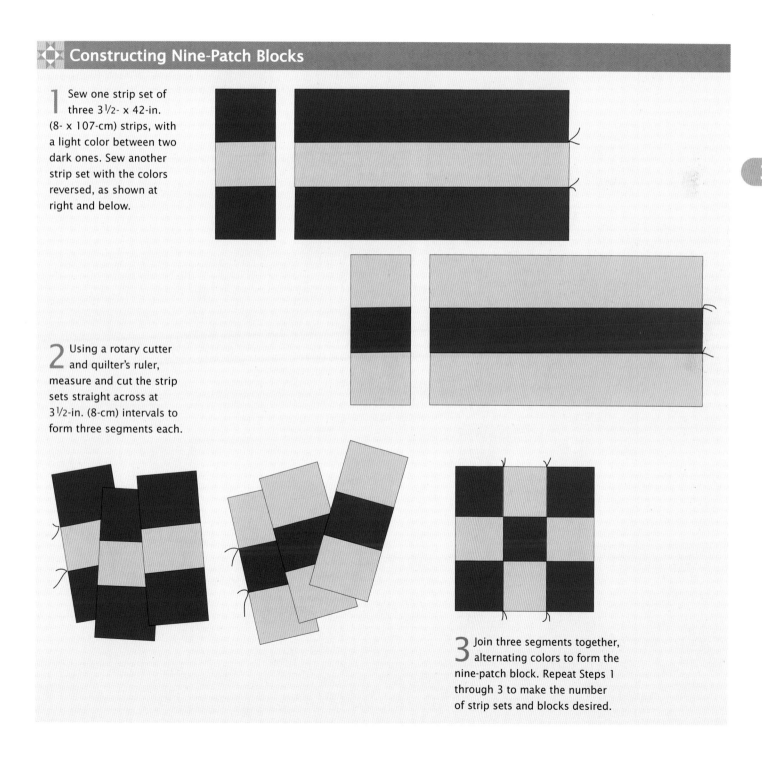

2 Using a rotary cutter and quilter's ruler, measure and cut the strip sets straight across at 3 1/2-in. (8-cm) intervals to form three segments each.

3 Join three segments together, alternating colors to form the nine-patch block. Repeat Steps 1 through 3 to make the number of strip sets and blocks desired.

◇ Strip-Pieced Double Irish Chain

This traditional 1½-in. (4-cm) finished block is made up of two alternating blocks, one consisting entirely of squares and the other of a center square surrounded by four smaller squares at the corners and four rectangles at the sides.

1 For the first block, assemble strip set I of five 2- x 42-in. (5- x107-cm) strips, in the following order: dark, contrasting, light, contrasting, and dark; strip set II with alternate contrasting and dark, starting and finishing with the contrasting; and strip set III with light, contrasting, dark, contrasting, and light.

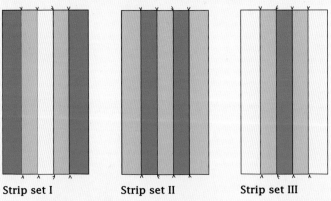

Strip set I   **Strip set II**   **Strip set III**

2 Using the rotary cutter and quilter's ruler, measure and cut the three groups of strips straight across at 2-in. (5-cm) intervals to form five-patch segments.

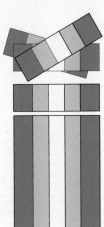

3 Join 5 five-patch segments together to form the Double Irish Chain block with the dark fabric patches, creating a diagonal cross, as shown at right.

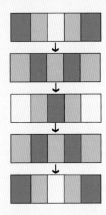

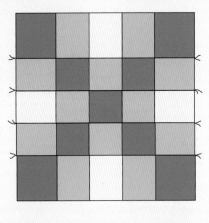

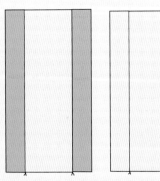

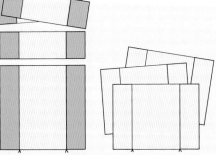

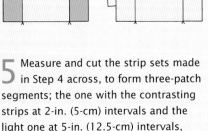

Strip set I   **Strip set II**

4 For the second (or alternate) block, assemble strip set I with a light 5-in. (12.5-cm) strip between two contrasting 2-in. (5-cm) strips. Sew strip set II with a light 5-in. (12.5-cm) strip between two light 2-in. (5-cm) strips.

5 Measure and cut the strip sets made in Step 4 across, to form three-patch segments; the one with the contrasting strips at 2-in. (5-cm) intervals and the light one at 5-in. (12.5-cm) intervals, as shown above.

6 Join the 3 three-patch units from Step 5 together to form the second (or alternate) block with the light segment between the ones with the contrasting corner squares. Assemble the blocks by alternating the first and second blocks, as shown on page 37, at lower left.

◆ Traditional Method Double Irish Chain

In this version, the patches are cut individually, rather than strip-pieced.

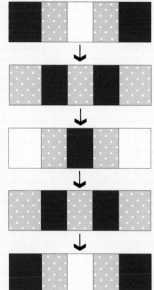

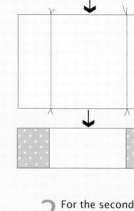

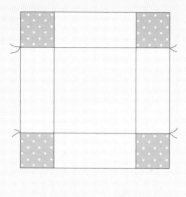

1 For the first block, cut 2-in. (5-cm) squares—nine dark, twelve in contrasting fabric, and four light. Assemble them in five rows of five, with a light square at the center of each side and the rest placed alternately, as shown above and at right. Repeat to make as many first blocks as desired.

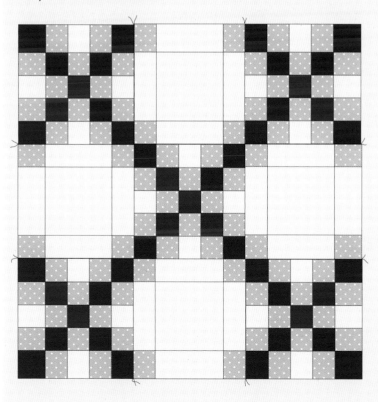

2 For the second (or alternate) block, cut a large 5-in. (12.5-cm) light square and four 2- x 5-in. (5- x 12.5-cm) light rectangles and four 2-in. (5-cm) contrast squares. Assemble them in three units with a small contrasting square on either side of a light rectangle at top and bottom, and a light rectangle on either side of the large square for the middle section, as shown above. Repeat to make as many second blocks as desired.

3 To create the effect of the Double Irish Chain pattern, alternate five of the first blocks with four of the second blocks. Each additional set of blocks will extend the cross pattern, which will cover the whole quilt top.

Log Cabin Patchwork

The basic method for this popular pattern consists of strips stitched around a center square. These blocks can be used singly or joined together in different formations to create a wide variety of quilt designs. It is one of the quickest and most effective strip-pieced patterns. Log Cabin patterns demand careful placement of the values of the fabrics to create the overall design. You can stitch the blocks individually or chain-piece them for greater speed and accuracy. It is best to cut strips across the width of the fabric and trim them to fit the block as you sew.

The Log Cabin block is particularly versatile because it can be adapted and altered in a number of ways. For example, the center square can be offset to one side or replaced with another geometric shape, such as a hexagon, triangle, or diamond. Another variation is the pineapple pattern, which forms triangles at each corner.

You can either draft the designs on squared graph paper or rearrange finished blocks to your satisfaction. To do this you will need to make up a number of blocks and pin them to a board or design wall to analyze your results.

38

Constructing a Log Cabin Block

1 Using a rotary cutter and quilter's ruler, cut two sets of 2½- x 42-in. (6- x 107-cm) strips in contrasting colors and a 2½-in. (6-cm) center square in another darker color.

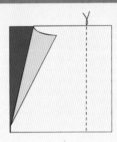

2 With right sides together, stitch a light strip along one side of the center square, maintaining a ¼-in. (6-mm) seam allowance. Trim off the excess and press the seam allowance away from the center square.

3 Working in a clockwise direction, stitch a second light strip across the trimmed end of the first strip and the second side of the center square. Trim and press as before.

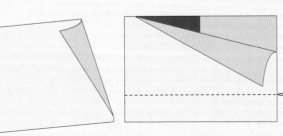

4 Continue with two dark strips along the third and fourth sides to complete the square. At each stage, check that the seam allowance is accurate and that the block remains square.

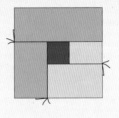

5 Always working in a clockwise direction, continue stitching two light and two dark strips on diagonally opposite sides of the block until you reach the desired size. Work the desired number of blocks in the same way.

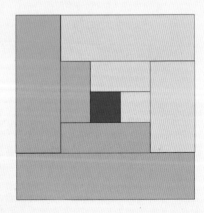

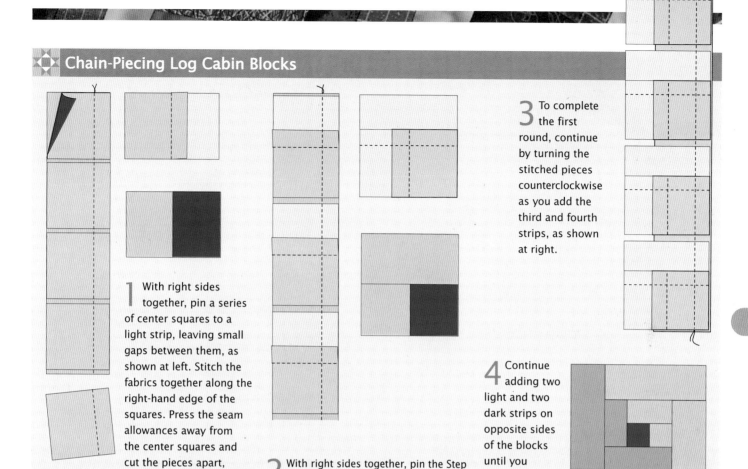

1 With right sides together, pin a series of center squares to a light strip, leaving small gaps between them, as shown at left. Stitch the fabrics together along the right-hand edge of the squares. Press the seam allowances away from the center squares and cut the pieces apart, trimming away the excess fabric on both sides of each center square. Press.

2 With right sides together, pin the Step 1 units to a second light strip, with the center square at the bottom, and stitch as before. Press and trim to size.

3 To complete the first round, continue by turning the stitched pieces counterclockwise as you add the third and fourth strips, as shown at right.

4 Continue adding two light and two dark strips on opposite sides of the blocks until you complete each of the blocks.

◇ Joining Log Cabin Blocks

1 For an arrangement of four blocks, stitch two blocks with right sides together, matching the seams and maintaining the 1/4-in. (6-mm) seam allowance. Press. Repeat with two more blocks and join the pairs of blocks to form a square, as shown at right and below. Press.

2 For larger projects, join a series of blocks with vertical seams to form horizontal rows and press. Then stitch the rows together to form a large rectangle and press the finished quilt top.

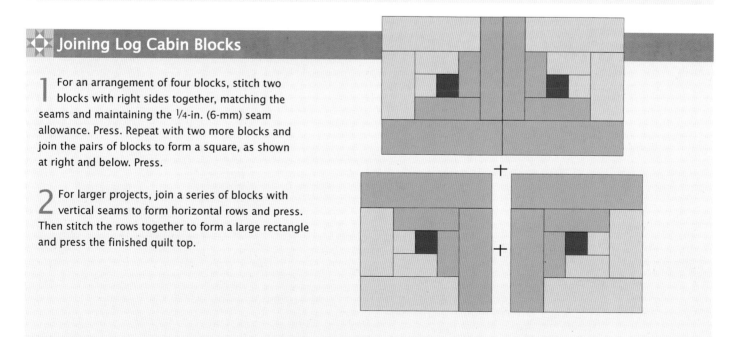

Traditional Log Cabin Designs

Starry Night

Starry Night is a simple design consisting of groups of four identical blocks, with the darker areas placed together to form a diamond shape. This group of four blocks can be used singly for a pillow or repeated for a quilt or throw.

Streak of Lightning

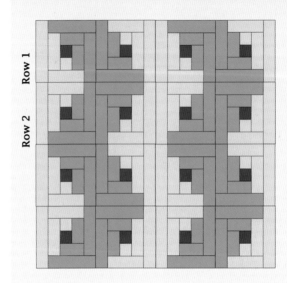

Row 1

Row 2

Streak of Lightning features a zigzag pattern. The first row is made up of pairs of blocks with the dark side at top right on the first block, and bottom left on the second. The second row mirrors the first, and these two rows are repeated down the length of the quilt.

Barn Raising

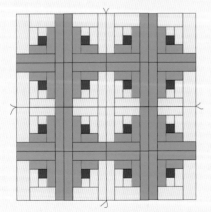

Barn Raising is a popular design for bed-size quilts. The four top-left blocks form a quarter of the entire pattern. For the top right-hand corner, the four blocks are the same as the adjacent quarter. The bottom half mirrors the top half so that a diamond pattern results.

Straight Furrows

The diagonal effect of Straight Furrows requires at least four rows of four blocks. For the first row, the dark side of the first block is placed at the bottom right, and the dark side of the second is at top left. For the second row, the first block has the dark at top left, and second has the dark at the bottom right. Continue placing blocks as shown at right to achieve the desired size of a quilt top.

40

Courthouse Steps

The Courthouse Steps differs from the basic Log Cabin block because the strips are placed alternately at the top and bottom, and at the right and left sides. The Courthouse Steps block is divided visually into four sections, producing a vertical or horizontal pattern, instead of the usual diagonal emphasis. The number of blocks you make will depend on the project—it could be four for a pillow or up to 64 or more for a large quilt.

◆ Constructing Courthouse Steps Blocks

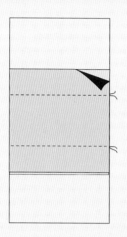 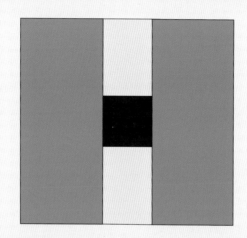 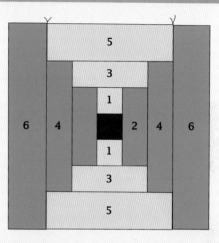

1 Cut two sets of 1½- x 42-in. (4- x 107-cm) strips in contrasting colors and a 1½-in. (4-cm) center square. With right sides together, stitch a light strip along the top edge of the square. Trim the excess and press the seam allowances away from the center square. Stitch a second light strip across the bottom edge of the center square. Trim and press as before.

2 Stitch the third and fourth dark strips along the two remaining sides of the segment from Step 1. Make sure that the seam allowances are accurate and the block is square. Press the seam allowances away from the center square.

3 Continue stitching two light and two dark strips on opposite sides of the block until you reach the desired size. Work the desired number of blocks in the same way.

4 Courthouse Steps blocks can be repeated across the width and length of a quilt for the traditional formation, or they can be alternated or placed in a random fashion for a more spontaneous effect, as shown at far right.

 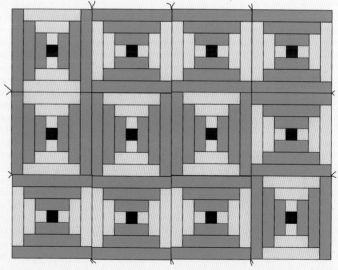

41

Rail Fence Pillow

This Rail Fence project is a very simple exercise in strip piecing. The method involves joining straight, rotary-cut strips together in groups of three (each one a different color), which are then cut into squares. The squares are then joined to form the pillow front. The pillow features five rows of five squares each, alternating the pink and blue colorways and the horizontal and vertical direction of the seams. The rows are then assembled to complete the square pillow front.

Cutting

1 Rotary-cut two 1³/₄-in. (4.5-cm)-wide strips across each of the three pink and three blue fabrics.

2 For the pillow backs, cut two 18³/₄- x 15-in. (49- x 38-cm) rectangles of pink fabric.

Note: Reserve the remaining pink fabric for piping.

Dimensions

Finished pillow is approximately 19 in. (49 cm) square.

Piecing the Strip Sets

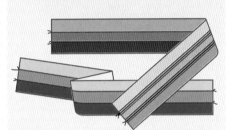

1 Machine-stitch 1³/₄-in. (4.5-cm)-wide strips together using a ¹/₄-in. (6-mm) seam allowance to form tricolored bands, grouping together the three pink fabrics and the three blue. Press the seam allowances open carefully, so that the seams lie perfectly parallel to each other.

2 Rotary-cut the strip sets into 4¹/₄-in. (11-cm) squares, making sure that the cutting lines are at right angles to the lower raw edge of the strip set. Cut a total of 13 pink and 12 blue squares.

Assembling the Pillow Front

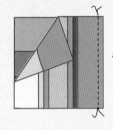 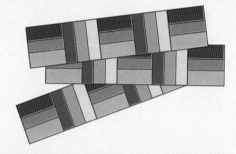

1 For the first row, arrange three pink squares and two blue squares, as shown below, and sew them together using a ¹/₄-in. (6-mm) seam allowance. Press. Make three of these rows.

2 For the second row, arrange three blue and two pink squares, as shown above right, and sew them together. Press. Make two of these rows. Press.

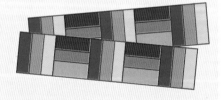

3 Stitch the five rows together, as shown at right, taking a ¹/₄-in. (6-mm) seam allowance. Press.

Equipment and Materials

- Three pink print fabrics in light, medium, and dark: ¼ yd. (23 cm) each
- Three blue print fabrics in light, medium, and dark: ¼ yd. (23 cm) each
- Solid pink fabric for the backing and piping: ¾ yd. (68.5 cm)
- Piping cord: 2½ yd. (229 cm)
- Quilter's chalk pencil
- Ruler
- Rotary cutter
- Basic machine sewing supplies and iron
- Pillow form: 19-in. (49-cm) square

Piping the Edge and Making Up the Pillow

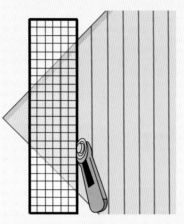
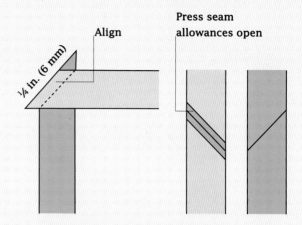

Align

Press seam allowances open

¼ in. (6 mm)

1 Rotary-cut approximately 3½ yd. (320 cm) of 1½-in. (4-cm)-wide bias strips to make the piping.

2 To join the strips, place two together, with right sides facing, and at right angles to each other, as shown above. Machine-stitch across the strips, as shown. Sew enough strips together to make the required length. Press the seam allowances open, as shown above right.

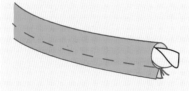

3 Wrap the wrong side of the fabric strip around the piping cord and, keeping the raw edges together, machine-baste close to the cord, as shown at left.

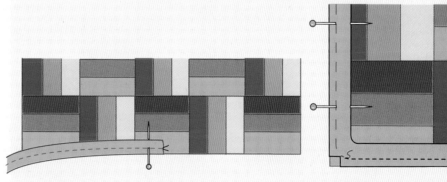

4 Place the piping on the right side of the pillow front, matching the raw edges, and baste it in place. Use a piping foot on your sewing machine and stitch as close to the piping as you can. It is best to begin about halfway across one side of the pillow, as shown above.

5 When you reach the first corner, snip the seam allowance of the piping in order to turn the corner smoothly. Machine-stitch up to the base of the snip, reverse-stitch for three stitches, then continue stitching the next side. Turn the remaining three corners in the same way. (Continued overleaf.)

43

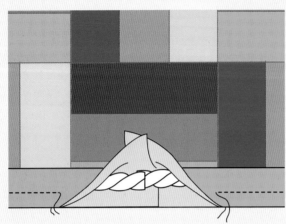

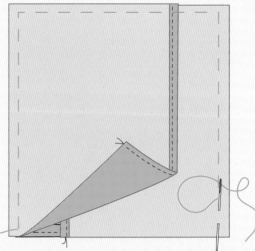

6 To join the piping, snip the excess cord so that the ends overlap slightly. Then trim the end of the fabric binding so that it overlaps the first end by approximately $^3/_4$ in. (2 cm).

8 For the pillow backs, fold and stitch a $^1/_4$-in. (6-mm) double hem along one long raw edge of each piece, and press. Place the pillow backs on the pillow front with right sides together, matching the raw edges around the outside and overlapping the hemmed edges at the center. Pin and baste around the edge of the pillow front and back, keeping the stitches close to the piping cord. Machine-stitch around all sides, using the piping foot and keeping your stitches as close to the piping as possible.

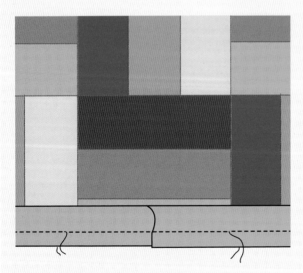

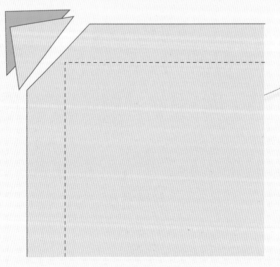

7 Unpick a few stitches at the beginning of the stitching, then fold back $^3/_8$ in. (1 cm) along the raw edge at the end of the binding. Tuck the raw end under the folded end and twist the ends of the cord together. Machine-stitch the join close to the cord as before, to finish the piping.

9 Trim diagonally across the seam allowance at each corner of the pillow, as shown above, and turn it to the right side. Insert a 19-in. (49-cm) pillow form.

Every quilter, from beginner to advanced, loves the classic Rail Fence pattern because of its simple, strong lines and ease of construction. When you need to make a gift for someone special in a short amount of time, try strip piecing and machine quilting this classic pillow design.

Traditional Patchwork

OF ALL QUILTING TECHNIQUES, PATCHWORK IS PROBABLY THE MOST POPULAR. SQUARES, TRIANGLES, AND DIAMONDS, AS WELL AS MORE COMPLEX SHAPES, ARE ARRANGED TOGETHER TO FORM DESIGNS WITH TRADITIONAL NAMES, SUCH AS CARD TRICK, BOW TIE, BROKEN DISHES, AND WINDMILL. THE BLOCKS ARE USUALLY SQUARE AND CAN BE USED SINGLY FOR ITEMS SUCH AS PILLOWS OR SMALL WALL HANGINGS, OR JOINED TOGETHER IN A VARIETY OF WAYS FOR QUILTS, LARGER WALL HANGINGS, OR LAP THROWS.

Patchwork blocks can be made up of any number of patches, but they are usually based on a grid, such as a four-patch, with four smaller squares stitched together to form a larger square. Nine-patch blocks have three rows of three squares, and five-patch have five rows of five squares. The squares can be subdivided horizontally, vertically, or diagonally to produce an infinite variety of different pieced designs.

Traditional blocks can be stitched by hand or machine, and as with all types of piecing, it is essential to keep a consistent seam allowance in order for the patches to fit together correctly. Identical blocks can be joined in rows or rotated, mirrored, or placed on-point. If you wish, you can use sashing, as seen at left, to separate the blocks, and add complementary patchwork or plain borders to enhance the quilt center.

The size of the blocks can be anything from 2 inches (5 cm) to 20 inches (50 cm) square—it all depends on what you are making and the scale you want.

This classic Churn Dash block takes on a new flavor with the addition of multiple pieced and plain borders.

Four-Patch Windmill Block

1 Cut out eight right triangles in the same size, four in plain fabric and four in a contrast print. Keep the lengthwise grain lines of the fabric aligned with a vertical edge of each patch and include a 1/4-in. (6-mm) seam allowance around each piece.

 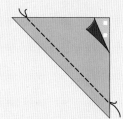

2 Join the triangles in pairs, one plain and one contrast, by placing them right sides together and stitching along the diagonal edge. Press the seam allowance toward the darker fabric and trim as shown.

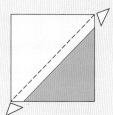 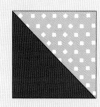

3 With right sides together, stitch two square patches together to form a rectangle, alternating the plain and contrast fabrics. Press the seam allowance as before. Complete another pair of patches. Stitch the two rectangles together with the points of the triangles meeting at the center. Press the seam allowance as before.

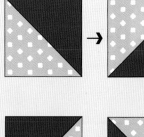 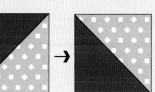 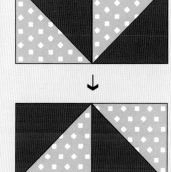

Adding Triangles to a Square

1 In order to take the seam allowance into consideration, the points of the triangle will slightly overlap the edges of the square. Mark the center of the diagonal edge of the triangle and on one side of the square.

2 Matching the center marks, pin the patches with right sides together and stitch along the seam line by machine. Press the seam allowance toward the darker fabric. Trim off the excess triangles, as shown.

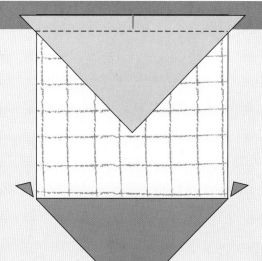
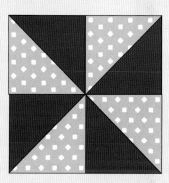

◈ Setting in a Patch at an Angle

1 Make a line of machine stay-stitching on the patch at the inner angle around the corner of the stitching line, and snip to the corner as shown at right.

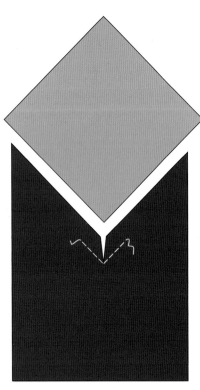

2 With right sides together, place and pin the insertion patch and stitch along the seam line toward the corner, stopping precisely at the clip in the stay-stitching.

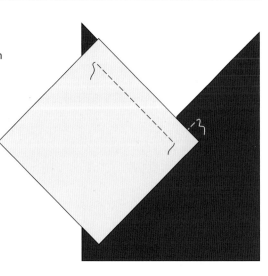

3 Pivot the work at the clip and continue stitching along the other side of the insertion square, as shown at right. Press the seam allowance away from the inserted patch so that it lies smoothly, as shown below.

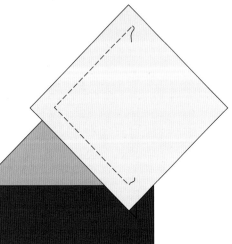

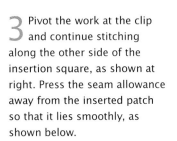

◈ Piecing Diamonds

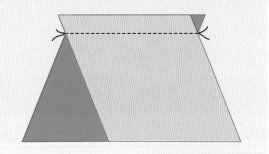

1 Position the two patches with right sides together and stitching lines aligned, as shown. Pin and stitch.

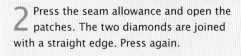

2 Press the seam allowance and open the patches. The two diamonds are joined with a straight edge. Press again.

◆ A Nine-Patch Texas Star Block

1 Using templates or by calculating your desired sizes, and using a rotary cutter, cut out four identical squares and four quarter triangles in light fabric and one central square in dark fabric. Cut four quarter triangles in a second light fabric and eight identical quarter triangles in a contrasting fabric. Make sure to include ¼-in. (6-mm) seam allowances in every piece, and keep the lengthwise fabric grain lines aligned with a vertical edge of each patch.

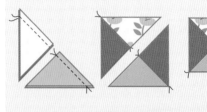

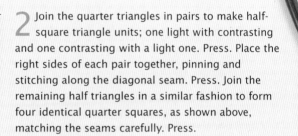

2 Join the quarter triangles in pairs to make half-square triangle units; one light with contrasting and one contrasting with a light one. Press. Place the right sides of each pair together, pinning and stitching along the diagonal seam. Press. Join the remaining half triangles in a similar fashion to form four identical quarter squares, as shown above, matching the seams carefully. Press.

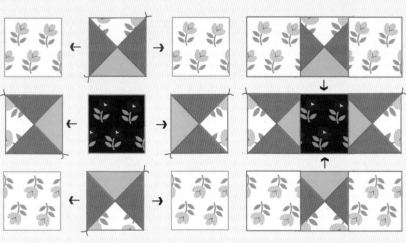

3 Arrange the seamed patches with the light squares at the corners and the dark square placed in the center. Stitch them together in three horizontal rows, as shown above, and stitch the three rows together, being careful to match the seams accurately. Press.

◆ A Five-Patch Fruit Basket Block

1 Cut out the desired-size patches in your chosen fabrics. Arrange the patches as shown at right. Press each seam allowance as you begin piecing.

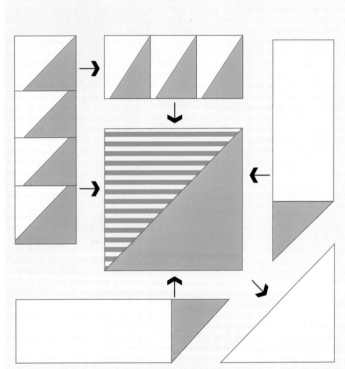

2 Join the 14 small triangles to make seven square units, and the two large triangles to make a large square unit, as shown above. Join a small triangle to each of the long rectangles at bottom left and top right, above.

3 Join three small squares in order to form the top horizontal row and four to form the left vertical row. Add the horizontal row to the top of the large center square, and then add the left vertical row to the left-hand side of the large square.

4 Add the rectangles with triangles to the bottom and right-hand edge and finish with the large triangle in the bottom right-hand corner. Press.

Setting Blocks Together

When designing a quilt, the size and number of blocks should be carefully considered. It is best to decide on the setting, or arrangement, of the blocks at the outset by drawing the design in miniature on graph paper. Choose blocks of a suitable size for the finished article—for full-size quilts, traditional blocks are often 12 in. (30 cm) square, while baby quilts or small wall hangings often feature smaller blocks. Borders and any sashing dimensions (*see* Setting and Finishing a Quilt, *pages 224–335*) should also be taken into consideration.

Blocks can be repeated horizontally and vertically, or rotated or mirrored for different effects. Repeating a block horizontally can add uniformity to a design, and often unexpected secondary patterns emerge where the blocks meet.

On-Point

Mirroring

Another common setting is to place the blocks on-point—that is, diagonally, which means that for a rectangular quilt, triangular setting triangles and blocks will have to be added at the sides and corners. This idea can be further extended with single rows of blocks placed vertically on-point, set with side and corner triangles. These are juxtaposed with similar rows that are set half a block higher or lower than their neighbor, a device that produces a zigzag background, such as the one shown above.

Alternating plain and pieced blocks can isolate intricately pieced blocks or allow space between blocks for quilting. Quite different effects can be achieved by mirroring or rotating pairs of asymmetrical blocks, as shown above. Blocks with a diagonal emphasis can be placed to produce a strong directional diamond or zigzag pattern across or down the design.

A Dash of Provence Quilt

This quilt, made from an assortment of print fabrics, uses a five-patch variation of the classic Churn Dash block. Although this block is repeated, the fabrics are varied. The strong block pattern stands out from a distance, while at close range the interplay of the printed fabrics adds interesting visual texture. The dominant navy and cream colors are accented by green and light blue fabrics from Provence in southern France, while the central medallion echoes and complements the blocks surrounding it. The main design is surrounded with a sawtooth border and framed with additional borders.

Dimensions

Finished quilt is approximately 50 x 40 in. (127 x 101 cm).

Materials and Equipment

- Assorted navy print fabrics: 1¾ yd. (157 cm) in total, or 14 fat eighths
- Assorted cream print fabrics: 1¼ yd. (115 cm) in total, or 10 fat eighths
- Green fabric: 1 fat quarter
- Light blue fabric: 1 fat quarter
- Cream print fabric for the inner border: ½ yd. (45 cm)
- Dark blue fabric for the outer border: ¾ yd. (68.5 cm)
- Backing fabric such as calico: 3¼ yd. (3 m), pieced and cut to 57 x 69 in. (145 x 177 cm)
- Medium-weight batting: 60 x 70 in. (152 x 180 cm)
- Cream and navy sewing thread
- Basic patchwork equipment

Preparation

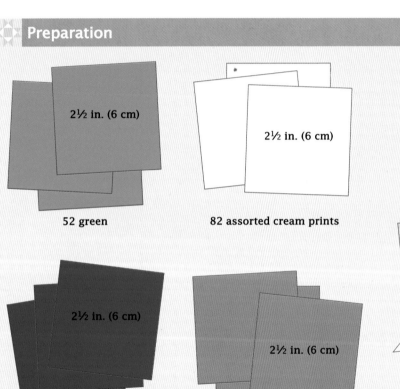

2½ in. (6 cm)

52 green

2½ in. (6 cm)

82 assorted cream prints

2½ in. (6 cm)

199 assorted navy prints

2½ in. (6 cm)

46 light blue

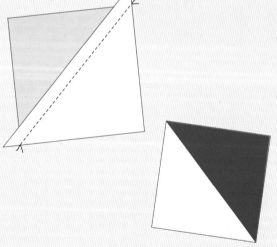

1 Using your rotary cutter, cut the number and color of 2½-in. (6-cm) squares of fabric shown above.

2 Using the triangular template on page 236, cut out 188 navy and 188 cream triangles.

3 Sew each navy triangle to a cream triangle along the diagonal, taking a ¼-in. (6-mm) seam. Press all of these toward the navy side so that you have 188 half-square triangles. Try to use as many different combinations of fabrics as you can to add variety.

Making Churn Dash Block A (Make 4)

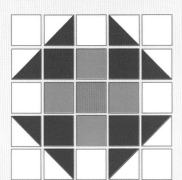

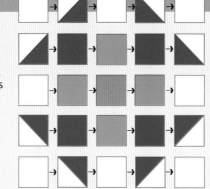

2 Arrange the squares as shown at left. Mix the fabric colors to get a random effect. Sew the squares together in horizontal rows of five squares, following the arrows, as shown at right.

1 For the first Churn Dash block, you will need:
8 cream squares
4 navy squares
8 navy and 8 cream half-square triangles
4 green squares
1 light blue square.

3 Sew the rows of five squares together as shown at right, matching the seam allowances. Press the seams to one side. Repeat this three times, so that there are four Churn Dash A blocks in all. They should all have the same colorways, but look slightly different because of the random arrangements of the cream and navy squares and half-square triangle units.

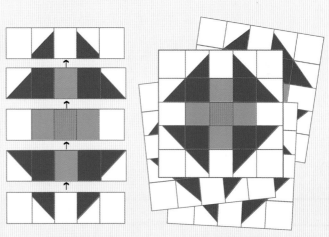

Making Churn Dash Block B (Make 2)

1 Now make two more Churn Dash blocks, but replace the greens with light blue. For each block, you will need:
8 cream squares
4 navy squares
8 navy and 8 cream triangles
1 green square
4 light blue squares.

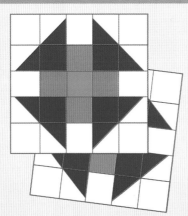

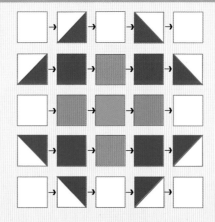

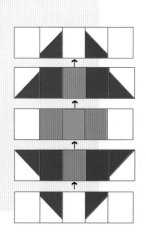

2 As you plan these blocks, mix up different cream and navy fabrics for variety. Piece these blocks together, as in the diagrams shown at right.

53

Making Churn Dash Block C (Make 4)

1 For these four modified Churn Dash blocks, you will need:

7 cream squares
4 navy squares
9 navy and 9 cream triangles
4 green squares
1 light blue square.

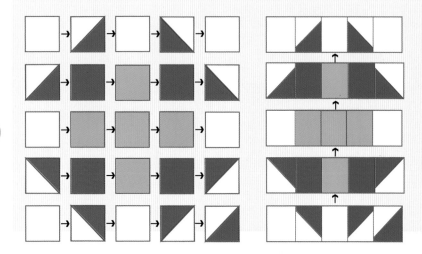

2 Again, mix the cream and navy fabrics at random. Then sew each block together following the arrows on the piecing diagrams shown at left. Press the seam allowances to one side.

Making the Medallion Center

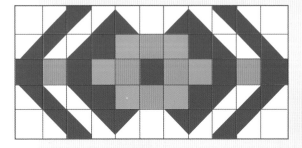

1 For the symmetrical medallion center design, you will need:

6 cream squares
9 navy squares
28 navy and 28 cream triangles
6 green squares
6 light blue squares.

2 Use the piecing diagram at right to sew it together. Press the seam allowances to one side.

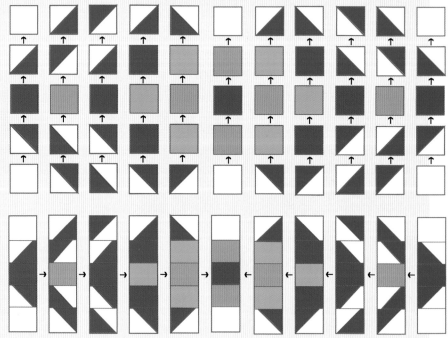

Making the Sashing

Each sashing strip is five navy print squares sewn in a row. Make 30 rows, arranging the navy prints randomly. Press the seam allowances to one side.

Assembling the Blocks with the Sashing

D Unit

1 Make a D unit by joining together:
2 A blocks
1 B block
10 sashing strips
8 light blue squares.
Press.

2 Sew the Step 1 units and pieces and blocks together, as shown in the piecing diagram at right. Then repeat, so that you have two D units.

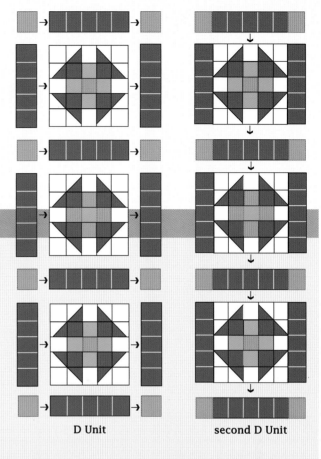

D Unit   second D Unit

E Units

1 Make an E unit by joining together:
2 C blocks
5 sashing strips
4 light blue squares.

2 Sew these together as in the piecing diagram, making sure that you arrange the asymmetric C blocks as shown. Then make another, so that you have two E units.

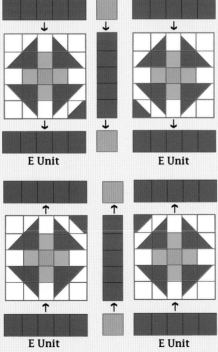

E Unit   E Unit

E Unit   E Unit

Making the center of the pieced top

Join the medallion from Steps 1 and 2 on page 54 to the two E units, as shown below. Remember that the E units are asymmetrical and need to be positioned so that the central piece you make is symmetrical. Press.

1 For the short sides of the quilt, make two rows of eight navy and cream half-square triangle units and another two rows of eight navy and cream units with the orientation reversed. For the long sides of the quilt make two rows of eleven navy and cream half-square triangle units and two rows of 11 navy and cream units with the orientation reversed.

Make two like this, and two in reversed direction

Make two like this, and two in reversed direction

2 Press the seam allowances toward the navy side.

3 Join the sawtooth borders to the green squares as shown below.

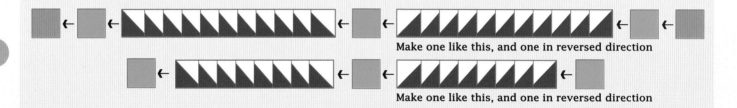

Make one like this, and one in reversed direction

Make one like this, and one in reversed direction

1 Sew the two shorter sawtooth borders to the long sides of the D units as shown. Press the seam allowances toward the sashing strips.

2 Sew the other sides of the D units to the center unit of the quilt top. Press.

3 Sew the two longer
sawtooth border
strips to the long edges
of the quilt center.
Press.

Adding the Inner Border

1 The central part of the quilt top should now measure about 54½ in. (138.5 cm) by about 42½ in. (108 cm), including the seam allowances.

2 Cut six 2½-in. (6-cm)-wide strips of the cream fabric for the middle border. Join the short ends of the strips together. Cut two strips the length of your quilt top (about 54½ in. (138.5 cm) and sew them to the long edges of the quilt top. Trim them even with the edges of the quilt center. Cut two strips approximately 46½ in. (118 cm) long and sew them to the shorter sides of the quilt. Press. Trim the ends of the border strips even with the edges of the quilt center.

Adding the Outer Border

For the outermost border, cut six 4-in. (10-cm)-wide strips of the navy fabric and sew the short ends together. Press. Sew the border lengths to the quilt in pairs, as for the inner border. You will need two lengths of approximately 58½ in. (149 cm) to sew to the long edges of the quilt top. Then you will need two lengths of about 54½ in. (138.5 cm) to sew to the shorter edges. Trim each border even with the quilt top to square up the quilt. This completes the quilt top. Press.

Layering the Quilt

1 Place the prepared backing wrong side up on a flat surface. Place the batting on top of the backing, and the quilt top on the batting, centering each. Pin from the center outward, then baste with large basting stitches, working in a grid from the center outward.

2 There is no need to mark lines for machine quilting if you follow the seams of the quilt. The quilting design used for the quilt pictured on page 59 is shown in black dotted lines below. Use navy or cream thread, or a color to match your choice of backing fabric.

Finishing

When you have finished quilting, trim the edges of the backing and batting to the size of quilt. There should be sufficient surplus in the outermost navy print border to give you some flexibility here. Bind the quilt with the navy fabric (*see* Edge Finishes, *pages 230–233*).

A rectangular quilt like this beautiful
Churn Dash variation makes a lovely
bed topper for a child's bedroom.

Foundation Piecing

BESIDES BEING A QUICK-AND-EASY METHOD OF PATCHWORK, FOUNDATION PIECING REQUIRES NO TEMPLATES. IN FOUNDATION PIECING, THE LINES OF A PATCHWORK DESIGN ARE MARKED IN REVERSE ON A PIECE OF FABRIC, NONWOVEN INTERFACING, OR PAPER. THESE LINES BECOME THE SEAM LINES FOR MACHINE STITCHING, WHICH IS DONE FROM THE UNDERSIDE OF THE MARKED FOUNDATION, GUARANTEEING STITCHING ACCURACY. THE FOUNDATION ALSO ADDS STABILITY TO THE APPLIED PATCHES, AND THE MARKED LINES ENABLE YOU TO STITCH PERFECT POINTS, EVEN ON THE TINIEST PATCHES.

Each fabric patch needs to be at least large enough to cover each shape, including ¼-in. (6-mm) or larger seam allowances all the way around. The grain of the fabric you use for each patch is somewhat less important than for regular machine piecing, because the fabric is anchored to the foundation with each seam you take. However, it is always a good idea to make sure that the grain lines along the edges of a block fall on either the crosswise or lengthwise grain, if possible.

You will need to work out the logical order in which to stitch the patches to the foundation. Some designs are best stitched from the center outward, while others can be sewn from side to side or diagonally across the block. For intricate designs, it may be necessary to stitch some patches together into sections before moving on with the block assembly.

Foundation Options

The foundation fabric itself can remain permanently in your work. This method is particularly suitable for borders of quilts where added weight gives stability. Fragile fabrics or small, intricate blocks can also benefit from a foundation of lightweight interfacing or cotton fabric. For a temporary foundation, you can use tracing paper, freezer paper, or tear-away interfacing, all of which are easy to remove after you finish stitching. Select a short stitch length on your machine to help with the removal.

The Mariner's Compass pattern may look difficult at first glance, but foundation piecing makes it both easy and fun to make.

The Basic Process

Follow these steps to learn how to do foundation piecing quickly and easily.

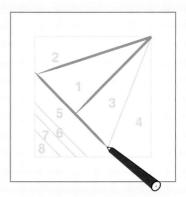

1 Trace the lines of the patchwork design in reverse onto a piece of foundation fabric, nonwoven interfacing, or paper, using the direct tracing method (*see page 124*) and allowing a wide margin all the way around the design. Work out the best piecing sequence and number each patch on the foundation.

2 Cut out the first patch larger than necessary, so that there is at least ¼ in. (6 mm) of fabric extending beyond the seam lines on all sides. Position and pin the first patch right side up in the appropriate place on the unmarked side of the foundation.

3 Cut the second patch larger than necessary, as for the first patch. Position and pin the second patch on top of the first patch with right sides together, as shown above.

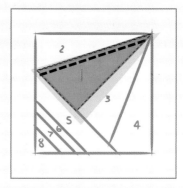

4 Turn your work over. With the marked side of the foundation facing you, stitch along the seam line between patch 1 and patch 2. Trim the seam allowance to ¼ in. (6 mm) from the stitched line, leaving all remaining edges untrimmed.

5 Turn your work to the right side again. Flip the second patch open, so that it is right side up and press it, making sure that it is large enough to cover the intended area.

6 Continue stitching, flipping, and pressing patches 3 through 8 in the same way. Position the crosswise or lengthwise grain lines of the outermost patches in alignment with the outer edges of the block. Make sure that enough fabric extends beyond the edges to allow for ¼-in. (6-mm) seam allowances. If you have used paper or tear-away interfacing as a foundation, carefully tear it away. Trim the edges of the block to include a ¼-in. (6-mm) seam allowance all around.

Irregular Blocks

Some blocks are impossible to piece in the conventional manner. This includes blocks that have a series of patches at right angles to one another or blocks with patches that need to be inserted at an angle. Follow these steps to foundation-piece these types of irregular blocks.

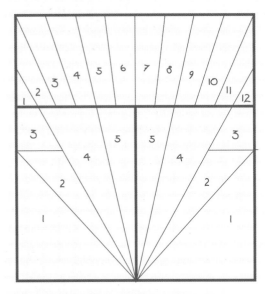

1 Divide the block into smaller, workable sections. Cut a separate foundation for each section, and number the stitching sequences, as shown above.

British Options

When you are conversant with the conventional method of foundation piecing, you can incorporate batting basted to the foundation fabric with patches stitched from the reverse side, as usual.

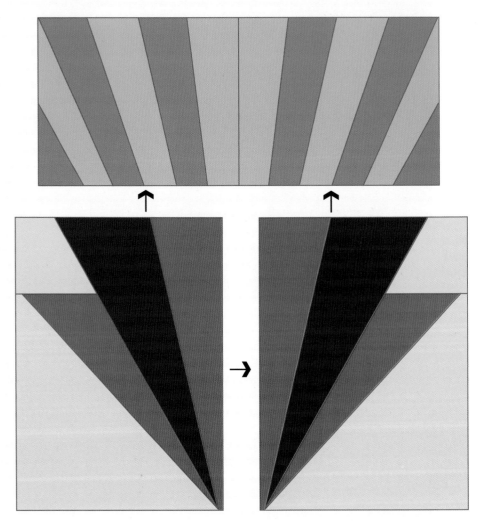

2 Stitch the appropriate patches in order on each foundation, as explained on page 61. If you have used temporary foundations, remove them now. Sew the three sections together, as indicated by the arrows, to form the complete block. Trim edges of sections and block to a ¼-in. (6-mm) seam allowance. Press the completed block.

Quilt-As-You-Go

Quilt-as-you-go foundation piecing combines the piecing and quilting process into a single operation. This technique involves stitching strips of fabric by hand or machine to a fabric foundation that has a layer of batting on top. This method is good for pillows and other small, single-square projects.

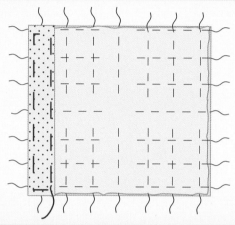

Vertical Strips

Follow these steps to attach strips of fabric vertically to a foundation-and-batting base.

1 Thread-baste a piece of batting to the right side of a foundation fabric in a grid, as shown at right. Baste the first fabric strip right side up along the left edge of the foundation-and-batting base, with the raw edges aligned.

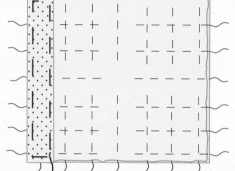

2 Place the second strip on top of the first with right sides together, and stitch along the inner edge through all layers. Flip the second strip open to the right side, as shown. Continue adding more strips across the batting in the same manner. Press as you go.

Diagonal Strips

Follow these steps to attach strips of fabric diagonally to a fabric-and-batting base.

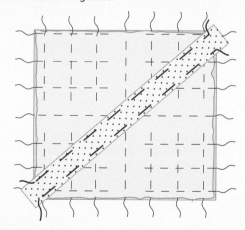

1 Thread-baste a piece of batting to the right side of a foundation fabric in a grid (see page 133). Cut fabric strips that are long enough to reach across and beyond the diagonal of the foundation-and-batting base. With the right side facing up, thread-baste both long edges of the first strip diagonally across the base, as shown above.

2 Position the second strip on top of the first, with right sides together. Referring to the basic process on page 61, stitch through all layers along the left long edge of the second strip. Flip the second strip open to the right side. Pin the second strip in place on the foundation base, pressing as you go. Continue adding more strips until you reach the corner of the base. Rotate your work and repeat to cover the rest of the foundation base in the same manner. Trim the excess fabric on all edges of the base to a 1/4-in. (6-mm) seam allowance beyond the finished block size.

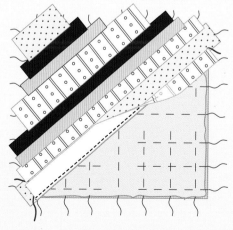

Mariner's Compass Wall Hanging

The Mariner's Compass patchwork pattern is a traditional design and has many variations—that is, the number and length of the points, or the size of the center circle. This small wall hanging is made from three basic compass squares that are joined together using a small semicircle and quarter circle as decorative motifs at the corners. Accurate cutting and stitching are essential to achieve the sharp points and smooth curves that are characteristic of this intricate design. A beginner should consider a small project like this one, or perhaps a pillow, before embarking on a full-scale quilt or a larger wall hanging.

Foundation Piecing

To use up odd-sized pieces of fabric, use the foundation-piecing patterns on pages 236–237, and follow the basic foundation-piecing techniques shown on pages 61–62. For the corner pieces, use the templates provided on page 237.

Cutting the Template Pieces

Copy the templates 1, 2, 3, 4, 5, 6, and 7 given on pages 236–237, then use the permanent marking pen to trace each onto template plastic. Each template includes a seam allowance of 1/4 in. (6 mm) on all sides. Cut out each template carefully along the marked lines.

Dimensions

Finished blocks are 12 in. (30 cm) square.

Finished wall hanging is 18 x 42 in. (46 x 107 cm).

Equipment and Materials

Note: Refer to the photo on page 69 for placement of colored pieces.

- Dark solid pink for points and binding: 1/2 yd. (46 cm)
- Mottled pink for circle background: 15 3/4 in. (40 cm) square
- Pale pink for points: 8 in. (20 cm)
- Bright pink print for center points: 23 1/2 in. (60 cm) square
- Cream tone-on-tone fabric for background: 15 3/4 in. (40 cm)
- Solid fabric for backing: 3/4 yd. (68.5 cm)
- Piece of batting: 22 x 46 in. (56 x 117 cm)
- Large sheet of template plastic: 18 x 20 in. (46 x 50 cm)
- Permanent marking pen for templates
- Marking chalk for fabric
- Ruler
- Basic machine sewing supplies and iron

Cutting the Fabric Pieces

For each Mariner's Compass block, you will need *three sets of each of the following*:

- Template 1: dark plain pink—cut 8 points
- Template 2: very pale mottled pink—cut 16 background pieces
- Template 3: pale pink—cut 4 points
- Template 4: bright pink print—cut 4 pieces
- Template 5: cream tone-on-tone—cut 4 pieces
- Template 6: bright pink print—cut 1 circle

For each quarter-circle corner section, you will need *four sets of each of the following*:

- Template 7: mottled pink—cut 2 pieces
- Template 7: bright pink print—cut 1 piece

For each semicircular edge section, you will need *four sets of the following*:

- Template 7: bright pink print—cut 2 pieces
- Template 7: mottled pink—cut 2 pieces
- Template 7: pale pink—cut 2 pieces

For the borders and bindings, cut strips as follows:

- narrow inner border cut two 14- x 1-in. (35- x 2.5-cm), and two 36- x 1-in. (95- x 2.5-cm) strips from dark solid pink

- wide middle border cut two 16 1/2- x 2-in. (42- x 5-cm), and two 37 1/2- x 2-in. (95.5- x 5-cm) strips from bright pink print

- narrow outer binding cut two 19 1/2- x 2-in. (49- x 5-cm), and two 40- x 2-in. (101- x 2-cm) strips from dark solid pink

Assembling the Three Main Blocks

Although the Mariner's Compass pattern seems complicated at first glance, and the method does rely on careful, accurate stitching, the assembly follows a simple, logical sequence. The template pieces have been numbered in sequence as a guide. Stitch all patchwork pieces with right sides together, taking a $1/4$-in. (6-mm) seam allowance.

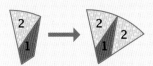

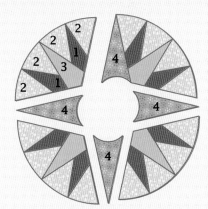

1 Begin the compass motif by joining piece 1 to one piece 2, then join another piece 2, as shown above. Make another section in the same way. Press seam allowances open.

2 Join the two resulting units to piece 3, as shown above. This forms the basic "quarter" of the compass design. Assemble another three quarter-sections in the same way, and press all seam allowances open.

3 Take up the remaining four pieces numbered 4 and join them to the Step 2 sections to form a circle, as shown at left. Remember that careful and accurate stitching is key to achieving a neat result. Press all seam allowances open.

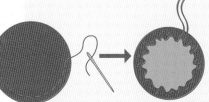

4 You will now see that the basic compass shape has a hole at the center. Take the remaining circular piece and work a small running stitch around the outside edge. Gather up the stitching around the circle template so the edge folds in on itself, as shown above; then secure the end of the sewing thread with a knot. Press. Remove the template.

5 Place the gathered circle over the center hole, and pin and baste in place, to cover all the raw edges neatly. Secure the folded curved edge of the circle in place using a small appliqué stitch in a matching thread color.

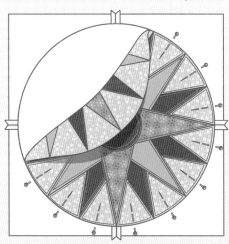

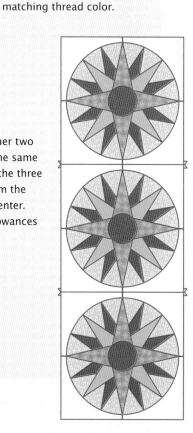

6 Join the short edges of the four cream background pieces to form a square with a large hole in the center, as shown at left. Pin each seam to the "north, south, east, west" points of the compass design to begin, then carefully pin the Mariner's Compass unit in place. Pin the convex edge of the compass circle to the concave edge of the background with right sides together. When the seam is complete, snip the curved edge of the background pieces so the seam allowance will lie flat when pressed.

7 Make another two blocks in the same way, then join the three together to form the wall-hanging center. Press seam allowances open.

Assembling and Applying the Corner Motifs

The motifs at each corner, and at the edges of the joining seams, are simply semicircles or quarter circles made from a wedge-shaped piece numbered 7.

1 For each corner piece, join two mottled-pink sections to a center dark pink print piece, then press the seam allowances open.

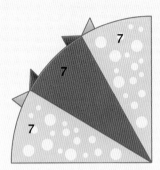

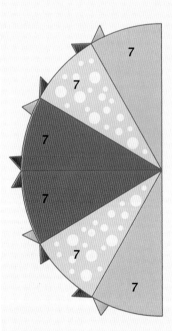

2 For each semicircular piece, join two dark pink print sections together to form the center, then join a mottled-pink piece to each side. Complete the shape by adding a pale pink section to each side. Press all the seam allowances open.

3 Place the resulting sections in position on the wall hanging, as shown at right, and pin and baste in place.

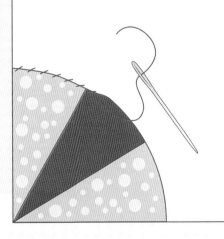

4 Use the tip of your needle to tuck the curved raw edge under, and appliqué the fold of each half and quarter circle neatly to the background fabric.

Adding the Borders

Note: The border and binding have a ¼-in. (6-mm) seam allowance included.

1 Take the two longest inner border strips and stitch to the side edges of the wall hanging with right sides together. Press the seam allowances open. Stitch the shorter strips to the upper and lower edges in the same way, and press the seam allowances open as before.

2 Take the two longest middle border strips and stitch to the side edges of the wall hanging with right sides together. Press the seam allowances open. Stitch the shorter strips to the upper and lower edges in the same way. Press, as before.

Quilting the Wall Hanging

Note: The border and binding have a ½-in. (12-mm) seam allowance included.

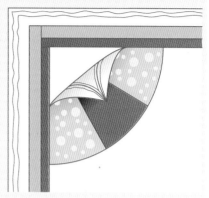

1 Cut out a 22- x 46-in. (56- x 117-cm) rectangle of batting and a piece of backing fabric the same size. Sandwich the batting between the backing fabric and the quilt top, as shown above, allowing 2 in. (5 cm) extra around all four sides of the quilt top. Thread-baste around the edge and at intervals of approximately 3 in. (7.5 cm) both vertically and horizontally to hold the layers secure, as shown below.

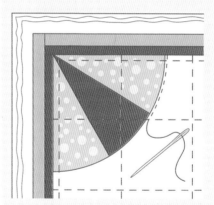

2 Using matching quilting thread, quilt along the seam lines of the three large circles, the four small semicircles, and the four quarter circles. Also quilt along the seam line between the inner narrow border strip and the wider middle border. Remove all the basting stitches when the quilting is complete. Trim the batting and backing even with the edges of the wall hanging.

67

Finishing

To complete the wall hanging, add binding to the outer edges to enclose the raw edges of the fabric and the batting.

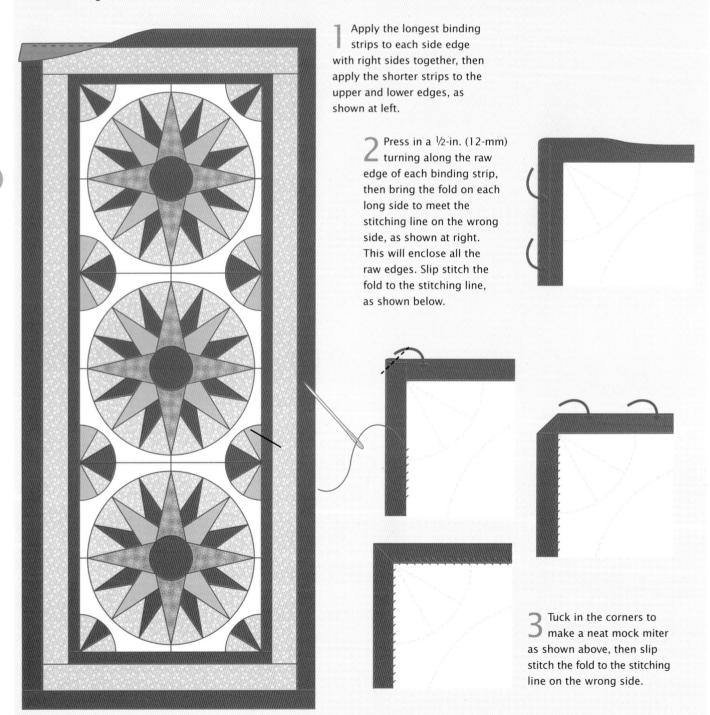

1 Apply the longest binding strips to each side edge with right sides together, then apply the shorter strips to the upper and lower edges, as shown at left.

2 Press in a ½-in. (12-mm) turning along the raw edge of each binding strip, then bring the fold on each long side to meet the stitching line on the wrong side, as shown at right. This will enclose all the raw edges. Slip stitch the fold to the stitching line, as shown below.

3 Tuck in the corners to make a neat mock miter as shown above, then slip stitch the fold to the stitching line on the wrong side.

The sharp points on these beautiful Mariner's Compass blocks will show off
your piecing skills to perfection. And they're so simple to make,
you may want to piece more than just one wall hanging!

English Paper Piecing

THIS TECHNIQUE, EPITOMIZED BY SUCH WELL-KNOWN HEXAGONAL PATTERNS AS GRANDMOTHER'S FLOWER GARDEN, IS A PERENNIAL FAVORITE WITH QUILTERS, BECAUSE MISTAKES CAN BE SPOTTED AT ONCE AND EASILY RECTIFIED. SOMETIMES KNOWN AS MOSAIC OR TEMPLATE PIECING, THE PAPER TEMPLATES ARE CUT TO THE EXACT FINISHED SIZE, KEPT INSIDE THE PATCHES WHILE THEY ARE SEWN TOGETHER, AND REMOVED LATER.

Window templates for English patchwork can be purchased from quilt shops, or you can cut your own (*see page 26*). Hexagons are useful shapes for English patchwork, as they can be fitted with other hexagons, triangles, and diamonds. Diamonds are used for the Tumbling (or Baby) Block pattern, as shown below, which gives a three-dimensional effect, or they can form six-pointed stars. These can be combined with hexagons, triangles, and trapezoids. You can work out the designs for all these on isometric graph paper (*see page 25*).

Extended honeycomb shapes can be used alone or with squares or triangles set on-point between them. If you are using octagons, you will need squares to fit them together.

Pentagons are more complicated, but 12 of these stitched together will form a three-dimensional ball shape often used as a baby's soft toy.

Paper templates can be made from freezer paper or lightweight typing paper. Although other fabrics can be used for English patchwork, it is best to start with cotton because this will enable you to fold the seam allowances crisply. Match the sewing thread to the darker of two adjacent patches or choose a neutral shade, such as gray or beige, that will blend with all of your chosen colors.

The Tumbling Stars pattern is a traditional favorite with quilters of all skill levels because of its three-dimensional look. In this pillow, it has been slightly adapted for a fresh look.

◈ Making Paper Templates

For beginners, a hexagon shape is the simplest to work with.

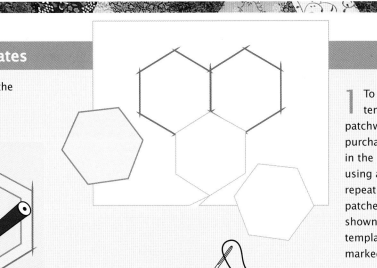

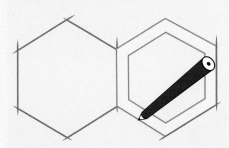

1 To make freezer paper templates for English patchwork, draw around a purchased hexagon template in the desired finished size using a sharp pencil, repeating for as many patches as you will need, as shown at left. Cut out the templates carefully on the marked lines.

2 Press the freezer-paper hexagon templates onto the wrong side of the fabric. Mark a ¼-in. (6-mm) seam allowance around each patch, as shown above.

4 Place two patches right sides together, aligning them accurately. Starting ¼ in. (6 mm) from the left corner, sew to the left corner, as shown at left.

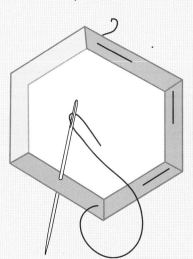

3 Fold the seam allowance over the first edge of the paper template and baste through all three layers, starting with a knot on the right side. Repeat along the second edge, taking a stitch across the fold at the corner. Continue folding and basting the remaining sides, as shown at left. Complete the other patches in the same way.

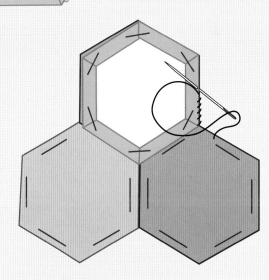

5 Bring the needle up through both layers of fabric, close to the edge, and take a tiny stitch over the folded edge, covering the previous stitches, bringing the needle out again to the right. Do not pull the thread too tightly or the seam will not lie flat. Take a tiny amount of fabric and do not pierce the paper. Continue stitching, covering the previous stitches. Fasten off securely with two or three stitches worked from right to left.

6 Add consecutive patches, joining adjacent edges in the same way. Continue with the same thread whenever possible. Leave the papers in the patchwork until the project is finished. Then remove the basting stitches, press, and remove the papers.

Hexagon Designs

Hexagons are very versatile shapes, since they can be made up into a number of different quilt designs that depend solely on the arrangement of the colors. Entire quilts are sometimes made up entirely of hexagon shapes, apart from the edges, which will need to have triangles or half-hexagons added to form straight edges. However, it is often quicker and easier to make up an entire patchwork "fabric" and cut off the excess parts to achieve the correct size and shape.

Fussy-Cut Motifs

With careful planning, printed fabrics can be cut so that a particular motif, such as a flower, is centered in a patch (*see page 22*). Striped fabrics can be cut and assembled to crea e directional e fects.

Grandmother's Flower Garden

Grandmother's Flower Garden usually consists of two (or three) concentric rows of hexagons surrounding a center hexagon in a contrasting color. The second or third row will serve as a division between other "flowers."

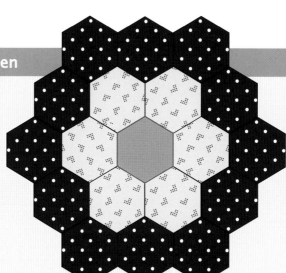

Field of Diamonds

Field of Diamonds develops the Grandmother's Flower Garden pattern with an additional hexagon at top and bottom, forming a diamond shape. Continue with more rows of hexagons to extend the size of the diamond.

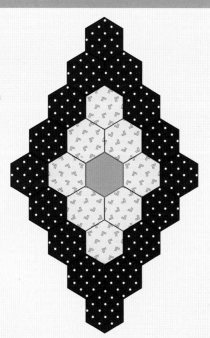

Ocean Wave

The Ocean Wave pattern makes an ideal border to combine with other hexagon patterns. The dimension of the design depends on the number of hexagons on each rise and fall, and the depth of the border can vary with the number of rows that you decide upon.

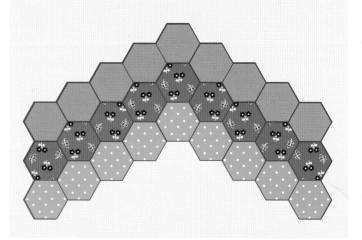

Diamond Patterns

Diamonds can be used alone or in combination with other shapes, such as triangles and hexagons. The most popular designs include Tumbling or Baby Blocks (*see page 74*) and Brick Pile and Inner City, also known as Right Angle. As they have a three-dimensional effect, they rely for their impact on the careful selection of correct color values.

Dealing with Points on Diamonds or Triangles

Although working with diamonds and triangles appears to present problems due to their pointed shapes, they can be paper-pieced without difficulty. Fold over the seam allowances as for other geometric shapes, leaving the excess fabric extended. When oversewing, simply ignore this excess, and it will lie flat without being stitched into the seam.

Inner City

Inner City is made up of nine diamonds, three each of dark, medium, and light fabrics, placed in such as way that they appear to be a collection of tall buildings with sunlight casting shadows to one side, as shown at right.

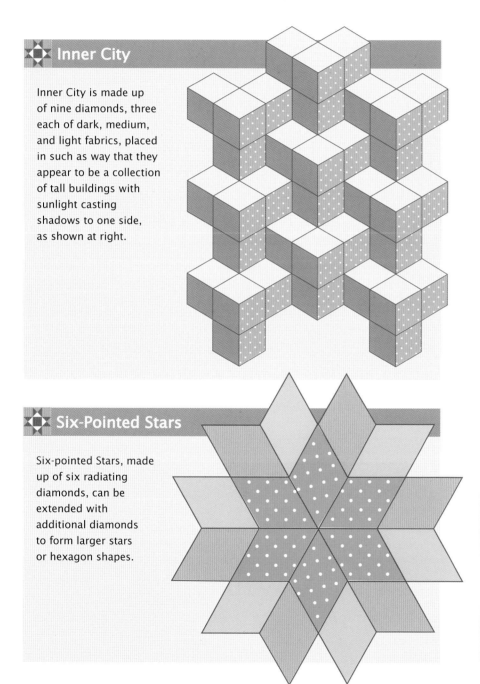

Six-Pointed Stars

Six-pointed Stars, made up of six radiating diamonds, can be extended with additional diamonds to form larger stars or hexagon shapes.

Brick Pile

For Brick Pile, diamonds are arranged in groups with two adjacent diamonds in the same fabric to emulate the top surface of the "bricks."

Tumbling Stars Pillow

This pillow is made using English paper piecing and the traditional pattern Tumbling Blocks. The Tumbling Block pattern has been modified slightly, using a careful arrangement of light, dark, and medium colors, and a light background color to give a more interesting three-dimensional effect. Look closely to see seven six-pointed stars, then look again to see the typical Tumbling Block shape made up of three diamond shapes. The central motif has been appliquéd to a self-patterned neutral background bordered with dark blue fabric. The pillow is hand-quilted in a diagonal grid pattern to follow the patchwork seam lines.

Dimensions

Finished pillow is approximately 20 in. (50 cm) square.

Fabric Choices

For this project, we used scraps of fabric in several different patterns and colors. Your design will be slightly different from the one featured because of the fabric scraps you choose.

Equipment and Materials

- Scraps of fabric with small patterns: 8 in. (20 cm) square; choose three light colors and three medium colors
- Solid or tone-on-tone dark blue fabric for pillow backs and border: 1¾ yd. (157 cm)
- Muslin for backing quilted piece: ½ yd. (45 cm)
- Cream print fabric for pillow front: ½ yd. (45 cm)
- Batting: ½ yd. (45 cm)
- Freezer paper
- Pencil
- Marking chalk (any kind)
- Ruler
- Sewing kit and iron
- Pillow form: 20 in. (50 cm) square

MEASUREMENTS FOR PILLOW PIECES

- For the borders, cut two 2- x 18½-in. (5- x 47-cm) strips and two 2- x 21½-in. (5- x 54.5-cm) strips
- For the cushion front, cut one 21½-in. (54.5-cm) square
- For the cushion backs, cut two 21½- x 15-in. (54.5- x 38-cm) rectangles
- Cut one 21½-in. (54.5-cm) square from muslin and batting
- For the cream background, cut one 18½-in. (47-cm) square

1 First trace the diamond-shaped pieces onto freezer paper using the template on page 238 (78 in total: 30 dark blue, 21 light-colored pattern, 27 medium-colored pattern). Cut out the diamond shapes. Press the waxy side of the freezer paper onto the chosen fabrics. Mark a ¼-in. (6-mm) allowance around each template on the wrong side of the fabrics. Cut out each diamond carefully, as shown at right.

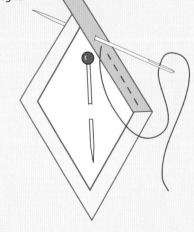

2 Baste the diamonds to the papers by folding the seam allowance over the uppermost right-hand edge, as shown at left. Baste through the fabric and the freezer paper, then finger-press the seam allowance at the top, where it extends beyond the paper, to make the folds flat.

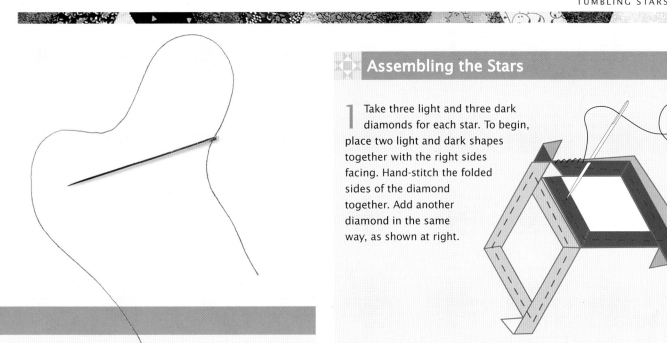

Assembling the Stars

1 Take three light and three dark diamonds for each star. To begin, place two light and dark shapes together with the right sides facing. Hand-stitch the folded sides of the diamond together. Add another diamond in the same way, as shown at right.

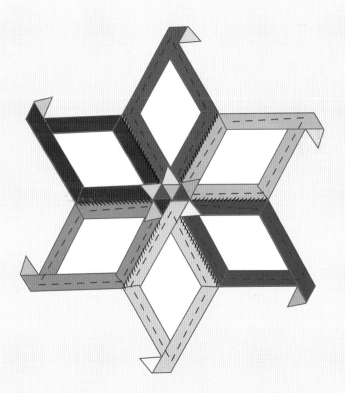

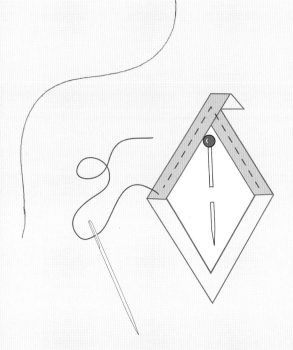

3 Fold the seam allowance on the opposite side, as shown above, and baste to the paper as before, finger-pressing the seam allowance where it extends. Continue in this way around all four sides. You will see that there is a little tab of fabric protruding from the top and lower points of the diamond.

2 Continue until the star shape is formed from the six diamond-shaped pieces. When joining the six pieces together, it is important to make sure that the bulk of fabric at the center be kept to a minimum. To do this, simply hold the extended tabs of fabric at the point of the shape out of the way; then sew only through the folded edge of the fabric. You will see that the tabs will form a neat spiral at the center of each star shape. Make seven of these stars.

Assembling the Central Motif

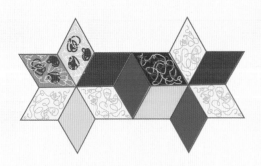

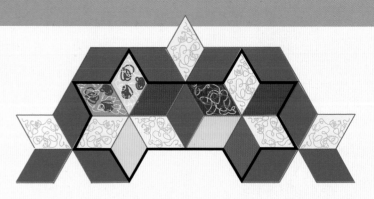

1 Begin assembling the central motif by joining two star shapes together with a dark blue diamond in between, as shown above. Make two more of these units.

2 Add ten more dark blue background diamonds to fill in the areas around the two star shapes, plus three medium diamonds at the top and side. You will see that already the central motif is beginning to form.

3 Now piece a star shape, as shown at left, that will form from the center of the motif. Stitch on six dark blue diamonds around the edges to form a larger hexagonal shape. Make two more of these units.

4 Stitch the Step 3 shape to the arrangement of diamonds in Step 2, as shown above.

5 Add another two star shapes and two blue diamonds (*see* Assembling the Stars *on page 75*), making sure that the positioning of the light and medium diamonds matches the others in order to keep the three-dimensional appearance balanced.

Applying the Border

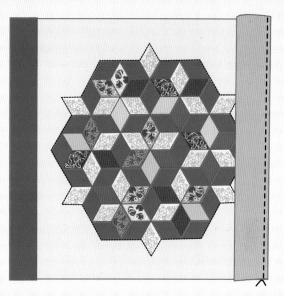

6 Finally, join the last two star shapes, and stitch to the main shape, filling in with dark blue background diamonds and the last three medium diamonds at the edge. Unpick all the basting stitches and remove the papers in readiness for the next stage.

1 Take the two shorter dark blue border strips and place them with right sides facing along the right- and left-hand sides of the pillow front. Machine-stitch the raw edges together, taking a $1/4$-in. (6-mm) seam allowance. Press the seams open.

Appliquéing the Motif to the Pillow Front

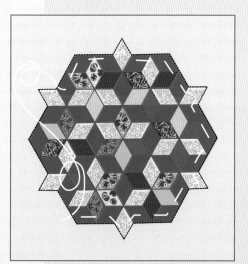

Place the patchwork motif centrally on the right side of the square that will form the pillow front. Pin in place, then baste around the edge to hold secure, as shown at left. Appliqué the outermost edges to the background, then remove the basting stitches.

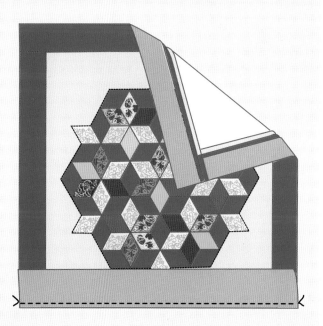

2 Sew the two remaining border strips to the upper and lower edges in the same way. Press both seam allowances open.

Quilting the Pillow

1 Cut a square of batting and a square of muslin 2 in. (5 cm) larger all around than the pillow front. Sandwich the batting between the pillow front and the muslin, then baste through all three layers to hold secure. Basting should be in a grid of horizontal and vertical lines, about 4 in. (10 cm) apart, as shown at right.

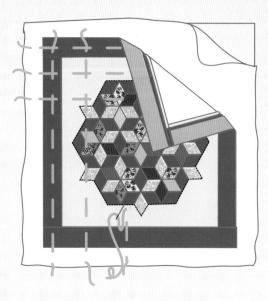

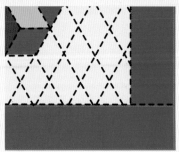

2 Hand-quilt around each of the diamond shapes, and continue in the form of a grid of diagonal diamond shapes to match the lines of the central motif in the background area. Finally, quilt along the seam lines of the dark blue border to complete the pillow front. Remove all basting threads.

Finishing

1 For the pillow backs, fold and stitch a narrow 1/4-in. (6-mm) double hem along one long raw edge of each piece and press.

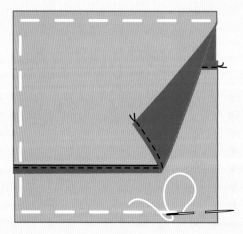

2 Place the pillow backs onto the front with right sides together, matching the raw edges around the outside and overlapping the hemmed edges at the center. Pin and baste around the outer edge. Machine-stitch, taking a 1/2-in. (12-mm) seam allowance.

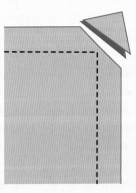

3 Trim diagonally across the seam allowance at each corner of the pillow then turn through to the right side. Press. Insert a 20-in. (50-cm) pillow form.

The Tumbling Stars pillow is a great way to use up
leftover squares of fabric to make a beautiful
accessory for any room.

Curved Patchwork

PATCHWORK BLOCKS THAT INCLUDE PIECED CURVED SHAPES MAY APPEAR TO PRESENT STITCHING DIFFICULTIES, BUT BY TAKING CARE WITH ACCURACY AND PIECING, YOU CAN ENJOY PIECING THEM AND ACHIEVE ANOTHER DIMENSION IN YOUR WORK. THESE DIFFER FROM APPLIQUÉ DESIGNS SUCH AS CLAMSHELLS (*SEE PAGES 100–101*) AND DRESDEN PLATE (*SEE PAGES 102–103*), WHICH ARE PREPARED AND THEN STITCHED TO THE BACKGROUND FABRIC.

Well-known designs, such as Drunkard's Path, Robbing Peter to Pay Paul, and Orange Peel, are all based on four-patch blocks and comprise two contrasting curved shapes pieced together. Although the Double Wedding Ring, made up of interlocking circular "rings," is in a unique category, it still demands the ability to stitch a convex piece into a concave shape. This is traditionally a hand-piecing method, but with care and practice, you can do curved piecing on a machine.

You can often purchase sets of two acrylic templates for the Drunkard's Path pattern in quilt shops, and you can also make your own templates from template plastic.

OPPOSITE The simple yet classic Drunkard's Path block design consists of convex and concave shapes. This piecing technique is easy to learn and the end result is very striking. For the best effect use contrasting colored fabrics.

Stitching a Quarter Circle into a Concave Shape

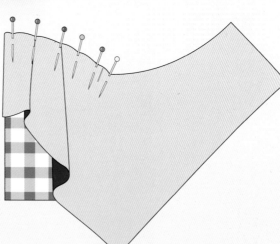

1 Cut a patch using a quarter-circle convex template, and another in contrasting fabric from a corresponding concave template. Make sure that the grain lines of the fabric are parallel with the straight edges of the templates. Fold each shape in half along the curved edge and finger-press or mark the center point of each.

2 Place the concave shape right sides together on top of the convex shape. Align the two straight edges at the left end and pin securely. Match the two center marks. Place more pins between, easing the excess fabric to fit the curve of the convex shape, as shown below.

3 Stitch a ¼-in. (6-mm) seam allowance by hand along the curved edge, as shown above. If you prefer to work by machine, ease the gathers and remove the pins as you go. Press the seam allowance toward the concave shape and check the accuracy of the finished square.

◇ Drunkard's Path Variation

The Drunkard's Path patch (*see pages 84–85*) can be used in a wide variety of different configurations, from a simple repeated fan shape to more intricate patterns, such as Wonder of the World, Mill Wheel, and Falling Trees. You can work out the designs on graph paper, and by reversing the colors and repeating or rotating the blocks, you can create a range of effects such as these.

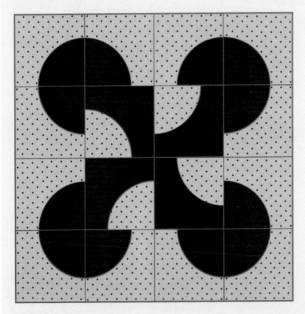

Wonder of the World

Falling Trees

Mill Wheel

◈ Curved Block Variations

Two four-patch blocks that rely for their effect on transposing light and dark fabrics are Orange Peel and Robbing Peter to Pay Paul. You can purchase templates for these or create your own using squared template plastic and a compass.

If you are not experienced at stitching curved seams, it is sensible to make each patch at least 3 in. (7.5 cm) square, particularly with Robbing Peter to Pay Paul, which has very narrow curved pieces to manipulate.

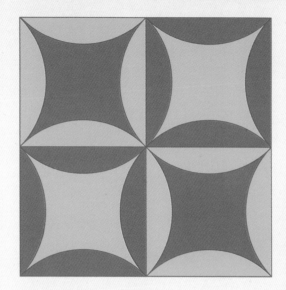

Robbing Peter to Pay Paul

Orange Peel

◈ Combining Curved and Straight-Edged Patches

One way you can vary patches with curved seams is to combine them with straight-edged shapes. There are several well-known designs, including Greek Cross and Tennessee Circle. You can also create your own using graph paper or squared template plastic, a quilter's ruler, and a compass.

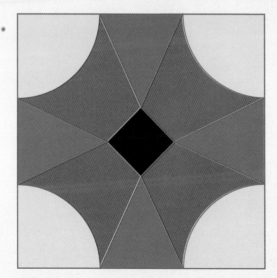

Greek Cross

Tennessee Circle

Drunkard's Path Pillow

This popular design is made up of sixteen square patches, all of which consist of a quarter-circle convex shape inserted into a concave shape, as shown below. The contrasting fabrics are reversed in half the patches, and the setting creates the meandering design.

Materials and Equipment

● Cream material: ⅙ yd. (15 cm)

● Blue fabric for pillow backs and piping: 2 yd. (183 cm)

● Piping cord: ¼-in. (6-mm) diameter

Dimensions

Finished pillow is approximately 16 in. (40.5 cm) square.

Constructing Drunkard's Path Block

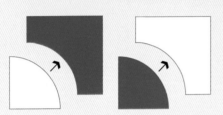

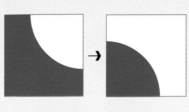

2 Make eight patches with light convex and dark concave shapes, and eight with the colors reversed, as shown at left. Press the seam allowances toward the concave shapes.

1 Using the templates on page 238, cut eight convex and eight concave shapes in light fabric. Cut the same number of each in dark fabric, and mark the center of the curves.

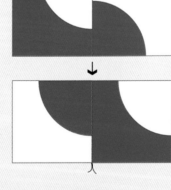

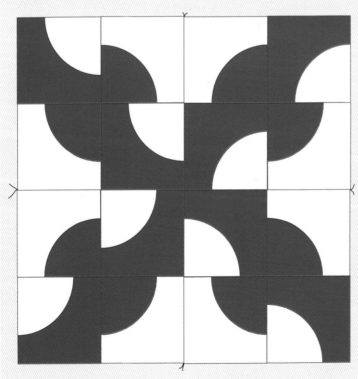

3 Piece the patches together in two rows, as shown above. Make a total of four identical four-patch blocks, matching the seams carefully. Then, turning each four-patch block 90 degrees, piece them together to make the 16-patch Drunkard's Path block shown at left. Press the seam allowances to one side as you go.

Two contrasting solid fabrics create a bold design
with a dramatic flair that will add sizzle to
any room in your home.

Folded Patchwork

THERE ARE SEVERAL PATCHWORK TECHNIQUES THAT RELY ON FOLDING FABRIC AND STITCHING IT TO A FOUNDATION FABRIC TO CREATE TEXTURED EFFECTS. THE FOLDED STAR (KNOWN IN ENGLAND AS SOMERSET PATCHWORK) CONSISTS OF SMALL SQUARES FOLDED INTO TRIANGLES, WHICH ARE ARRANGED TO FORM STAR-SHAPED, KALEIDOSCOPIC PATTERNS. CATHEDRAL WINDOW AND ITS VARIATIONS SIMULATE THE LOOK OF STAINED GLASS, WITH INTRICATELY FOLDED SQUARES AND CONTRASTING INSERTED PATCHES THAT FORM THREE-DIMENSIONAL PATCHWORK. JAPANESE FOLDED PATCHWORK INVOLVES COMBINING BATTING AND FABRIC CIRCLES, AND JOINING THE PATCHES TOGETHER AS YOU GO.

Although the following methods of folded patchwork can be relatively time-consuming, they are very effective for small items, such as pillows, bags, and accessories. If you wish to use them for larger projects, such as quilts, throws, or wall hangings, consider increasing the scale of the folded patchwork and use fine cotton fabrics that will not add too much weight to the finished project.

Folded Star

This type of patchwork does not need to be quilted, because the layers of patches form a thick, finished fabric in themselves. The edges are usually finished with binding or surrounded by other patches or fabric strips. As you learn the following technique, mount the foundation fabric in an embroidery hoop or other frame to keep it taut.

Making a Folded Star

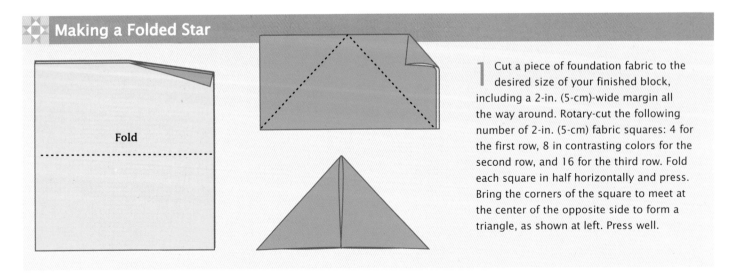

Fold

1 Cut a piece of foundation fabric to the desired size of your finished block, including a 2-in. (5-cm)-wide margin all the way around. Rotary-cut the following number of 2-in. (5-cm) fabric squares: 4 for the first row, 8 in contrasting colors for the second row, and 16 for the third row. Fold each square in half horizontally and press. Bring the corners of the square to meet at the center of the opposite side to form a triangle, as shown at left. Press well.

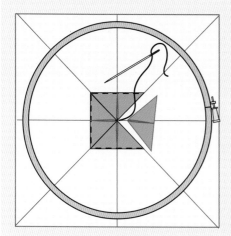

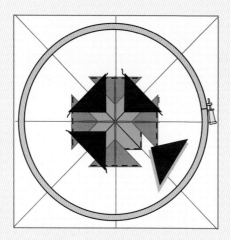

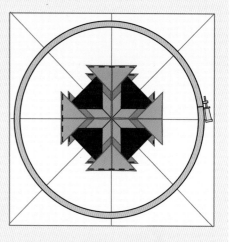

2 At the center of the large foundation fabric square, draw a square that is the size of the finished block. Mark diagonal, vertical, and horizontal lines meeting at the center. Mount the fabric in an embroidery hoop or frame. Using the marked lines as guidelines, pin four triangles with their points touching at the center, as shown above. Slip stitch the points to the foundation fabric and use the running stitch to hold the raw edges in place.

3 For the second row, stitch eight prepared triangles in two contrasting fabrics to the foundation fabric, overlapping the raw edges of the first row. Make sure that the triangles all radiate correctly from the center point. Slip stitch the triangles in place, as shown above. Do the same for the third row.

4 In the same manner, add four more triangles, one on each side.

Combining Hand and Machine Methods

You can attach the points of the triangles with slip stitches, and replace the running stitches along the raw edges with machine zigzag stitching.

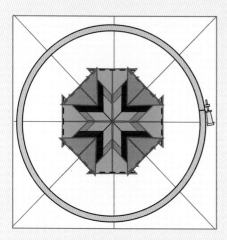

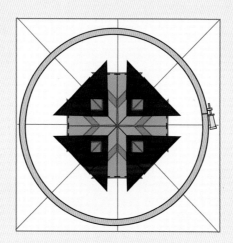

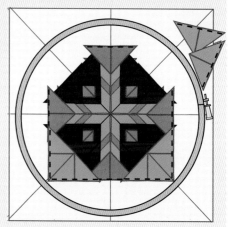

5 Add four more triangles, one at each corner, as shown above.

6 Add eight more triangles, two at each corner, radiating from the center, as shown above.

7 Continue adding triangles to fill the gaps. If you wish to form a square, add two triangles to each corner, as shown at bottom above. Finish with binding or insert the design into a framework of fabric sashing or border strips.

Cathedral Window Patchwork

Referred to in England as Mayflower patchwork, Cathedral Window patchwork is made up of squares that are folded, re-folded, and joined together with a contrasting-fabric insert that covers the seams. You can feature different print fabrics or isolated motifs, such as a flower, in the inserts, or replace the inserts with embroidery, lace, or beadwork.

Stitching by Hand

2 Fold the four corners of each square to meet in the center. Press and baste the corners in place, as shown above right.

3 Fold the four corners of each square again, bringing them to meet in the center, as shown at right.

1 Cut four 8½-in. (22-cm) solid-colored squares. Fold and press a ¼-in (6-mm) hem around all four sides of each square and thread-baste it in place, as shown above.

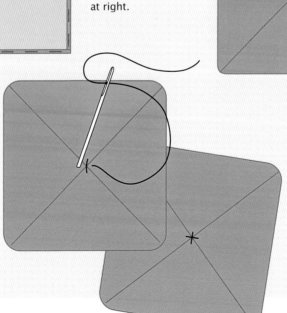

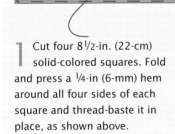

4 Press the squares and secure the corners through all the layers with slip stitches or a small cross-stitch, as shown at left.

88

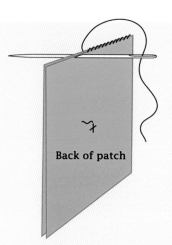

Back of patch

5 With right sides together, oversew two squares together along one edge, as shown at left, matching the corners. Repeat to make a second pair of squares.

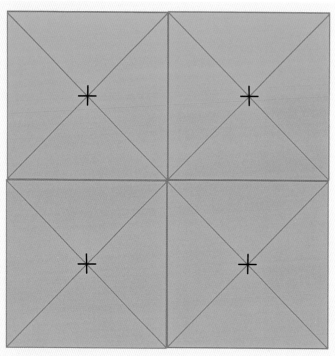

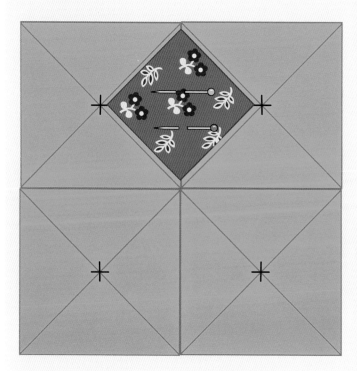

6 Oversew the two pairs of squares together, as shown above.

7 Cut four squares of contrasting-print fabric, the diagonals of which are only slightly smaller than the vertical seam to be covered. Position and pin an insert square on-point over a seam, as shown above.

8 Curl the folded edges of neighboring squares over the insert squares on all four sides, and slip stitch them in place with thread that matches the solid-colored fabric, as shown at right. Fill each area between the solid-colored squares with inserts. At the edges of the project, either include triangular inserts or leave those areas without inserts.

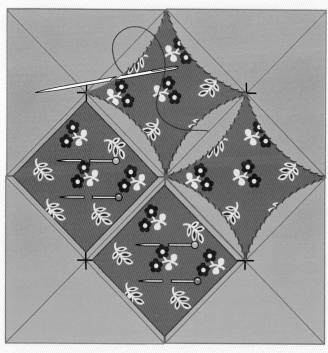

◇ Stitching by Machine

The machine method of Cathedral Window patchwork differs slightly from the hand method, but both create projects that need no binding, backing, or quilting.

1 For 4-in. (10-cm) finished squares, cut as many 8½-in. (22-cm) squares as your project requires. Fold each square in half with right sides together, and sew the short edges with a ¼-in. (6-mm) seam allowance, as shown below. Trim the corners, as shown.

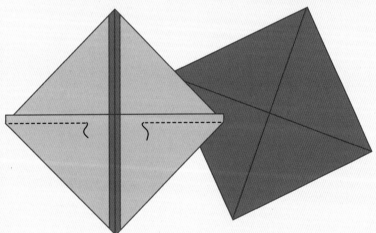

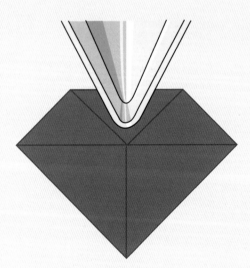

2 Separate the raw edges of each square, bringing the two seams together at the center. Pin and stitch the raw edges together, leaving a gap for turning the square right side out, as shown above. Trim the corners of the seam allowances. Turn the square right side out, pushing out the corners gently. Slip stitch the opening closed.

3 Press the square lightly, taking care not to stretch the edges. Fold the corners to the center, so they meet at the center point of the seams, and press creases, as shown above; these will serve as stitching lines for the next step.

4 Open up the pressed folds and position one square next to another with wrong sides together. Sew the two squares together along the creased lines, as shown at right. Fold the triangular flaps back to the center again, as shown at right. Continue adding more squares in the same manner to form a horizontal row in the size needed for your project. Repeat to make as many horizontal rows as necessary.

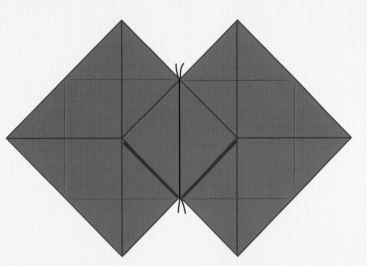

Consider Size

The Cathedral Window technique produces one of the heaviest types of quilts possible. Rather than using it to make a bed-size quilt, consider this method for much smaller items, like table runners or small wall hangings.

91

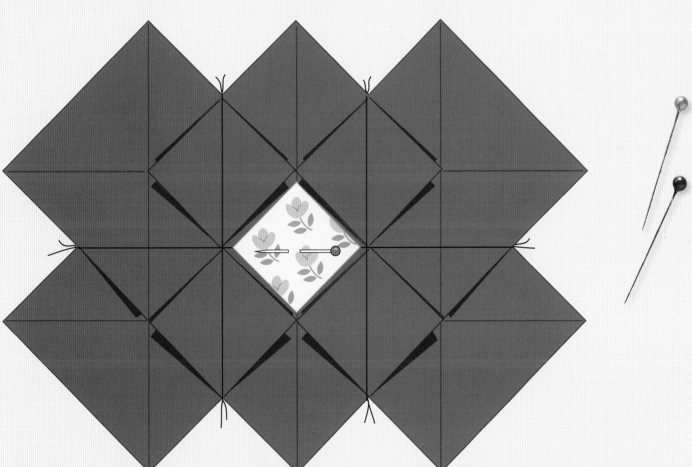

5 Stitch the horizontal rows together in the same manner as the squares. Fold the triangular flaps to the center again and stitch them in place by hand or machine, referring to Step 4 of Cathedral Window "Stitching by Hand" on page 88. Add contrasting inserts to cover the seams and finish as for the hand method. The corners are folded in, resulting in a square, straight edge. Stitch the folds in place with decorative machine-stitching, if desired.

Secret Garden

This technique is similar to Cathedral Window patchwork; however, the inserts do not cover the seams, but are revealed like four-petaled flower shapes inside each square.

Making Secret Garden Folded Patchwork

1 For 4-in. (10-cm) finished squares, cut 8½-in. (22-cm) solid-colored squares. Baste a ¼-in. (6-mm) hem around each square. Fold and press the squares as for Cathedral Window, as shown at left (*see page 88*). Repeat the folding process, this time without stitching the triangles to the center of each square.

2 Cut a square of contrasting fabric to fit between the pressed lines on the folded squares. Pin and baste it in place, as shown at left.

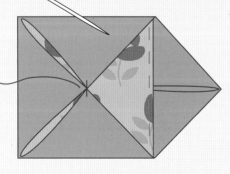

3 Fold the four triangular flaps down to meet in the center of the square and secure them with a single cross-stitch, as shown above.

4 Curl the eight folded edges up to reveal the contrasting insert fabric in each square and slip stitch them in place, using thread that matches the solid-colored fabric. To assemble the number of completed squares required for your project, oversew them together on the wrong side (*see page 89*).

Japanese Folded Patchwork

This type of folded patchwork incorporates batting into its construction, so it requires no further batting or backing. You will need both circular and square templates: the diagonal measurement of the square must be the same as the diameter of the circle, then add a ¼-in. (6-mm) seam allowance to the circle. Choose very thin batting and two contrasting cotton fabrics.

Hexagons

This technique can be adapted to make hexagons, which can be joined to form patterns like Grandmother's Flower Garden (see page 72). Simply use a hexagon-shaped template rather than a square one, and stitch six curved edges, rather than four.

Making Japanese Folded Patchwork

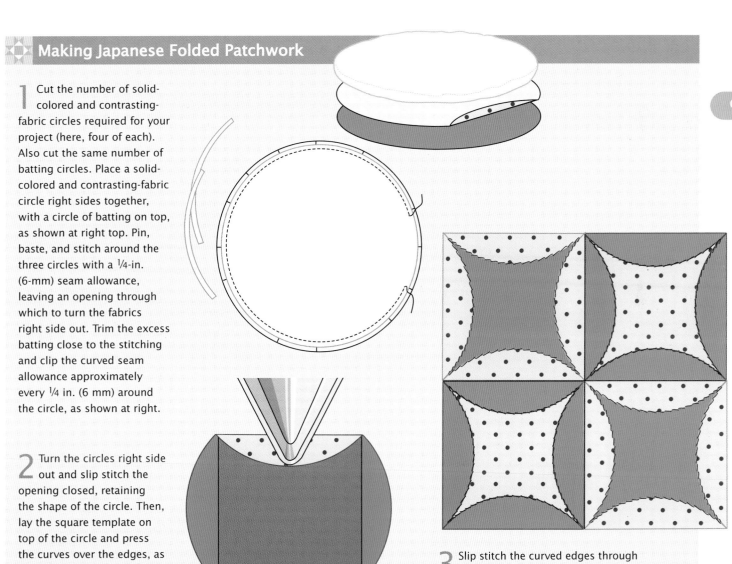

1 Cut the number of solid-colored and contrasting-fabric circles required for your project (here, four of each). Also cut the same number of batting circles. Place a solid-colored and contrasting-fabric circle right sides together, with a circle of batting on top, as shown at right top. Pin, baste, and stitch around the three circles with a ¼-in. (6-mm) seam allowance, leaving an opening through which to turn the fabrics right side out. Trim the excess batting close to the stitching and clip the curved seam allowance approximately every ¼ in. (6 mm) around the circle, as shown at right.

2 Turn the circles right side out and slip stitch the opening closed, retaining the shape of the circle. Then, lay the square template on top of the circle and press the curves over the edges, as shown at right. Then remove the template. Prepare half of the circles with the solid fabric facing up and the other half with the print fabric facing up.

3 Slip stitch the curved edges through all layers. To join the completed patches, oversew them together on the wrong side (see page 89).

93

Secret Garden Glen Quilt

The inspiration for this quilt is the Kelburn Country Park, a beautiful country estate located on the west coast of Scotland; it was designed to give the impression of a stream meandering through the landscape. It combines the two techniques of Secret Garden for the larger patches and Cathedral Window for the smaller ones (*see pages 88–9, 92*). The original quilt was made in a selection of coordinating butterfly-printed fabrics in different colorways, with inserts in a wide variety of colors and fabrics. You can use scraps or remnants to achieve a similar effect or devise your own version of a landscape. The total fabric yardage is given as a guide only.

Dimensions

Small cathedral window blocks are 2 in. (5 cm) square.

Big secret garden blocks are 4 in. (10 cm) square.

Finished quilt size is 43 in. (109 cm) square.

Cutting

Trace the templates onto fabric for the Secret Garden (8-in./20-cm square), Cathedral Window (4-in./10-cm square) and the inserts, 4-in. (10-cm) square for the Secret Garden, and 1-in. (2.5-cm) square for the Cathedral Window (*see page 238*) or use a rotary cutter and mat to cut them from the fabrics.

Equipment and Materials

- Selection of co-ordinating butterfly printed fabrics for the Secret Garden patches, the Cathedral Window inlays, borders and bindings: 3¼ yd. (3 m) total
- Scraps of blue, cream, pink, light green, medium blue, yellow, orange silk and dark brown/green silk.
- Selection of fabrics for sky and water Cathedral Window patches: 2¼ yd. (206 cm) total
- Selection of fabrics for flower Cathedral Window patches: 3½ yd. (320 cm) total
- Selection of fabrics for background Cathedral Window patches: 2¼ yd. (206 cm) total
- Backing fabric: 47 in. (119 cm) square (or 4½ yd./4 m of 54 in./137 cm fabric for a seamless backing)
- Batting: 6 x 44 in. (15 x 112 cm) for the borders
- Size 11 seed beads in colors to match the fabrics, approx. 400
- Size 10 quilting needle
- Basic patchwork equipment and iron

For the Secret Garden Blocks and Inlays

- Blue/cream butterfly fabric, cut nine 8½-in. (22-cm) squares
- Blue silk, cut four 4-in. (10-cm) squares
- Cream silk, cut five 4-in. (10-cm) squares
- Pink/cream butterfly fabric, cut four 8½-in. (22-cm) squares
- Pink silk, cut four 4-in. (10-cm) squares
- Light green silk, cut one 4-in. (10-cm) square
- Black/green butterfly fabric, cut twelve 8½-in. (22-cm) square

- Green/brown silk, cut twelve 4-in. (10-cm) squares
- Orange/beige/blue butterfly fabric, cut nine 8½-in. (22-cm) squares
- Yellow silk, cut five 4-in. (10-cm) squares
- Orange silk, cut four 4-in. (10-cm) squares
- Dark blue butterfly fabric, cut three 8½-in. (22-cm) squares
- Medium blue silk, cut three 4-in. (10-cm) squares

For the Secret Garden Borders and Bindings

Blue/cream butterfly fabric, cut four strips 1½ in. (4 cm) wide, across width of fabric
Black/green/brown butterfly fabric, cut four strips 1½ in. (4 cm) wide, across width of fabric

For the Cathedral Window Blocks and Inlays

- Cream sky fabrics, cut sixteen 4½-in. (11.5-cm) squares
- Blue sky fabrics, cut thirty-three 4½-in. (11.5-cm) squares
- Dark blue sky fabrics, cut twenty-one 44½-in. (11.5-cm) squares
- Pink flower fabrics, cut twelve 4½-in. (11.5-cm) squares
- Purple flower fabrics, cut twenty-one 4½-in. (11.5-cm) squares
- Yellow flower fabrics, cut eleven 4½-in. (11.5-cm) squares
- Orange flower fabrics, cut nine 4½-in. (11.5-cm) squares
- Dark brown flower fabrics, cut ten 4½-in. (11.5-cm) squares
- Multiflower fabric, cut fourteen 4½-in. (11.5-cm) squares
- Green ground fabrics, cut sixty-six 4½-in. (11.5-cm) squares
- Brown ground fabrics, cut thirty-six 4½-in. (11.5-cm) squares

- Blue/cream butterfly fabric, cut sixty-nine 1-in. (2.5-cm) squares
- Pink/cream butterfly fabric, cut fifty-one 1-in. (2.5-cm) squares
- Dark blue butterfly fabric, cut twenty-five 1-in. (2.5-cm) squares
- Orange/blue/beige butterfly fabric, cut seventy-one 1-in. (2.5-cm) squares
- Black/green/brown butterfly fabric, cut one hundred and thirty 1-in. (2.5-cm) squares

Making and Joining the Patches

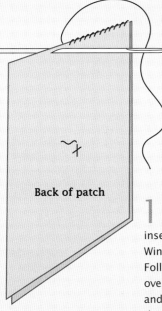

Back of patch

1 Make 37 large Secret Garden patches including their inserts and 252 small Cathedral Window patches without inserts. Following the chart on page 96, oversew the patches together and then add the inlays over the Cathedral Window patches.

2 Add the inserts over the Cathedral Window seams, making graduated transitions in color and fabric to form the design. Leave the outermost patches without inserts.

Adding the Top and Bottom Borders

1 Cut two strips of fabric and two of batting for the top and bottom borders, each 1½ x 40½ in. (4 x 103 cm).

2 Pin, baste, and stitch a strip of batting to each strip of fabric, along the length and the two short ends, using a ¼-in. (6-mm) seam allowance. Trim the excess batting close to the seam, as shown at right.

3 Press the seam allowances over the batting and oversew the borders along the folded edge to the top and bottom of the quilt.

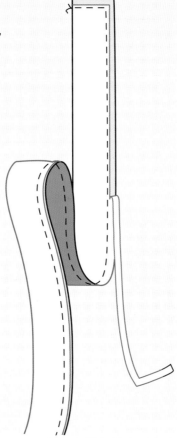

Adding the Side Borders

Note: In the original quilt the side borders have been pieced to blend with the fabrics of the quilt, but you can use solid fabrics if you prefer.

1 Cut two strips of fabric (or pieced fabric) and two of batting for the side borders, each 1½ x 43 in. (4 x 109 cm).

2 Complete the side borders in the same way as the top and bottom borders, and stitch them to the sides of the quilt.

Finishing

1 Lay the quilt on the backing fabric wrong sides together, and pin the layers together securely. Tie beads on all the corners of the Cathedral Window patches. Thread a needle with a thread matching the bead color. Coming up from the back at the corner of the Cathedral Window, pick up a bead and go back down again in the same place as you came up. Double-knot the thread at the back. Cut off the thread to a length of approximately 1 in. (2.5 cm).

2 Bind the edges of the quilt (*see page 230*).

Secret Garden Glen Chart

Use this chart as a guide to block placements for the Secret Garden Glen quilt.

Use the Secret Garden Glen quilt as a durable, yet decorative,
table topper, as shown here, or as a wall hanging in
another room in your home.

Applied Patchwork

THERE ARE SEVERAL METHODS OF PATCHWORK THAT INVOLVE PREVIOUSLY PREPARED PATCHES APPLIED TO A FOUNDATION OR BACKGROUND FABRIC TO FORM A VARIETY OF DIFFERENT DESIGNS.

For crazy patchwork, the foundation fabric is completely covered, while for other patterns, such as Clamshells and Dresden Plates, the background fabric remains visible and should be chosen to complement the patchwork fabrics. Although these applied patchwork techniques are usually done by hand, they can also be adapted for machine stitching to create different effects, especially with the array of decorative stitches now available on today's sewing machines.

Crazy Patchwork

Fabrics in different weights and fiber contents, such as velvets, corduroy, brocade, or satin, are all suitable for crazy patchwork. However, if your finished project will be laundered, it is best to use fabrics of a similar type.

Using a Fabric Foundation

Cut a piece of foundation fabric in the shape and size of your finished project, adding at least a 1-in. (2.5-cm) margin all the way around. Arrange randomly shaped fabric patches on the foundation with right sides up, overlapping the raw edges of each piece slightly. When you are happy with your arrangement, pin the patches in place so that you can make any final adjustments to the design before basting. Then baste the patches in place, so that they remain firmly in place while you are stitching.

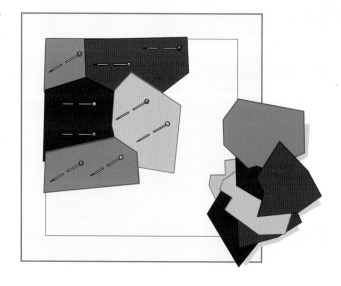

Using Iron-on Interfacing as a Foundation

Cut a piece of iron-on interfacing in the size and shape of your finished project, adding at least a 1-in. (2.5-cm) margin all the way around. Arrange the patches as shown at right. Set an iron to a temperature suitable for the fabrics you are using and press them in place. Turn your work over and press it again, to adhere the pieces firmly to the interfacing.

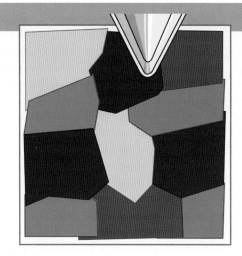

99

 ## Stitching the Patches

Choose embroidery threads that blend or contrast with the fabrics in your quilt, and work embroidery stitches through all layers by hand or machine so that the patches are anchored securely to the foundation. Crazy patchwork is not usually quilted, since it is so thick with seams. You can add a backing and tie the layers together, if you wish.

Feather Stitch

Bring the needle out a short distance from the raw edge of the patch to your left and insert it into the patch on the right. Holding the thread toward you, bring the needle up through the loop of thread, slightly below and to the right of the edge of the left-hand patch. Pull the thread all the way through. Make another feather stitch below and to the left, then again to the right. Repeat as desired between patches.

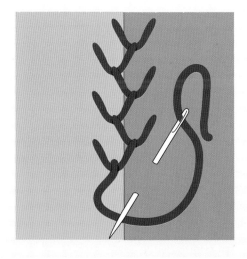

Herringbone Stitch

The herringbone stitch is worked from left to right. Bring the needle up through the lower of the two fabrics and take a diagonal stitch into the upper fabric. Bring the needle out a short distance to the left of the insertion point and take a diagonal stitch into the lowermost fabric. Repeat as desired between patches.

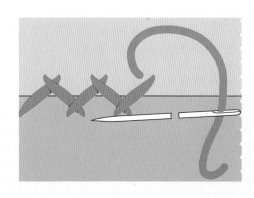

Other Embroidery Stitches

Cretan stitch, double feather or closed feather stitch, open chain, buttonhole, or cross-stitch can all be used to add variety to crazy patchwork. If you prefer machine embroidery, try satin, open zigzag, or other decorative stitches to cover the raw edges of the patches.

Clamshells

Also known as the Fish-scale pattern, Clamshell patchwork is suitable for decorating pillows, bags, and table linens. Clamshells are usually appliquéd to a background fabric, but you can also use them to cover a fabric foundation.

Try both the freezer-paper method and the iron-on interfacing method on page 99 to see which you prefer. Both methods produce smooth, accurate curves, although interfacing tends to stiffen the patches slightly.

◆ Freezer-Paper Method

Follow these steps to prepare Clamshell patches with freezer paper.

1 Use the full-size template on page 239 to mark as many Clamshell patches as needed for your project onto freezer paper.

3 Clip the seam allowance along the curved edge of each patch, as shown at right, stopping just short of the template. Fold the curved seam allowance over the freezer paper and press it in place as shown above right, creating a smoothly curved top edge on each patch.

Commercial Templates

You can also make Clamshell patches using purchased acrylic or plastic templates. Visit your local quilt shop and check out the various sizes and options available.

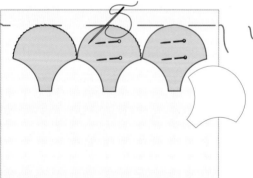

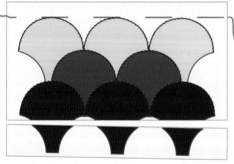

2 Press the templates onto the wrong side of the fabric with the shiny side facing down, making sure that the straight grain of the fabric runs vertically through the center of each patch. Allow 1/2 in. (12 mm) around each template. Cut out the Clamshell patches with a 1/4-in. (6-mm) seam allowance.

4 Mark a horizontal line on the background fabric with a water-erasable pen, basting stitches, or a piece of chalk. Pin a row of Clamshell patches in place along this line with the right sides up and the sides touching, as shown above. Blind stitch (see page 159) the Clamshell patches to the background fabric along the top, curved edges. Remove the freezer-paper templates.

5 Add additional rows of Clamshell patches as desired, overlapping the curved edges and keeping the alignment of each row correct. Half-clamshell patches can be added at the end of each row, or the outer sides can be cut off and bound. The shapes in the final row can be turned under and stitched in place or cut off, as shown above, and bound with the edges of the quilt.

Iron-On Interfacing Method

Press iron-on interfacing to the reverse side of the Clamshell patches, making sure that the interfacing lies just inside the ¼-in. (6-mm) seam allowances. Clip and fold the top seam allowances over the edges of the interfacing and thread-baste them in place with tiny stitches (for a neat edge and to hold the curve in place), ending with a knot on the right side. Continue as for the freezer-paper method on page 100, removing the basting stitches after you finish appliquéing the Clamshell patches to the background fabric.

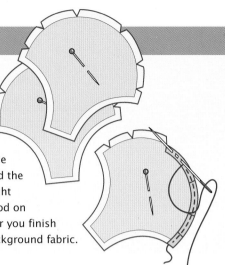

Machine Stitching Option

If you prefer machine stitching along the curved edges of the Clamshell patches, experiment with various effects. Try straight and zigzag stitching, and investigate the decorative stitching capabilities of your sewing machine.

 ## Clamshell Variations

Try some of these variations to explore the versatility of Clamshell patchwork.

Diagonal Rows

Arrange the colors of the Clamshell patches on the background fabric so that they form diagonal rows, or group two pairs of patches together in adjacent rows to form diamond-shaped areas of color, as shown below. Appliqué all adjacent patches together. Press.

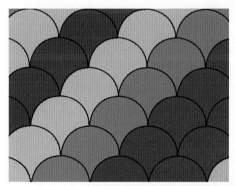

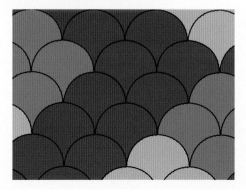

Mosaic

For the Mosaic pattern, place two Clamshell patches with their short, straight edges together, and another pair at right angles to the first pair, filling in the gaps with the curved edges of adjacent patches, as shown at right. Appliqué all adjacent patches together. Press.

Double Axehead

Take the Mosaic variation idea one step further, using templates that are shaped like an apple core, rather than actual Clamshell templates. Alternate them vertically and horizontally in each row to create the Double Axehead pattern, as shown at right. Appliqué all consecutive patches together. Press.

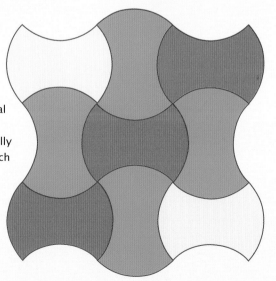

Dresden Plates and Fans

Dresden Plates and Fans are suitable for quilts, throws, and wall hangings. A single Dresden Plate motif is also ideal for round pillows, place mats, or basket covers. Based on segments of a circle, the outer edges of both types of designs can be curved, scalloped, or pointed, and they usually feature a small circle at the center to cover the narrow ends of the segments. You can stitch both Dresden Plates and Fans by hand or machine, or combine the two techniques.

◆ Iron-On Interfacing Method

You can prepare the segments of a Dresden Plate or Fan block using either the freezer-paper method (*see page 100*) or the iron-on interfacing method (*see page 101*). There are also commercial templates available, or you can make your own templates by using a protractor to work out the divisions of the circle. Whichever preparation method you prefer, follow these steps to make a Dresden Plate block. For a Fan block, follow the same steps, using fewer segments, and add a quarter-circle instead of a circle to the narrow ends of the segments.

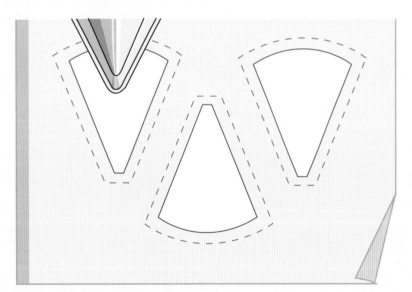

1 Using templates (*see page 239*), mark as many segments and center circles as you need on the dull side of a piece of iron-on interfacing. (Here, you will need to mark four light segments, four dark segments, and one circle.) Cut the shapes out on the marked lines. Press the interfacing shapes shiny side down onto the wrong side of your fabric, making sure that the straight grain of the fabric runs vertically through the center of each patch. Allow at least 1/2 in. (12 mm) around each patch for adding a 1/4-in. (6-mm) seam allowance, as shown above.

2 Cut out the segments and circle with a 1/4-in. (6-mm) seam allowance around each one. Clip the seam allowance around the top, curved edge of each segment, stopping just short of the interfacing. Prepare the circle in the same manner, as shown at right.

3 With right sides facing, sew two segments together along the outer edge of the interfacing, starting 1/4 in. (6 mm) from the edge of the fabric at the top edge, and ending at the narrow edge of the quarter-circle, as shown below.

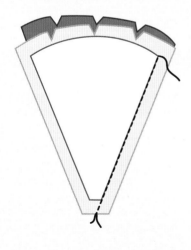

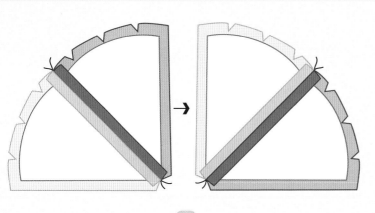

4 Join the remaining segments in pairs to create three more quarter-circles, pressing the seam allowances open as you go. Join two pairs to create a half-circle, as shown at right above. Repeat. Join the half-circles to create the Dresden Plate shape. Check the accuracy of your seam allowances at each stage.

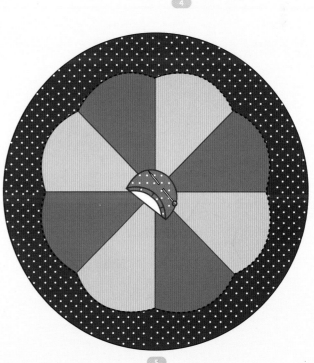

5 Fold the seam allowance along the top of the curved edges of the segments to the wrong side, using the interfacing to produce smooth curves. Thread-baste the seam allowances in place, starting with a knot on the right side. Pin, baste, and stitch the outer edges of the segments to the background fabric, and pin and stitch the prepared circle in the center, as shown at right.

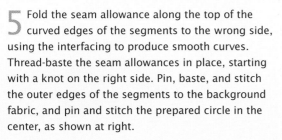

Freezer-Paper Method

If you use the freezer paper method (*see page 100*) to prepare the segments and circles or quarter-circles for a Dresden Plate or Fan block, press the freezer-paper shapes onto the wrong side of your fabric. Stitch the segments together and press the seam allowances over the top edges of the freezer paper shapes. Remove the freezer paper before stitching the shapes onto the background fabric.

Dresden Plate Variations

Besides featuring different numbers of segments in a Dresden Plate block, it is possible to vary the edges by including symmetrical or asymmetrical points, or varying the height of the curves. These can be combined to produce a wide range of effects, as shown here.

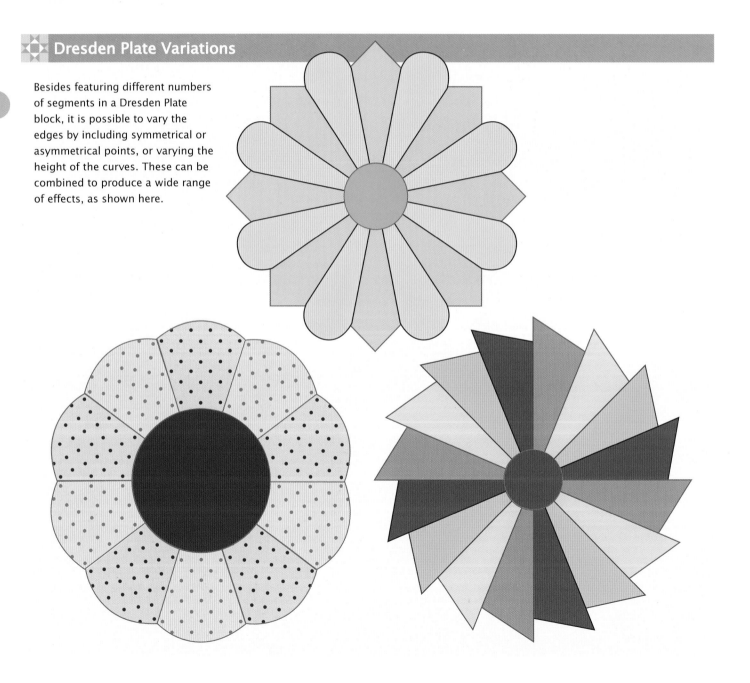

Fan Pattern Variations

The Fan pattern outline can be used in similar ways as the Dresden Plate pattern, and the segments can be stitched either with or without the small quarter-circle at the apex. Because the basic Fan design consists of a quarter-circle stitched on a background square, you can arrange Fan blocks in an infinite number of ways, including the Mohawk Trail, Falling Trees, and other interesting configurations shown here.

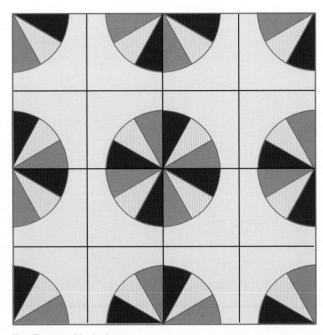

Fan Pattern Variation

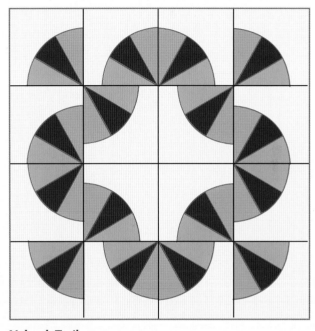

Mohawk Trail

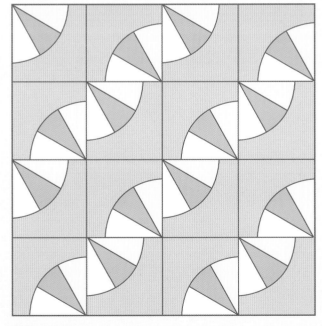

Falling Trees

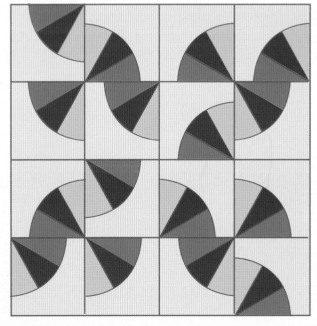

Fan Pattern Variation

Crazy Patchwork Pillow

Crazy patchwork is one of the most exciting forms of patchwork—you never know what you're going to get in the end! There are no rules here—the goal is to do whatever you feel looks best. You can combine any type of fabric with lace, trim scraps, beads, charms, or hand embroidery. Here we have used cotton fabric scraps and "strings" (the skinny strips of fabric that are left over from cutting out larger pieces). This crazy patchwork features rows of decorative herringbone stitch worked by hand in black thread over the major seams. The pieces are shown on the template; the scraps are shown in Step 1.

Dimensions
Finished pillow size is approximately 20 in. (50 cm) square.

Equipment and Materials
- Large scraps of colorful fabrics
- Assorted strips of fabrics
- Solid fabric for pillow backs: ½ yd. (45 cm)
- Black embroidery floss
- Freezer paper
- Scissors for fabric
- Pencil
- Quilter's chalk pencil
- Ruler
- Rotary cutter (if desired)
- Basic sewing supplies and iron
- Pillow form: 20 in. (50 cm) square

Piecing the Center Rectangle

The center rectangle is formed from shaped pieces 1, 2, 3, and 4, which are cut from a larger piece made from big, random scraps stitched together. The seams may be straight or curved, depending on the scraps you have, or a combination of both straight and curved seams.

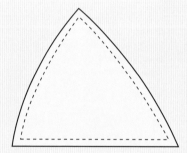

1 Trace the pillow template (the center rectangle) full size on freezer paper (*see page 71*). Cut out pieces 1, 2, 3, and 4 on the drawn lines. Retrace each piece on another piece of freezer paper, adding a ½-in. (12-mm) seam allowance to each edge, as shown at left.

2 Stitch together large scraps (about hand size), with right sides together, taking a ¼-in. (6-mm) seam allowance, clipping the seam allowances where necessary, so that curved edges lie flat. You can make one large piece to accommodate the entire center rectangle or smaller ones to fit each pattern section separately.

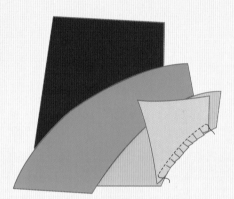

Fabric Choices
For this project, we have pieced-together scraps of fabric in several colors. Your own design will be different, because this style of patchwork depends on the fabric scraps that you have at your disposal. However, see the pattern template on page 239 for basic pattern measurements.

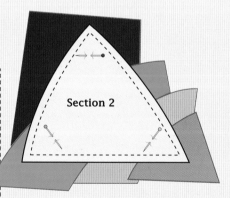

Section 2

3 Pin pattern sections 1 through 4 to the pieced fabrics and cut each one out, as shown above right. Use the picture of the pillow on page 109 as a piecing guide.

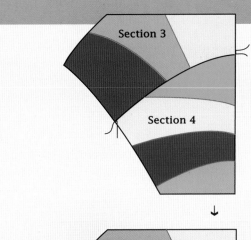

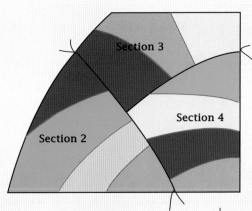

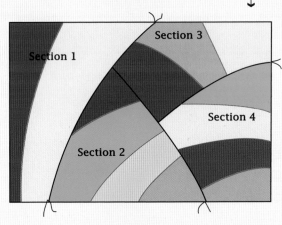

4 Put the pieces together in the following sequence. Join sections 3 and 4 first, then join them to section 2, then join them to section 1, as shown above.

5 Press all the seam allowances flat and trim the center rectangle to 13 x 20 in. (33 x 50 cm).

Piecing the Upper and Lower Bands

The upper and lower bands are cut from a wider strip of fabric made up of random fabric strings, using freezer paper as a foundation.

1 Cut two strips of freezer paper, each 10 in. (25 cm) wide and 22 in. (56 cm) long, for the upper and lower band foundations. Place two strips of fabric, right sides together, onto one foundation, as shown. Machine-stitch through the fabric and the paper, taking a ¼-in. (6-mm) seam allowance. Open out the fabric and finger-press the seam flat.

2 Continue to add strips of fabric to the paper foundation in the same way, using either a random method or a specific sequence of colors, until you cover the other end of the foundation. Repeat with the second foundation.

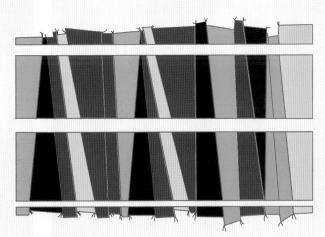

3 Trim the upper and lower bands to 4½ x 20 in. (11.5 x 50 cm), as shown at left. You may now remove the freezer paper.

107

Assembling the Pillow Front

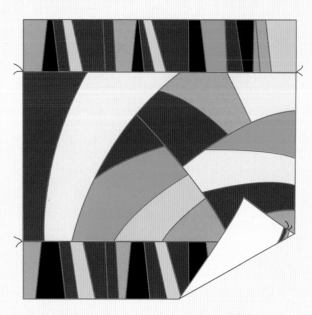

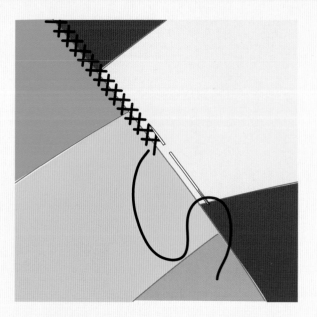

1 Pin the upper and lower bands to the center rectangle, with right sides together. Machine-stitch, taking a ½-in. (12-mm) seam allowance. Press the seams open.

2 Thread a needle with three strands of black embroidery floss and, from the right side, begin the decorative herringbone stitch over the seam between the two sections. Work this stitch as shown above, from left to right, taking care to make the stitches even.

Assembling the Pillow

1 For the pillow backs, first cut two 15- x 20-in. (38- x 50-cm) rectangles from solid fabric. Fold and stitch a double ¼-in. (6-mm) hem along one long raw edge of each piece. Press.

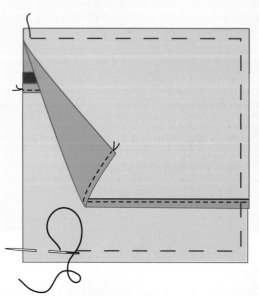

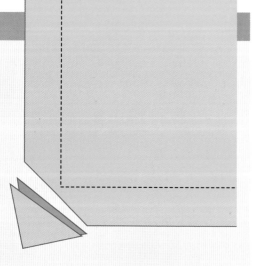

2 Place the pillow backs onto the pillow front with right sides together, matching the raw edges around the outside and overlapping the hemmed edges at the center. Pin and baste around the outer edge, then machine-stitch, taking a ½-in. (12-mm) seam allowance.

3 Trim diagonally across the seam allowance at each corner of the pillow and turn it to the right side. Press. Insert a 20-in. (50-cm)-square pillow form.

108

Combine various scraps of fabric in your
favorite colors to make a crazy-patch pillow
that adds a beautiful accent to any room.

Machine Quilting

ALTHOUGH HAND QUILTING IS THE TRADITIONAL WAY OF SECURING THE LAYERS OF A PATCHWORK QUILT
TOGETHER, AND IS VALUED BY MANY PEOPLE FOR ITS AESTHETIC BEAUTY, A SEWING MACHINE ACCELERATES
THE QUILTING PROCESS WITHOUT COMPROMISING THE BEAUTY OF THE FINISHED PIECE.

For machine quilting, it is best to use a fairly thin batting and work on small projects before embarking on a major piece of work. Get to know your sewing machine thoroughly and purchase a few accessories, such as an even-feed foot, which rides over layers of fabric with ease. A quilting guide will enable you to work rows of parallel stitching easily, and a darning foot will be needed for free-motion quilting. For couching, you will need a braiding or embroidery foot, through which you thread a thick yarn to be held in place with zigzag stitching.

Preparation for Machine Quilting

As for hand quilting, careful preparation for machine quilting will result in a lovely finished quilt, so take care with marking fabrics, basting, and layering to ensure that the article will retain its shape during the machine-quilting process. Set a long stitch length and the correct tension on your machine by moving the tension disk (or dial) to ensure that the upper and lower threads are similarly tensioned.

This Oh, My Stars! quilt in fresh
reds and greens makes a lovely
bed topper or wall hanging to
grace any room.

Starting and Finishing Machine Quilting

To start or finish a line of stitching in the center of the work, do not work reverse stitches in the normal way, but leave long ends of thread. Later, thread each one singly onto a needle and finish by winding the thread around the needle two or three times to create a French knot. Insert the needle into the batting layer only and pass the knot through. Bring the needle out of the fabric approximately ½ inch (12 mm) and clip the thread.

◆ Quilting Patchwork or Appliqué

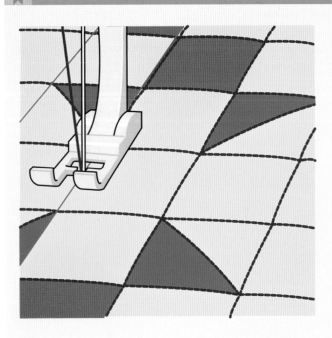

For Better Support

For a large-scale project such as a quilt, place a table to the left of your machine. Roll up the left-hand side of your work and secure the rolled quilt with bicycle clips while stitching the right-hand area. Repeat the process in reverse for the left side of the quilt.

1 For in-the-ditch quilting (*see page 137*), follow the seam lines, making sure that the needle pierces the fabric as closely as possible to the patchwork or appliqué seam. If you prefer to work outline or echo quilting (*see page 137*), use the width of the machine foot as a guide or alter the needle position as desired.

Purchasing Presser Feet

If your sewing machine did not come with suitable presser feet or attachments for machine quilting, check your local machine dealership to purchase the ones you need.

◆ Stitching a Grid

1 Attach an even-feed foot and quilting guide to your machine. Using a ruler, mark a line on the top fabric from top to bottom through the center. Starting at the center top, work a row of stitches along the marked line toward the bottom edge.

2 Align the bar of the quilting guide with the stitched line and work a second row of stitches to the right of the first, also from top to bottom. Repeat lines of stitching until you reach the right edge.

3 Keeping the work the same way around, insert the quilting guide to the right of the presser foot and, still stitching from top to bottom, work rows of stitching to the left edge.

4 Turn the work around and repeat the process with rows of stitching at right angles to the first set of rows.

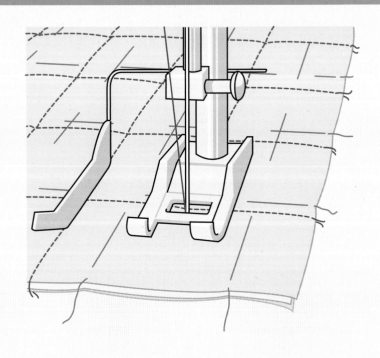

Free-Motion Quilting

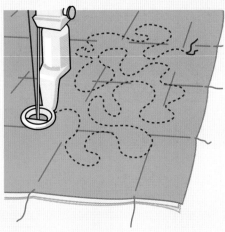

1 Attach a darning foot and disengage the feed dogs on your machine. This will enable the fabric to be moved in any direction. Set the stitch length and width to 0.

2 Lower the presser bar and bring both threads to the surface. Insert the needle and start stitching, moving the fabric as if you are "drawing" meandering curves with the needle.

3 To work the "vermicelli" stitch, as shown at right, work a series of smaller loops and curves to completely cover the surface of the area to be quilted. This will throw the unstitched areas into relief.

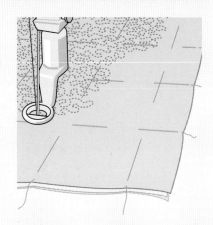

Meander quilting

Vermicelli stitch

113

 ## Couching

1 Attach a braiding or embroidery foot and thread an embroidery yarn through its hole. As you work narrow zigzag stitches, they will automatically couch the embroidery yarn in place.

2 Finish by taking both threads to the back of the piece and work them into the batting layer.

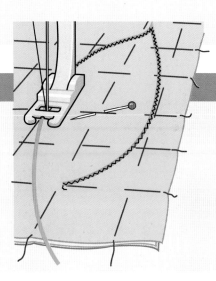

 ## Trace-and-Tack Quilting

1 This is similar to the hand method of transferring a quilting design (*see page 127*), so transfer the design to tracing paper.

2 Thread-baste the quilt layers in a grid pattern. Then pin the paper design on top of the prepared fabrics through all layers.

3 Machine-stitch through all layers, following the lines marked on the paper. When you have finished, carefully tear away the paper to reveal the quilted lines.

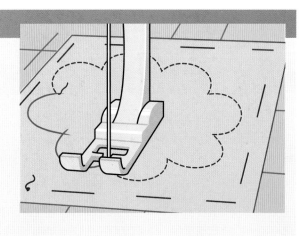

Oh, My Stars! Quilt

Reds and greens always make a lovely combination, because they are directly opposite each other on the color wheel. This quilt, made by Cathy Kucenski, features Manor House fabrics by Gail Kessler for Andover Fabrics (*see Resources, page 251*) in a lush, Edwardian setting, shown on page 111.

Equipment and Materials

- Red tone-on-tone print fabric: 1 yd. (91.5 cm)
- Background dot fabric: ⅔ yd. (61 cm)
- Large-scale floral print: 1½ yd. (137 cm)
- Green fabric: 1⅓ yd. (120.5 cm)
- Fabric for quilt backing: 1⅓ yd. (120.5 cm)
- Batting: 44 in. (112 cm) square
- Sewing needle
- White cotton thread for basting

Dimensions

Blocks are approximately 9½ in. (24 cm) square.

Finished quilt is approximately 42½ in. (108 cm) square.

Piecing the Star Blocks

Follow these cutting and piecing steps to make each section of the Star blocks.

For the Star-Point Units

1 From the floral print, cut eighteen 4¾-in. (12-cm) squares.

2 From the red fabric, cut nine 4¾-in. (12-cm) squares.

3 From the dot fabric, cut nine 4¾-in. (12-cm) squares.

For the Corner Units

1 From the red fabric, cut two 2¼- x 44-in. (5.5- x 112-cm) strips and two 1¾- x 44-in. (4.5- x 112-cm) strips.

2 From the dot fabric, cut two 1¾- x 44-in. (4.5- x 112-cm) strips and two 2¼- x 44-in. (5.5- x 112-cm) strips.

Piecing the Star-Point Units

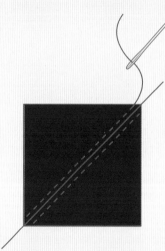
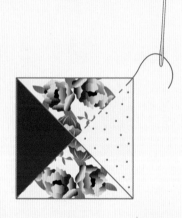

1 Place nine 4¾-in. (12-cm) red squares on top of nine 4¾-in. (12-cm) floral print squares, with right sides together. Mark a diagonal line from corner to corner on each of the red squares. Sew a seam ¼ in. (6 mm) on each side of the marked line, as shown above. Cut each pair of squares apart on the marked diagonal line. Press the seam toward the floral-print fabric in each half-square triangle unit.

2 Repeat Step 1 with nine 4¾-in. (12-cm) dot squares and the remaining nine floral-print squares. Sew one half-square triangle unit from Step 1 to one half-square triangle unit from Step 2, as shown above. Repeat with the remaining half-square triangle units for a total of 36 star-point squares. Press.

Assembling the Star Blocks

1 Sew the 2¼- x 44-in. (5.5- x 112-cm) red fabric strips to the 1¾- x 44-in. (4.5- x 112-cm) dot fabric strips. Press the seam allowances toward the red strips. From these two strip sets, cut a total of 36 segments, each 2¼ in. (5.5 cm) wide, as shown above.

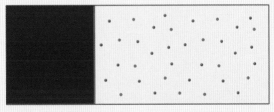

2 Sew the 1¾- x 44-in. (4.5- x 112-cm) red fabric strips to the 2¼- x 44-in. (5.5- x 112-cm) dot fabric strips. Press the seam allowances toward the red strips. From these two strip sets, cut a total of 36 segments, each 1¾ in. (4.5 cm) wide, as shown above.

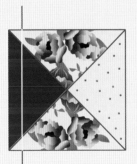

3 Before assembling the quilt top, you will need to trim these 36 star-point square units to 3½- x 4-in. (8- x 10-cm) units, as shown above, so that they will line up with the four-patch corner units.

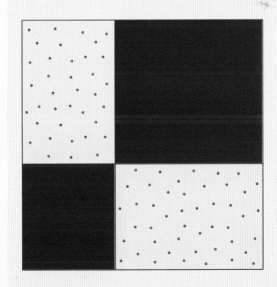

3 Sew a Step 1 unit to a Step 2 unit, as shown at left, to make a corner unit. Repeat with the remaining Step 1 and Step 2 units, for a total of 36 corner units. Press. Each corner unit should measure 3 in. (7.5 cm) square.

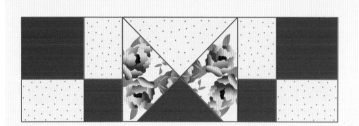

1 Lay out the pieces for each Star block in rows, as shown in
Steps 1, 2, and 3, and sew the rows together in the order
shown. *Note: Trim the star-point units to line up with the
corner units, as shown on page 115.* Make sure that the corner
units and the star-point units are all facing the correct direction
as you sew each row together. For the top row of the block,
sew together two corner units and one star-point unit, as
shown above. Press.

2 For the middle row, sew together two star-point
units and a center square, as shown above. Press.

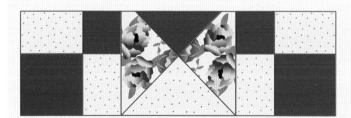

3 For the bottom row, sew together two corner units
and one star-point unit, as shown above. Press.

4 Repeat steps 1 through 3 to make
the remaining nine Star blocks. Press
the completed Star blocks.

From the green sashing fabric, cut six 2- x 9½-in. (5- x 23-cm) strips, and two 2- x 32-in. (5- x 81-cm) strips.

Adding the Sashing Strips to the Quilt Center

1 Sew two 2- x 9½-in. (5- x 23-cm) green fabric strips between three Star blocks, as shown above. Press the seam allowances toward the sashing strips. Repeat to make two more of these rows.

2 Referring to the quilt diagram at right, sew the two 2- x 32-in. (5- x 81-cm) green sashing strips horizontally between the three rows of blocks. Press the seam allowances toward the sashing strips.

117

For the First Border

From the green fabric, cut four 2- x 36-in. (5- x 95-cm) strips.

Adding the First Border

1 Find the midpoint of a 2- x 36-in. (5- x 95-cm) green sashing strip and pin it to the midpoint on one side of the quilt. Pin the rest of the sashing strip to the edge of the quilt center. There will be extra fabric at the ends of the border to allow for mitering the corner seams.

2 Beginning and ending 1/4 in. (6 mm) from the edge of the quilt center, sew the sashing strip to the quilt center, using a 1/4-in. (6-mm) seam allowance. Referring to the quilt diagram on page 117, repeat to add the first border strips to the remaining three edges of the quilt center. Press the seam allowances toward the first border.

3 Miter the corner seams of the first border, referring to page 231. Trim and press the corner seam allowances open.

Adding the Second Border

Sew each of the four 4 1/2-in. (11.5-cm) second-border strips to the edges of the quilt center in the same manner as for the first border, referring to the quilt diagram on page 117. Press the seam allowances toward the second border.

For the Backing and Binding

1 From the backing fabric, cut a 44- x 44-in. (112- x 112-cm) square. Press.

2 From the green binding fabric, cut five 2 1/2- x 44-in. (6- x 112-cm) strips.

Finishing

1 Lay the quilt backing on a flat surface, with the wrong side facing up.

2 Place the 44-in. (112-cm) batting square on top of the quilt backing, smoothing out any wrinkles.

3 Position the quilt top over the batting, smoothing out any wrinkles. Thread-baste the three layers of the quilt sandwich together by hand, using a sewing needle and the white cotton thread.

4 Quilt by machine, as desired.

5 Sew the short ends of the binding strips together with diagonal seams. Trim the seam allowances to 1/4 in. (6 mm) and press them open. Fold the binding in half lengthwise, and press. Sew the binding to the edges of the quilt, mitering the corners, referring to page 231.

6 Add a label and display sleeve to the back of the quilt, if desired.

The symmetry of the star blocks in this quilt gives it a very planned, structured appearance. The red and green color complements are used in different proportions, which enhances the quilt's strong visual appeal.

Hand Quilting

QUILTING PRODUCES A DECORATIVE AND TEXTURAL EFFECT THAT CAN BE USED EITHER ON PLAIN FABRIC OR TO EMBELLISH PATCHWORK AND APPLIQUÉ. ALTHOUGH SLOWER THAN MACHINE QUILTING, IT IS SATISFYING AND ENJOYABLE TO WORK.

Traditional quilting designs vary from simple outlines that hold the layers of a quilt sandwich together to elaborate patterns that take many hours to stitch. Plain quilts, known as wholecloth quilts, rely on intricate hand quilting to create interest and beauty. In addition to traditional hand quilting, trapunto and Italian quilting can add variety and stretch your creativity.

Successful hand quilting relies on careful preparation, including transferring the design to the fabric, basting the layers of the quilt sandwich together, and using a hoop or frame to hold the quilt sandwich. It is also essential to gather the quilting needles you like best (*see page 14*) and find a thimble that fits your finger comfortably before you take your first stitch.

The fundamentals of hand quilting remain much as they were four hundred years ago.

Preparation

Hand quilting relies for its effect on the play of light on the surface of the quilt, so pale and shiny fabrics will reflect the light more than dark, dull colors.

Backing fabrics should be a similar weight and fiber content as the top fabric. Light- or medium-weight calico and plain or printed cottons are all suitable.

Choose a thread with a fiber content similar to that of the fabric—cotton with cotton and silk with silk. For greater strength and more impact, cotton quilting thread is the obvious choice. For decorative effects, you may choose to use specialty threads containing metallic or rayon fibers.

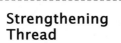

Strengthening Thread

To strengthen a fine cotton, silk, or poly/cotton thread, draw it through a block of natural beeswax prior to stitching.

 ## Preparing the Quilt Sandwich

If the finished quilted article needs to be washable, launder the fabric before you begin, or use preshrunk material. Most cottons will need to be washed, dried, and carefully ironed to ensure that the warp and weft of the fabric lie straight (*see page 31*). For a purely decorative piece, the fabric will only need pressing. It is advisable to allow at least 2 in. (5 cm) of fabric and batting all around the quilting design for any adjustments, and for framing or mounting.

Joining Pieces of Batting Together

To join two widths of batting, butt them together and stitch with a loosely worked herringbone stitch, as shown below. For thick batting, work a second row of herringbone stitch on the reverse side (*see also page 99 for herringbone stitch*).

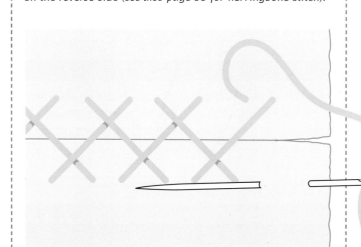

Batting

When choosing batting, consider the fiber content and the thickness. Synthetic polyester is available in several lofts. It is lightweight, washable, and dry-cleanable. Needle-punched polyester batting is firm and dense, with little loft, which makes it a good choice for small projects. Batting made from natural fibers such as silk, wool, and cotton are good choices if you wish to keep the fabric content of the project the same throughout. All types of batting are easy to handle but need careful laundering according to the manufacturer's instructions.

Enlarging Designs

 Using a Grid System

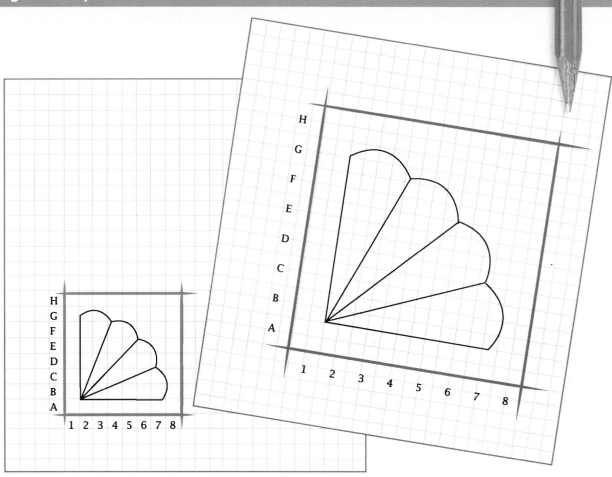

Positioning a Design

There are two ways of positioning a quilting design on the fabric. You can judge it by eye, or if you wish the design to be placed symmetrically, follow these steps.

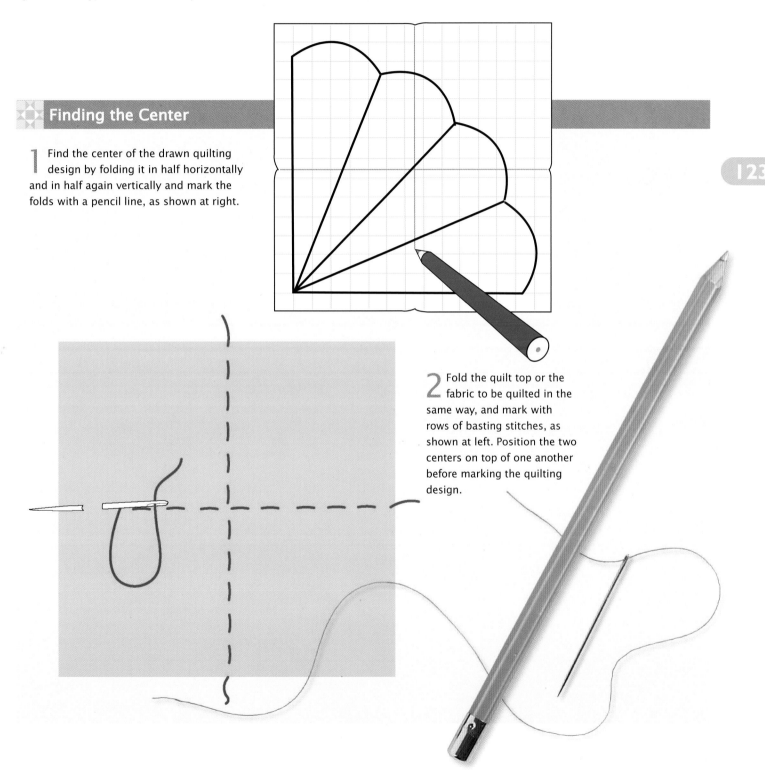

◈ Finding the Center

1 Find the center of the drawn quilting design by folding it in half horizontally and in half again vertically and mark the folds with a pencil line, as shown at right.

2 Fold the quilt top or the fabric to be quilted in the same way, and mark with rows of basting stitches, as shown at left. Position the two centers on top of one another before marking the quilting design.

Transferring a Quilting Design

Quilting designs need to be transferred to the fabric in the quilt top before the quilt is layered into a quilt sandwich, framed, or put in a hoop. There are a number of different methods, ranging from simple tracing to the use of a light box, templates, or stencils. Fabric markers of various types are available (*see page 16*). Whichever one you use, always mark the design very lightly.

Direct Tracing Using a Light Box or Window

A light box is a good investment if you intend to work on dark fabrics. Simply tape your quilting design to the lit glass surface, then tape the fabric on top. Provided the fabric is not too thick or dark, the design will show clearly and can be traced with ease, using a removable fabric marker or pencil.

If you do not own a light box and are working on a fairly small scale, the design with the fabric on top can be taped to a lit window and traced in the same way.

Direct Tracing

This method is suitable for transferring a quilting design to light fabrics that allow you to place the design underneath and trace directly onto the fabric.

Outline the design on paper in black permanent pen. Using masking tape, tape the design to a work surface, then tape the fabric in position on top. Trace the design onto the fabric.

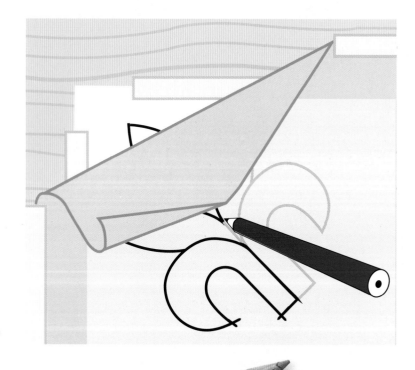

124

Pricking and Pouncing

This transfer method is suitable for intricate designs. It is also useful for repeat motifs because the tracing can be reused a number of times. Make a pricker using a sharp needle with the eye inserted into a cork. Pounce powder is traditionally crushed chalk, which can be purchased at quilt shops or in stick form at art shops. An alternative is dressmaker's chalk, which is available in several colors at fabric stores.

Making a Pounce Pad

Roll up an 8- x 4-in. (20- x 10-cm) piece of felt lengthwise, fold in half, and secure ends with a cotton thread, as shown below.

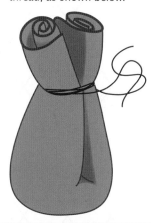

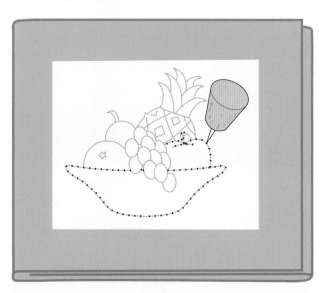

1 Trace the design onto tracing paper. Place it right side down on a padded surface, such as a folded towel. Use a pricker to prick holes at regular intervals along the lines of the design. You could also stitch the design on a sewing machine without thread. If the design is complex, it helps to lower the feed dogs or use a free-motion foot on the machine when you do this.

2 Turn the pricked tracing to the right side and position it on the fabric, securing it with masking tape.

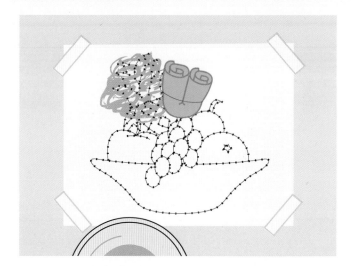

3 Dip the folded edge of the pounce pad into the pounce powder and rub the powder through the holes, using a circular motion. Take care not to smudge the design.

4 Remove the tracing paper and connect the dots using a quilter's pencil. Gently pat away any excess pounce powder.

Masking Tape

For a design made up of long, straight lines, you can use a ruler and your chosen fabric marker. A useful alternative is to use masking tape, which is available in several widths from paint stores, art stores, and hardware shops. Quilt shops stock a very narrow ¼-in. (6-mm) width.

¼ in.
(6 mm)

1 in.
(2.5 cm)

2 in.
(5 cm)

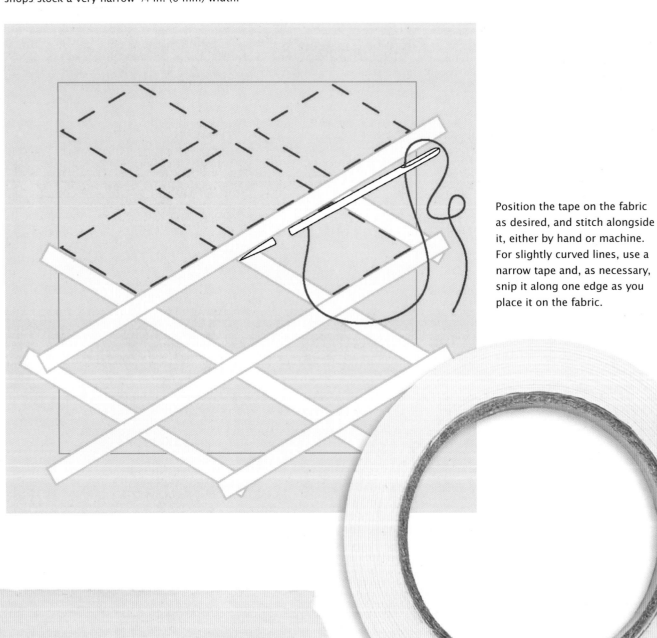

Position the tape on the fabric as desired, and stitch alongside it, either by hand or machine. For slightly curved lines, use a narrow tape and, as necessary, snip it along one edge as you place it on the fabric.

126

Alternative Methods

Tracing and Basting

This method of transferring a design is not often used for hand quilting, but is suitable for bold hand-quilted designs or when using a highly textured fabric that could not otherwise be easily marked. A version of this method can be used for machine quilting (*see page 113*).

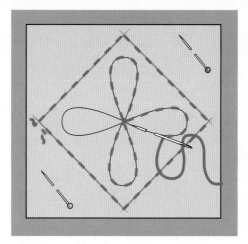

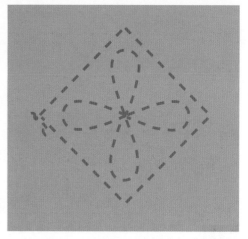

1 Draw the quilting design on tracing paper. Position and pin the tracing on top of the fabric.

2 Beginning with a secure knot and a backstitch, work small running stitches along the marked lines of the design, through both the paper and the fabric. Finish with a double backstitch.

3 Tear away the tracing paper to reveal the basted line, being careful not to undo the stitching. Slightly scoring the tracing with the point of a needle can help the removal of the paper. The basting is removed later as the quilting progresses.

127

Dressmaker's Carbon Paper

Available in several colors, dressmaker's carbon paper is used in a similar way to ordinary carbon paper. It is best to mark lightly on dark fabrics. Choose a color that will show up easily on your fabric, and test before using to ensure that the marks will wash or iron out.

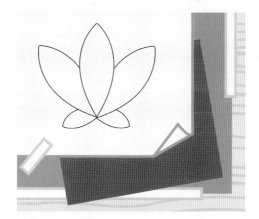

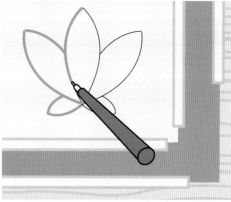

1 Tape the fabric right side up with masking tape on a hard work surface. Place the traced design in position on top of the fabric, holding it temporarily in place with tape.

2 Slip the carbon paper, colored side down, between the tracing and the fabric, as shown above, and secure with masking tape.

3 Using a spent ballpoint pen, a tapestry needle with a blunt lip, or a similar blunt instrument, draw over the marked lines, pressing firmly. Make sure that you do not lean your hand on the tracing, as smudges from the carbon paper can result.

Stencils and Templates

Stencils and templates are very useful ways to mark quilting designs. They are particularly good for repeat designs and often have registration marks or notches along the edges to help position them accurately.

Stencils

Plastic commercial quilting stencils are available in a wide range of designs, such as flowers, leaves, wreaths, and hearts. Background designs can be created with simple diamonds or lattice patterns, and border stencils are available in traditional cables, scrolls, feathers, and waves.

Quilting stencils have slits along the outlines of the motif through which the design is marked on fabric. Position the stencil and draw through the slits with a fine removable fabric marker or pencil. Remove the stencil and connect the broken line, if desired.

Templates

Unlike stencils, which can define the inner and outline details of a quilting motif, templates are simple plastic shapes around which the design is marked. Geometric shapes, such as circles, squares, triangles, and diamonds, are all suitable as templates, together with simple shapes, such as hearts or leaves.

1 Position the template on the fabric or paper, and draw around it with your chosen marker. For a continuous or all-over design, overlap the previously drawn motif and mark around it again.

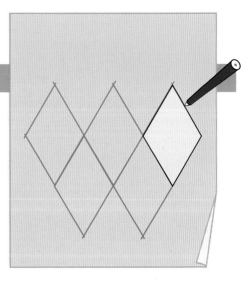

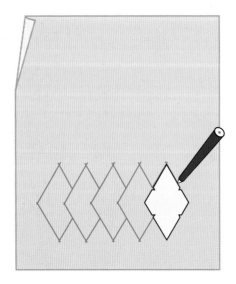

2 For a continuous-line design, position the template on the fabric and mark around it. Using the registration marks or notches on the template, reposition for the second and subsequent repeats to create a regular pattern or border design.

128

Cutting Your Own Stencils

Your own drawings or those taken from photographs or other printed matter can be adapted and simplified to create quilting designs. It is a simple task to cut your own stencils from soft, opaque or transparent plastic. This allows you to cut channels easily and accurately with a single- or double-bladed X-Acto knife, and the plastic will stand up to repeated use.

1 Trace the design onto stencil plastic using a black permanent marking pen. Mark where to cut slits along the outline of the design and any internal details, leaving a "bridge" between the slits so that the stencil will not fall apart when cut.

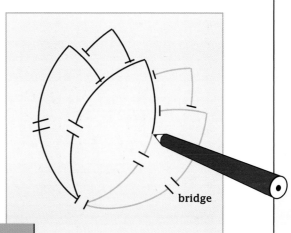

bridge

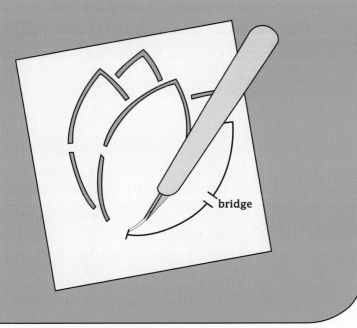

bridge

2 Place the stencil plastic on a cutting mat and carefully cut 1/8-in. (3-mm) slits along the marked lines, using a double-bladed craft knife.

Hoops and Frames

Although some people prefer to quilt without supporting the quilt, hand quilting is often more successful if the work is mounted in a hoop or frame. There are a number of different hoops and frames; whichever type you select, the quilt top and back should be pressed and the design marked before you layer the quilt sandwich. Care should be taken that the quilt sandwich is not distorted in any way.

Visit your local quilt shop and ask for information and opinions about floor frames from people who work there and have experience with many different brands.

130

Circular, oval, or square hoops are similar to those used for embroidery but are deeper and stronger. The outer hoop is adjusted with a screw. Small hoops are good for small projects, especially if the whole design can be positioned within the hoop. A larger quilting hoop can be used for bigger projects, but will need to be relocated as the quilting progresses. If you do this, make sure that you do not distort or damage previously stitched areas of the design. Whenever you finish a quilting session, remove your work from the hoop, as creases or an impression of the hoop may occur overnight. Binding the inner hoop with the bias strips of muslin, as shown at right, will protect delicate fabrics, prevent undue creasing, and provide a better grip.

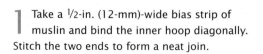

1 Take a ¹/₂-in. (12-mm)-wide bias strip of muslin and bind the inner hoop diagonally. Stitch the two ends to form a neat join.

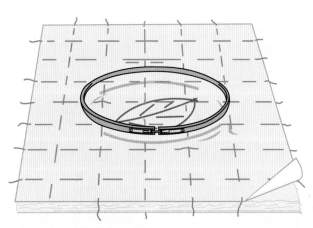

2 Adjust the screw of the outer hoop so that it fits loosely over the inner hoop, allowing sufficient space to accommodate the thickness of the quilt sandwich.

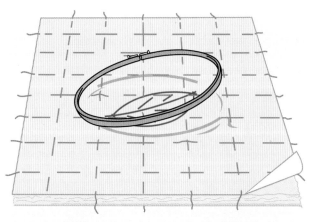

3 Place the basted quilt sandwich over the inner hoop and press the outer hoop down over the inner one. The grain of the fabric should be straight and not unduly taut. Tighten the screw to hold the quilt sandwich in place.

Tubular Hoops

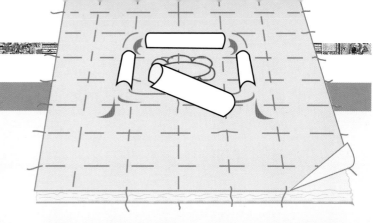

Unlike traditional circular or oval quilting hoops, plastic PVC frames have four sets of tubular PVC pipes that make up a rectangle or square. Their advantage is that there is less likelihood of the quilt sandwich being stretched on the bias. Lay the prepared quilt sandwich over the frame, and clamp the outer tubes in place, as shown at right.

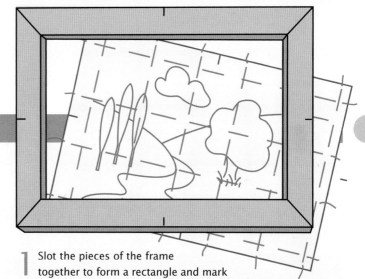

British Options

Stretcher Frames

Like tubular frames, stretcher frames are suitable for rectangular items, such as small wall hangings, pillows, or appliqué pictures, provided that the quilting design can be contained within the frame. Stretcher frames consist of four mitered pieces of soft wood that fit together to form a rectangle or square. Pairs of sides in different lengths are available at needlework shops and can be interchanged with sides in other lengths. A soft-wood, flat profile picture frame can be used as an alternative.

1 Slot the pieces of the frame together to form a rectangle and mark the center of each side. Make corresponding marks on the edge of the quilt sandwich.

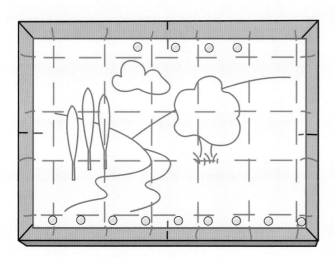

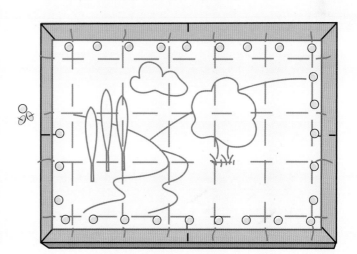

2 Starting at the top, align the center marks and secure the fabric with a thumb tack. Continue pinning at 1-in. (2.5-cm) intervals, working toward the corners. Turn the frame and fasten the bottom edge in the same way, stretching the fabric taut.

3 Complete the other two sides. Pin the center points and continue toward the corners, pinning first one side, then the other, to tension the fabric evenly.

Frames

A traditional full-size floor frame is expensive and can sometimes be too large to be accommodated in a home. However, the smaller tapestry frames used by embroiderers for needlepoint and surface embroidery are similar and can be used with or without a floor stand. They come in various sizes and are made up of two rollers, each with webbing attached. These are held apart with side stretchers that have split pins or pegs to adjust the size. To tension the sides of the fabric, lengths of fabric tape (available in quilt and sewing stores) are pinned in zigzag formation along the length of the side stretchers, as shown in Step 4. It is common when using this type of frame to frame the backing fabric first and then baste the batting and quilt top on top.

1 Mark the center point of the webbing on the rollers, and make a corresponding mark at the center top and bottom of the backing fabric.

2 Fold over the top edge of the backing fabric and pin it along the webbing, as shown below. Overcast the two together with strong thread, starting in the center and working outward, first to one side and then to the other, as shown in Step 3. Repeat by stitching the bottom edge to the webbing on the opposite roller.

Side stretcher

2

3 To assemble the frame, roll any excess length of backing fabric onto the bottom roller. Insert the side stretchers and secure them with the split pins or pegs so that the fabric is evenly tensioned but not too taut.

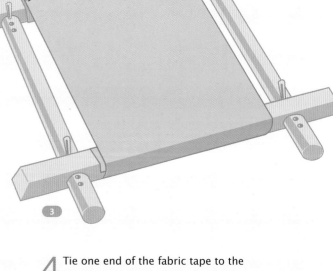

3

Roller

4

4 Tie one end of the fabric tape to the bottom roller and take it diagonally across onto the backing fabric. Pin in place and take it diagonally over and around the side stretcher, pinning it again on the edge of the backing. Continue along the length of the side stretcher, as shown at left, pulling the tape evenly, and tie off around the top roller. Repeat with a second piece of fabric tape along the other edge.

5 Add the batting and quilt top in the same manner, as shown in Step 4.

Basting

After the design has been transferred to the top fabric, you will need to baste the three layers of the quilt sandwich together. Failure to secure the layers properly will mean that they are likely to move while you are quilting and the finished quilt will be distorted. Basting guns, which hold the layers together with plastic tacks, are now available. For large-scale projects, these can be a quick alternative to hand basting.

 ## Basting with Safety Pins or Thread

Using Safety Pins

Place the batting on top of the backing fabric. Then position the quilt top on top, with right side up. Align the grain lines of the quilt top and backing. Pin the layers together with quilter's safety pins, smoothing out any wrinkles from the center.

Using Thread

Thread an embroidery (or crewel) needle, size 5, with white cotton sewing thread and, starting in the center, work a row of large basting stitches, about 2 in. (5 cm) in length, to the lower edge and then another row to the top edge. Follow this with a similar horizontal row from side to side through the center. Working outward, make rows of basting stitches about 3 in. (7.5 cm) apart in grid formation until the surface is entirely covered.

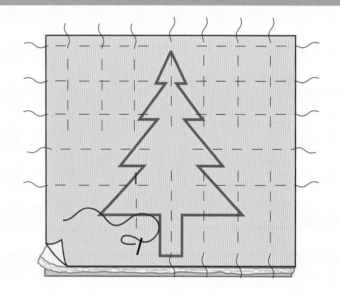

 ## Alternative Method

Basting with the Backing Fabric Framed

When you are using a tapestry frame, it is helpful to frame the backing fabric (*see page 132*) before adding the batting and quilt top. Preparation for trapunto and corded quilting (*see page 145*), which require only two layers, can be done in the same way, so that the filling stands out in relief on the top fabric.

Place the backing fabric in a quilting hoop so that it lies taut. Place the batting and the quilt top loosely on top. Smooth, pin, and baste in a grid as for normal thread basting.

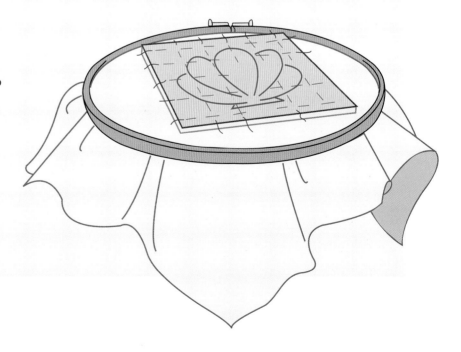

Stitching Direction

Start your quilting stitches in the center of the project and gradually work outward, smoothing the surface as you go. Complete each section of the design systematically. If the design features long background lines, stitch them all in the same direction.

The Hand-Quilting Process

For quilts, where the back needs to look as good as the front, you will need to start and finish your quilting stitches in such a way as to be strong but unobtrusive. For items where the look of the backing is unimportant, such as pillows or garments that will eventually be lined, you can begin and end the stitching simply by making a double-back stitch on the backing fabric.

Choose an appropriate quilting thread for your project (*see page 14*) and select a quilting (betweens) needle that will comfortably accommodate it. To strengthen the thread and prevent it from twisting, run it across a block of natural beeswax.

The traditional hand-quilting stitch is a simple running stitch. It gives a clear definition to the design, accommodates the thickness of the batting with ease, and is easy and fun to work. It is essential to work with a consistent tension, an even stitch length, and a similar distance between each stitch. This evenness of stitching is, in fact, more important than the actual size of the stitches themselves. Working a perfect row of quilting stitches will require a little practice to achieve your own rhythm.

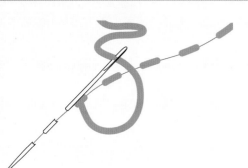

Running Stitch

Working from right to left (or left to right if you are left-handed), bring the needle in and out of the layers of fabric at regular intervals, making small, evenly spaced stitches. Depending on the thickness of the batting, you should be able to pick up two or three stitches at a time.

Stab Stitch

Although similar to the running stitch, the stab stitch is worked singly. Bring the needle vertically up and down through the layers, pulling the thread tight to make a precise stitch on the surface.

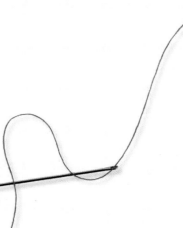

Threads

Decorative stitches add dimension and color to many types of quilts. A variety of threads can be used—pearl cotton and cotton floss, metallic thread, and rayon and silk ribbon threads—depending on how creative you feel. Always add decorative stitches before layering and basting the quilt because specialty threads are usually not strong enough to pull repeatedly through a quilt sandwich.

British Methods

Work decorative stitches like these on the quilt top, before layering it into a quilt sandwich for further quilting.

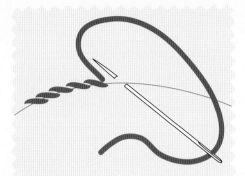

Stem Stitch

This stitch produces a continuous ropelike line. Working from left to right (or right to left if you are left-handed), bring the needle just above the stitching line and take it down a short distance along the stitching line. Keeping the thread loosely above the stitching line, bring the needle up again halfway along the length of the first stitch. Pull the thread tight and repeat. Secure with a double backstitch at the back of the work.

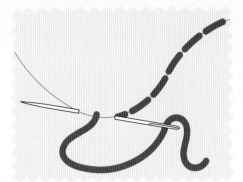

Backstitch

Backstitch makes a continuous line, similar to machine stitching. Bring the needle up a short distance from the starting point, then take a small stitch back to the starting point through the layers of fabric. Bring the needle out ahead of the first stitch and repeat. Secure with a double backstitch at the back of the work.

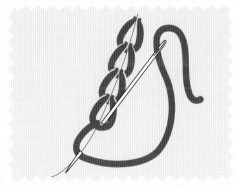

Chain Stitch

This makes a line of interlocked loops and is worked toward you from top to bottom. Bring the needle out on the stitching line and insert it again in the same hole, leaving a loop. Bring the needle up through the loop below the starting point—as far as you want the stitches to be long—and repeat. To finish, take a small vertical stitch over the bottom of the last loop to secure. Secure with a double backstitch at the back of the work.

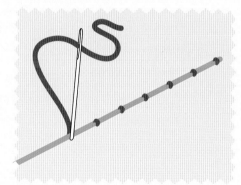

Couching

At the beginning of the stitching line, bring the thread to be couched up onto the surface of the quilt top. Thread a second thread and bring it up a short distance along the stitching line. Hold the couched thread taut and take a small vertical stitch over it with the second thread. Repeat vertical stitches at regular intervals over the couched thread. Take both threads to the back of the work and fasten off. Secure with a double backstitch at the back of the work.

How to Hand-Quilt

1 To begin, thread the needle with about 18 in. (46 cm) of thread and make a small knot a short distance from the end. Insert the needle through the quilt top and batting, as shown at left. Tug the thread gently so that the knot pulls through the backing into the batting, as shown below. Begin stitching.

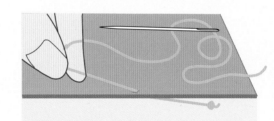

Thimbles

Most quilters find that a thimble on the middle finger of the hand on top of the work (usually your dominant hand) is helpful. You may also wish to use one on the first finger of the hand underneath the work to prevent being pricked and to assist in pushing the needle up.

2 Make a row of small, even running stitches through all layers, using the thimble to guide the needle from the top and a finger below the quilt to direct it back to the surface. You can pick up several stitches on the needle at one time.

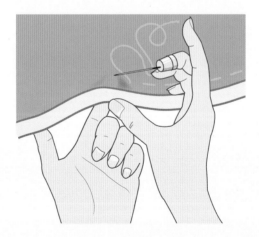

3 To finish a line of quilting, wind the thread around the needle twice, then insert in the batting layer. Run the needle away from the stitching, staying inside the batting layer only. Bring the thread to the right side of the quilt sandwich, pop the knot beneath the surface, as show at right, and clip the thread close to the surface of the fabric.

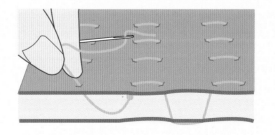

136

Quilting without Marking

Although patchwork projects are often quilted with elaborate patterns and traditional designs, there are several easy ways to secure the layers of batting and fabric together that do not require marking.

In-the-Ditch Quilting

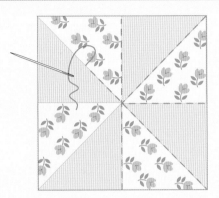

This method of stitching involves quilting along the seam lines through all layers of the quilt sandwich. This adds texture, but does not impinge on the overall design.

Outline Quilting

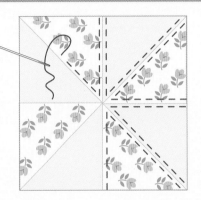

Quilt ¼ in. (6 mm) from one or both sides of the patchwork seams. An appliqué motif can also be outlined. There is no need to mark the design, as it can be judged by eye.

Echo Quilting

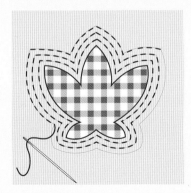

Echo quilting involves doing several lines of quilting following the shape of a motif. This technique is especially common in Hawaiian quilts.

Seed Quilting

Also known as stippling, seed quilting involves small, straight stitches worked randomly over the surface. The density of the stitching can be varied to produce flat or less flat textures.

137

Two Choices Quilt

Two traditional blocks, "Grandmother's Choice" and "Sister's Choice," in gentle blues and whites combine to create this lovely quilt designed by Cathy Kucenski. By placing certain fabrics in specific areas of the blocks, you can see beautiful secondary patterns emerge. All fabrics in this quilt are by Gail Kessler for Andover Fabrics (*see Resources, page 251*).

Equipment and Materials

- Large floral-print fabric: 5/8 yd. (58 cm)
- Small floral-print fabric: 5/8 yd. (58 cm)
- White-dot fabric: 5/8 yd. (58 cm)
- Blue-dot fabric: 5/8 yd. (58 cm)
- Striped fabric: 5/8 yd. (58 cm)
- Floral checkerboard-print fabric: 1/4 yd. (23 cm), checks are 1 in. (2.5 cm) square

- Striped floral-print fabric: 1 3/4 yd. (157 cm)
- Backing fabric: 3 1/2 yd. (320 cm)
- Binding fabric: 1/2 yd. (45 cm)
- Batting: 60 in. (152 cm) square
- Sewing needle
- White cotton thread for basting

Dimensions

Finished blocks are 15 in. (38 cm) square.

Finished quilt is approximately 56 in. (142 cm) square.

Grandmother's Choice Blocks

Follow these steps to cut and piece five Grandmother's Choice Blocks for this quilt.

Piecing the Grandmother's Choice Blocks

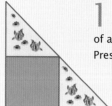

1 Start by sewing two small floral-print triangles to adjacent sides of a blue-dot square, as shown. Press. Make 20 of these units.

2 Sew one Step 1 unit to a large floral-print triangle. Press. Make 20 of these units.

3 For the top row of the block, sew two Step 2 units to a 3 1/2- x 6 1/2-in. (8- x 16.5-cm) striped rectangle, as shown above. Press the seam allowances toward the striped fabric. Make one of these rows for each of the five blocks.

Cutting for Grandmother's Choice Blocks

1 From the blue-dot fabric, cut twenty 3 1/2-in. (8-cm) squares.

2 From the small floral print, cut twenty 3 7/8-in. (10-cm) squares. Cut these squares in half diagonally.

3 From the large floral print, cut ten 6 7/8-in. (17-cm) squares. Cut these squares in half diagonally.

4 From the striped fabric, cut twenty 3 1/2- x 6 1/2-in. (8- x 16.5-cm) rectangles.

5 From the white-dot fabric, cut five 3 1/2-in. (8-cm) squares.

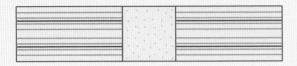

4 For the middle row of the block, sew the short edges of two 3¹/₂- x 6¹/₂-in. (8- x 16.5-cm) striped rectangles to opposite edges of a 3¹/₂-in. (8-cm) white-dot square, as shown above. Press the seam allowances toward the striped fabric. Make one of these rows for each of the five blocks.

5 For the bottom row of the block, sew two Step 2 units to the long edges of a 3¹/₂- x 6¹/₂-in. (8- x 16.5-cm) rectangle, as shown above. Press the seam allowances toward the striped fabric. Make one of these rows for each of the five blocks.

6 Sew the rows from Steps 3, 4, and 5 together to complete each of the five Grandmother's Choice blocks, as shown above. Press the completed blocks.

Sister's Choice Blocks

Follow these steps to cut and piece four Sister's Choice Blocks for this quilt.

1 From the white-dot fabric, cut sixteen 3¹/₂-in. (8-cm) squares.

2 From the blue-dot fabric, cut sixteen 3¹/₂-in. (8-cm) squares and sixteen 3⁷/₈-in. (10-cm) squares.

3 From the small floral print, cut sixteen 3¹/₂-in. (8-cm) squares and sixteen 3⁷/₈-in. (10-cm) squares.

4 From the striped fabric, cut sixteen 3¹/₂-in. (8-cm) squares.

5 From the large floral print, cut four 3¹/₂-in. (8-cm) squares.

◈ Piecing the Sister's Choice Blocks

1 Place a 3⁷/₈-in. (10-cm) blue-dot square on top of a 3⁷/₈-in. (10-cm) small floral-print square, with right sides together. Mark a diagonal line from corner to corner on the top square. Sew a seam ¼ in. (6 mm) in on each side of the marked line. Cut each pair of squares apart on the marked diagonal line. Press the seam allowances toward the blue-dot fabric. Make 32 of these half-square triangle units, as shown at left.

2 The blocks are assembled in horizontal rows. For the top row, sew together in the following order: a 3¹/₂-in. (8-cm) white-dot square, a half-square triangle unit from Step 1, a 3¹/₂-in. (8-cm) small floral-print square, a half-square triangle unit from Step 1, and a 3¹/₂-in. (8-cm) white-dot square. Press. Make eight of these rows, as shown above. Four of them will be used in Step 6.

3 For the second row, sew together in the following order: a half-square triangle unit from Step 1, a 3¹/₂-in. (8-cm) blue dot square, a 3¹/₂-in. (8-cm) striped square with the stripes placed vertically, a 3¹/₂-in. (8-cm) blue dot square, and a half-square triangle unit from Step 1. Press. Make a total of eight of these rows. Four of them will be used in Step 5.

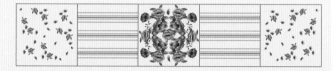

4 For the third row, sew together in the following order: a 3¹/₂-in. (8-cm) small-floral square, a 3¹/₂-in. (8-cm) striped square with the stripes placed horizontally, a 3¹/₂-in. (8-cm) large floral square, a 3¹/₂-in. (8-cm) striped square with the stripes placed horizontally, and a 3¹/₂-in. (8-cm) small floral square. Press. Make four of these rows, as shown above.

5 For the fourth row, simply reverse the position of one of the rows from Step 3, as shown above. Press. You will need to do this for the fourth row in each of the four blocks.

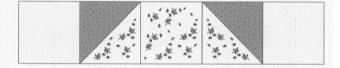

6 For the fifth row, simply reverse the position of one of the rows from Step 2, as shown above. Press. You will need to do this for the fifth row in each of the four blocks.

7 Sew the five rows from Steps 2 through 6 together to complete each of the four Sister's Choice blocks. Press the completed blocks.

Putting It All Together

Follow these steps to assemble the quilt center and add the borders to the quilt top.

Cutting for the First Border

From the 1-in. (2.5-cm) checkerboard-floral-print fabric, cut five 1½- x 44-in. (4- x 112-cm) strips.

Adding the First Border

1 Referring to the quilt diagram below and the photo on page 143, sew the short ends of the 1½- x 44-in. (4- x 112-cm) floral-checkerboard strips together. Press the seam allowances open. Sew the strip to the top edge of the quilt center, trimming it even with the edges of the quilt center. Repeat for the first border at the bottom of the quilt.

2 Sew the remaining first-border strip to the sides of the quilt, trimming the ends of the border even with the edges of the quilt center. Press the seam allowances open. If desired, you can sew a seam between each 1-in. (2.5-cm) checkerboard square in the first border to make it look as though it has been pieced.

141

Assembling the Quilt Center

Referring to the quilt diagram and the photo on page 143, sew the blocks together in three horizontal rows, alternating the block positions, as shown at right. Press the completed quilt center.

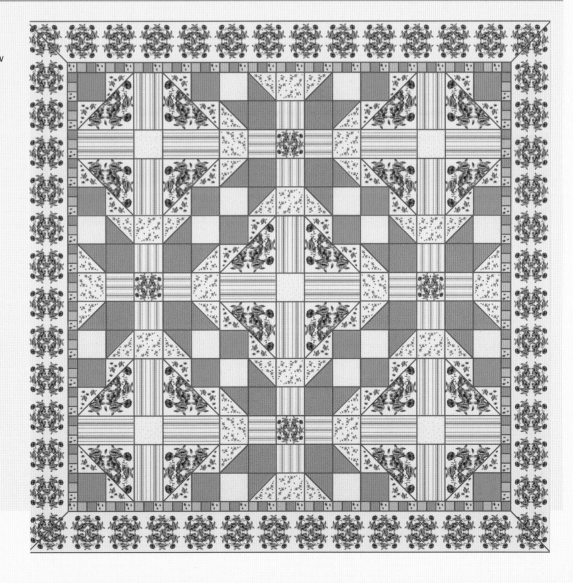

Cutting for the Second Border

From the floral-striped fabric, cut four 5- x 60-in. (12.5- x 152-cm) border strips.

Adding the Second Border

1 Find the midpoint of one second-border strip and pin it to the midpoint on one side of the quilt center. Pin the rest of the second-border strip to the edge of the quilt center. There will be extra fabric at the ends of the border to allow for mitering the corner seams.

2 Beginning and ending ¼ in. (6 mm) from the edge of the quilt center on each side of the quilt top, sew the second border strips to the four edges of the quilt top, using a ¼-in. (6-mm) seam allowance.

3 Referring to page 231, miter the corner seams of the second border. Press the corner seam allowances open.

Finishing

1 Cut the 3½ yd. (320 cm) of backing in half on the crosswise grain. Remove the selvages and sew the two lengths of fabric together along the lengthwise grain. Press the seam allowance open. Cut the backing to a 60-in. (152-cm) square. Lay the quilt backing on a flat surface, with the wrong side facing up.

2 Place the 60-in. (152-cm) batting square on top of the quilt backing, smoothing out any wrinkles.

3 Position the quilt top over the batting, smoothing out any wrinkles. Baste the three layers of the quilt sandwich together by hand, using a sewing needle and the white cotton thread.

4 Quilt by hand in the ditch of the patchwork seams, or as desired.

5 Sew the prepared binding to the edges of the quilt, mitering the corners (*see page 231*).

6 Add a label and display sleeve to the back of the quilt, if desired.

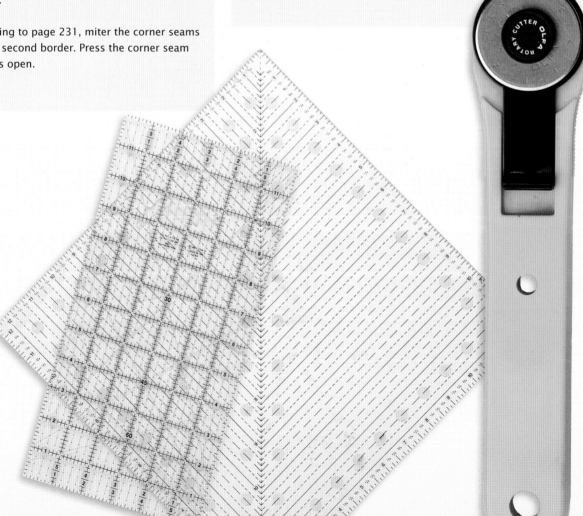

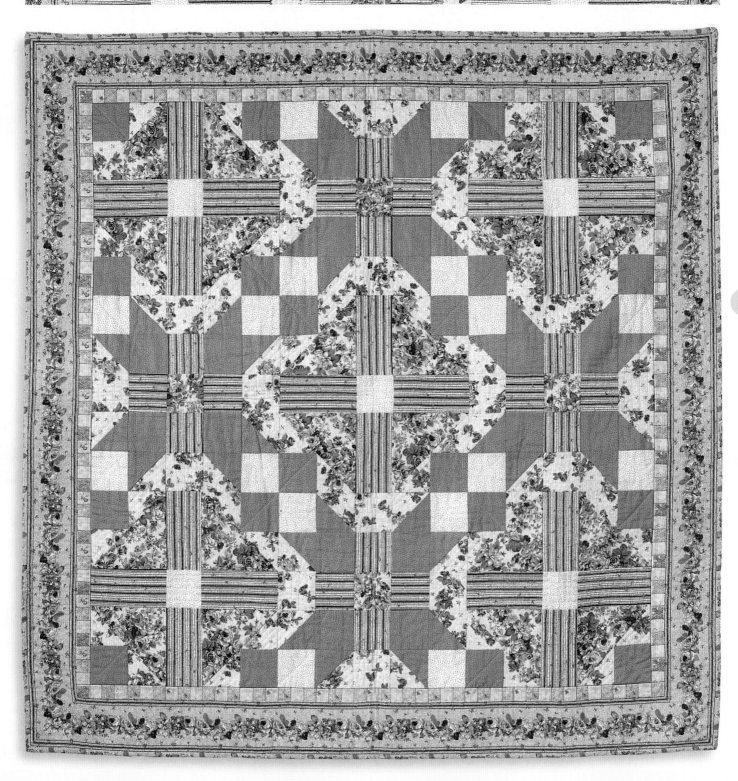

This combination of two traditional blocks creates a
unique quilt design with a feeling of yesteryear.

Trapunto and Corded Quilting

BOTH TRAPUNTO AND CORDED QUILTING REQUIRE JUST TWO LAYERS OF FABRIC. YOU CAN DO EITHER TECHNIQUE BY HAND OR MACHINE. CHOOSE A SOLID-COLORED COTTON OR SILK AS THE TOP FABRIC AND A SOLID-COLORED FOUNDATION FABRIC OF SIMILAR WEIGHT IN THE SIZES NEEDED FOR YOUR PROJECT.

You can transfer designs for either of these methods to the top fabric using a template or trace directly onto the fabric, using a light box for a dark fabric if necessary. Unless you plan to back the project, use these techniques only for items where the reverse side does not show, such as pillows or lined garments.

The padding in this heart-and-leaf wreath design enhances the shapes against a background of gentle hills and valleys created by the hand-quilted cross-hatched grid.

Trapunto

Known in England as stuffed quilting, trapunto features individual curved motifs, such as flowers or the pear shown below.

Stitching by Hand

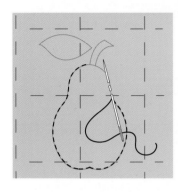

1 Mark the design lightly on the top fabric. Cut a piece of foundation fabric at least 2 in. (5 cm) larger all around than the top fabric. Thread-baste the two layers of fabric together in a grid to the edge of the motif. Place the foundation fabric in a hoop or frame, allowing the top fabric to hang free. Quilt the design by hand, using the running stitch, the backstitch, or a decorative stitch (see pages 134–135).

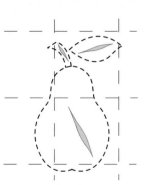

2 Loosen the tension on the foundation fabric slightly. On the reverse side, cut a small diagonal slit at the center of the pear, stem, and leaf, making sure not to cut the top fabric or the quilting stitches.

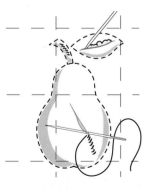

3 Gently insert small pieces of batting through the slits, using a blunt instrument, such as a tapestry needle. Check the front side of your work to make sure it is smooth and rounded. Oversew the edges of the slits together on the back, as shown at left.

Transparent Top Fabrics

For a delicate effect, try using a transparent top fabric, such as organza or voile, and insert strongly colored yarn to create the raised designs.

Stitching by Machine

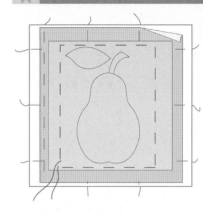

1 Trace the design onto tracing paper. Pin and baste the top and foundation fabric together in a grid (see page 133). Baste the traced design on the top fabric, as shown at left.

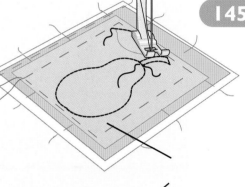

2 Machine-quilt along the marked lines of the design through the tracing paper and fabrics, leaving long thread tails wherever you start or end a line of stitching, as shown at right.

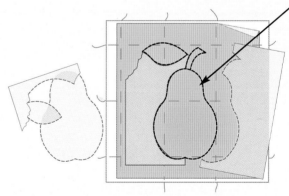

3 When you finish quilting, carefully tear away the tracing paper, as shown above. Slit, stuff, and complete the motif as for trapunto by hand. Finish by threading a needle with each of the thread tails and take the threads to the wrong side of your work. Do two or three backstitches with each thread on the foundation fabric, and clip the threads.

145

Corded Quilting

Also known as Italian quilting in England, corded quilting can be used alone or combined with trapunto. For corded quilting, the design is also marked on a top fabric and basted to a foundation. Parallel lines of quilting stitches are worked and then padded with yarn to form a pattern of raised channels.

◇ Stitching by Hand

Follow these steps to do corded quilting by hand.

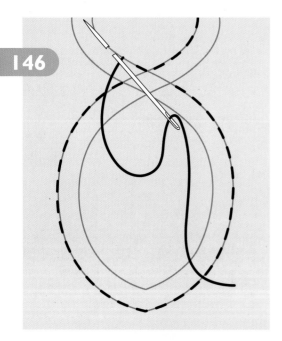

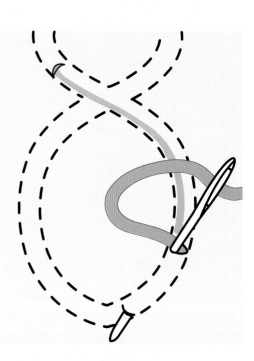

1 Mark the design lightly on the top fabric, as for trapunto (*see page 145*). Baste the top and foundation fabrics together in a grid. Place the foundation fabric in a hoop or frame, leaving the top fabric hanging free. Hand-quilt along the double lines of the design, using the running stitch or the backstitch and making sure that the threads do not cross each other at intersections, as shown above.

2 Loosen the tension on the foundation fabric slightly. Thread a large-eyed tapestry needle with yarn that matches the color of the top fabric. On the reverse side of your work, insert the needle between the stitching lines, taking care not to pierce the top fabric. Bring the needle out again through the foundation fabric when the curved channel restricts its progress, and reinsert it through the same hole to continue, as shown at right.

3 On sharp curves, bring the needle out of the foundation fabric approximately every inch. At intersections, cut the yarn and begin again on the other side, as shown at left. Leave the yarn ends loose to avoid puckering. Snip off the ends of each strand of yarn to finish.

Stitching by Machine

There are several ways of doing corded quilting by machine. The first method is to machine-stitch two parallel lines and then thread yarn through them from the wrong side of your work. If you prefer, you can also mark the design on the wrong side of the foundation fabric, remembering to reverse any design that is asymmetrical or directional. An alternate technique is to machine-quilt a design that is marked on tracing paper, as for trapunto by machine (*see page 145*). Use a needle to take long threads to the back of the work by hand. Tear away the papers, then thread the yarn between the parallel lines, as for the hand method.

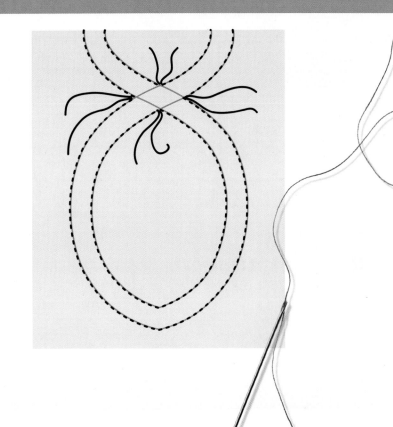

Using a Double Needle

A quick and accurate way to machine-quilt channels for corded quilting is to use a double needle. These are spaced at either 1/8-in. or 3/16-in. (3- or 4-mm) intervals. Using two spools of thread, thread the double needle, making sure that the threads are not twisted and are separated by the tension disk. Transfer the design to the top fabric as for the hand method (*see page 146*). Machine-stitch along the marked lines, stopping at intersections and leaving long thread tails, which will be secured on the wrong side of your work by hand. Thread a large-eyed tapestry needle with yarn and finish as for the hand method (*see page 146*).

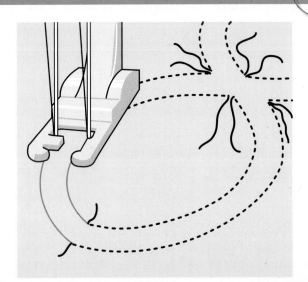

Trapunto-Quilted Pillow

This pillow combines both the stuffed and corded quilting methods for the central wreath and heart motif, which creates a highly three-dimensional appearance on the fine diagonal quilted grid. Trapunto is quite an interesting technique that requires both patience and perseverance, but the results are worth every minute you spend doing this beautiful stitching.

Cutting for the Pillow

For the pillow front, cut one 16-in. (40.5-cm) square of peach fabric.

For the batting, cut one 16-in. (40.5-cm) square.

For the backing, cut two 16-in. (40.5-cm) squares of muslin.

For the pillow backs, cut two 15- x 11-in. (38- x 28-cm) rectangles of peach fabric.

Dimensions

Finished pillow is approximately 14½ in. (36 cm) square.

Piping

Reserve the remaining peach fabric for the piping —approximately 1¾ yd. (160 cm) long.

Equipment and Materials

- Peach fabric: 1 yd. (91.5 cm)
- Muslin: ½ yd. (46 cm) for backing
- 1 oz. (25 g) batting: ½ yd. (46 cm)
- Skein of thick white yarn
- Thick tapestry needle
- ¼-in. (6-mm)-diameter piping cord: 1¾ yd. (160 cm)
- Large sheet of plain paper
- Pencil
- Silver-colored pencil (Berol Verithin number 753)
- Pencil sharpener
- Masking tape
- Peach quilting thread
- Acrylic ruler
- Rotary cutter
- Cutting mat
- Basic sewing supplies
- Iron
- Pillow form: 14 in. (35 cm) square
- Piping foot for sewing machine

Transferring the Pattern

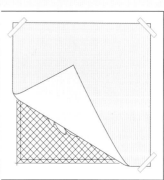

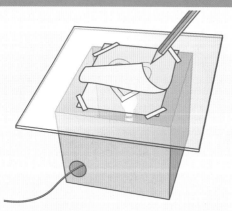

1 Trace the pattern given on page 240 to full size on a sheet of plain paper. Place the paper underneath the peach fabric square and secure the corners of the fabric to it, using pieces of masking tape.

2 If you have a light box, place the fabric and paper on it and trace the design onto the fabric using the silver pencil. Alternatively, tape the fabric and paper to a window in daylight. The light should be sufficient to enable you to see the design lines through the fabric easily.

Make Your Own Light Box

You can also make a temporary light box from a large cardboard box with a small lamp inside and a sheet of glass on top. Cut a hole on one side of the box for the lamp cord.

Working the Corded Motifs

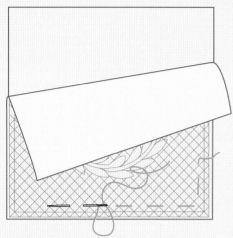

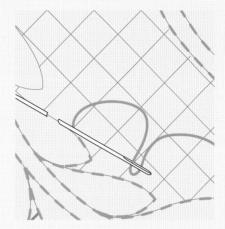

1 Place the fabric with the traced design onto one of the 16-in. (40.5-cm) squares of muslin, and baste the two layers together around the edges so that the layers don't shift while you work.

2 Using small running stitches and quilting thread, stitch along both lines of the central heart-shaped motif and all lines of the leafy wreath motif, working as accurately as you can. Make sure you finish the threads securely and neatly on the muslin side of the work with a backstitch.

3 Take the tapestry needle and thread it with a length of the thick white yarn. Turn the work over and make a small hole between the stitching lines of the heart shape, as shown above. Do not cut the muslin— simply use the blunt point of the needle to make a hole in the loosely woven threads of the fabric.

4 Pass the yarn along the channel, bringing it out though the muslin at points where the design curves, or at corners, and reinsert it into the same exit hole to continue to negotiate the curved shape. Fill the entire shape with the yarn in this way.

5 When you reach your starting point, snip off the end of the cord close to the muslin backing and tuck the cord neatly into the channel with the tip of the tapestry needle. Work the circle at the center of the leafy wreath in the same way.

Quilting the Background Grid

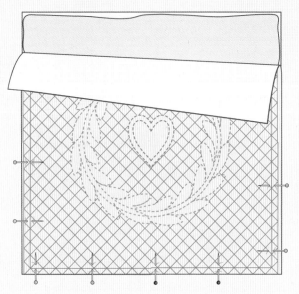

1 Sandwich the batting square between the top fabric layers and the second muslin square. Pin and thread-baste through all three layers around the edges so that they do not shift while you quilt the background grid.

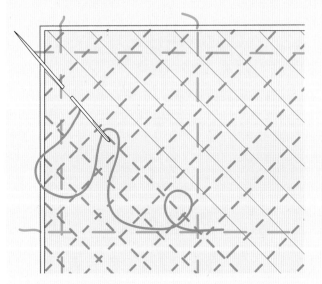

2 Using small running stitches, quilt through all three layers, following the marked diagonal lines. Work from the center outward, making sure that you keep the stitching lines parallel. Always fasten off the ends of each thread securely on the muslin side of the work with a backstitch. Trim the finished quilted piece to 15 in. (38 cm) square, to match the backing.

Working the Stuffed Motifs

1 Working from the muslin side of the layered fabrics, make a small slit at the center of the heart motif. Use a tapestry needle to stuff small pieces of batting through the slit to pad out the shape

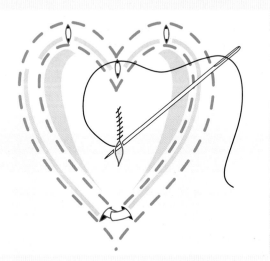

2 Slip stitch the slit closed with the peach sewing thread, as shown above, so that the padding does not escape. Pad each of the leaves around the circular wreath in the same way.

◇ Piping the Edge and Assembling the Pillow

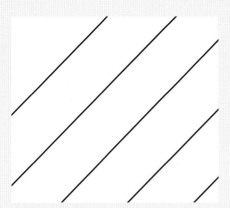

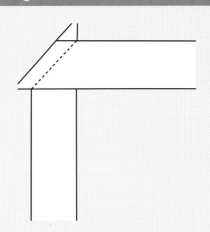

Rotary-cut 1¹/₂-in. (4-cm) bias strips.

1 You will need to cut approximately 1³/₄ yd. (160 cm) of 1¹/₂-in. (4-cm)-wide bias strips to make the piping (*see page 148*). Sew enough strips together to make the required length. Open out the remaining peach fabric and lay it flat on your work surface. Using a ruler and rotary cutter, cut as many 1¹/₂-in. (4-cm)-wide bias strips as required.

2 To join the bias strips, place two together, with right sides facing and at right angles to each other, as shown above. Machine-stitch diagonally across the pieces; trim the seam allowance to ¹/₄ in. (6 mm).

3 After joining all the bias strips together in this way, press the seams open, as shown above, taking care not to stretch the fabric.

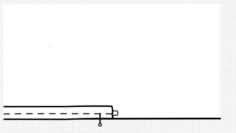

4 Insert a piping foot on your sewing machine. Wrap the wrong side of the bias strip around the piping cord and, keeping the raw edges together, machine-baste as close to the cord as possible, as shown above.

5 Place the piping on the right side of the pillow front, matching the raw edges, and baste it in place. Use a piping foot on your sewing machine and stitch as close to the piping as you can. It is best to begin to stitch about halfway across one side of the pillow.

6 When you reach the first corner, snip into the seam allowance of the piping in order to turn the corner smoothly. Machine-stitch up to the base of the snip, then reverse-stitch for three stitches, then continue stitching around the next side of the pillow. This strengthens the corner. Stitch the remaining three corners in the same way.

Piping the Edge and Assembling the Pillow (continued)

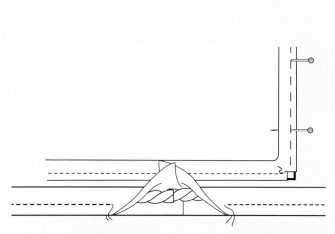

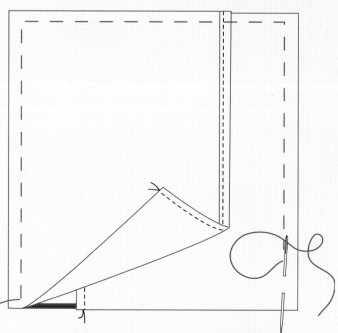

7 To join the ends of the piping, snip the excess cord so that the ends overlap slightly, as shown above. Trim the end of the fabric strip so that it overlaps the first end by approximately ¾ in. (2 cm). Unpick a few stitches at the beginning of the stitching, then fold back ⅜ in. (1 cm) along the raw edge at the end of the binding. Tuck the raw end under the folded end and twist the ends of the cord together.

9 For the pillow backs, fold and stitch a ¼-in. (6-mm) double hem along one long raw edge of each piece. Press. Place the pillow backs on top of the pillow front, with right sides together. Match the raw edges around the outside and overlap the hemmed edges at the center. Pin and baste around the outer edge, keeping the stitches close to the piping cord. Machine-stitch close to the piping as before, using the piping foot on your machine.

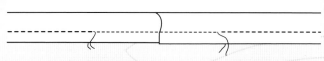

8 Machine-stitch the join close to the cord, as shown above, to finish.

10 Trim diagonally across the seam allowance at each corner of the cushion, then turn through to the right side. Insert the pillow form.

Trapunto designs stand out effectively in relief against a background of gentle hills and valleys created by hand-quilted cross-hatching. The piping around the edge of the pillow echoes the raised texture of the central trapunto design.

Hand Appliqué

APPLIQUÉ IS OFTEN COMBINED WITH PATCHWORK AND QUILTING TO PROVIDE A CONTRAST IN PATTERN OR TEXTURE. IN THE SIMPLEST OF TERMS, IT IS THE STITCHING OF FABRIC SHAPES TO A PLAIN OR PIECED BACKGROUND. BALTIMORE ALBUM QUILTS, WITH THEIR INTRICATE MOTIFS, FLOWERS, AND BIRDS, ARE PARTICULARLY ASSOCIATED WITH THIS METHOD.

Appliqué designs should be fairly bold so that the shapes are easy to assemble and stitch. There are a number of ways to prepare and stitch appliqué shapes, depending on your personal preference, the types of fabrics, and the design. Fabrics that do not fray can be stitched without seam allowances. For needle-turn appliqué, it is necessary to cut a template the same size and shape as the finished shape and then add seam allowances when cutting the fabric. These seam allowances are turned to the back of the shape, ready for stitching. Freezer paper or iron-on interfacing can also be used to help define the accuracy of the shapes.

Here, repeat motifs look particularly lovely around a quilted center star design, with an angled appliquéd border design that complements the central quilted shape.

Most appliqué projects consist of precise shapes taken directly from the original design. If this is complex, the traced templates can be numbered to correspond with those on the original to identify them and to designate the order of assembly.

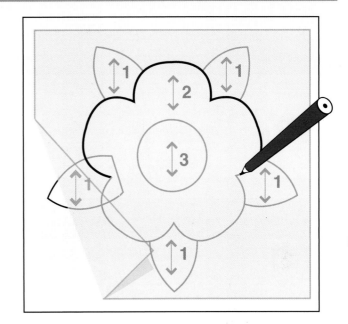

1 Trace the design and, if necessary, number each shape to coincide with that on the original, as shown at right.

2 Cut out each shape and use it as a pattern for cutting out the fabric patches according to the appliqué method you have chosen (*see pages 156–157*). Assemble and stitch the various elements of the design in a logical order, overlapping shapes as necessary, as shown at left.

◈ Raw-edge Appliqué

Fabrics that do not fray, such as felt or Ultrasuede, can be cut and stitched without seam allowances. Pin the template right side up on the front of the fabric and cut out. Position the appliqué shape on the background fabric and pin or baste in place. Stitch the shape, using your chosen hand-appliqué stitch.

156

◈ Basic Needle-Turn Appliqué

Sometimes known as the blind stitch, this traditional appliqué method is used for shapes made from fabrics that fray and for those fine enough to allow a seam allowance to be folded under. Iron-on interfacing or freezer paper can be inserted to produce a sharper-edged turning line if you wish.

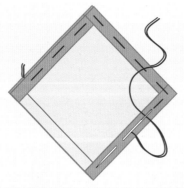

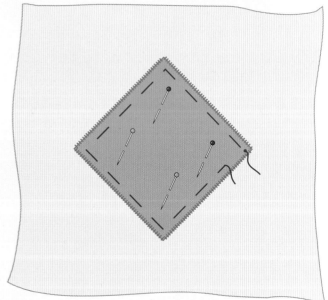

1 Pin the paper template right side down on the back of the fabric. Mark around the template and cut the shape out, adding 3/16-in. (4-mm) seam allowance, as shown above.

2 Fold and press the seam allowance to the wrong side, using the paper as a guide. Snip, notch, or trim the seam allowance on curved edges as necessary. Remove the paper and baste the seam allowance in place around the entire shape, as shown above.

3 Pin or baste the prepared appliqué shape in place on the background fabric. Secure with the blind stitch, as shown above, and remove the basting stitches.

Using Freezer Paper Inside Appliqué Shapes

Freezer paper and similar products sold by quilt shops are useful aids for giving precision to appliqué shapes, as they produce a sharp edge over which the seam allowance can be folded. Care should be taken in removing the paper.

1 Trace the appliqué shape onto freezer paper with the shiny side down. Cut out the template without turning lines. Using the template, cut out the fabric, adding seam allowances as shown at right.

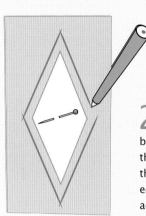

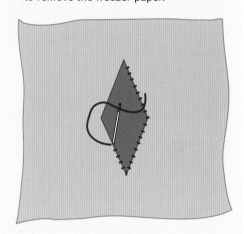

2 Position the freezer paper centrally, shiny side up, on the back of the cut fabric shape. With the point of a dry, hot iron, push the seam allowance up and over the edge of the freezer paper so that it adheres, as shown above.

3 Stitch the shape in place, as shown below. Cut away the background fabric underneath the appliqué shape to remove the freezer paper.

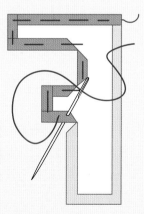

Preparing Appliqué Shapes with Iron-On Interfacing

Although appliqué shapes were not traditionally backed, fusible interfacing can be a useful aid because it helps to produce a sharp edge. As the interfacing is retained permanently within the shape, it adds extra thickness, which should be taken into consideration when deciding to use this method.

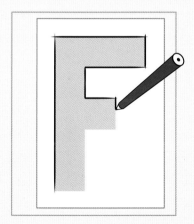

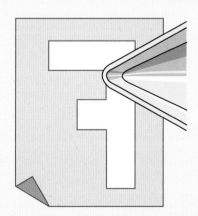

1 Either use a template or make a direct tracing from a design, marking the shiny side of the fusible interfacing, as shown above. Cut out on the marked line as for freezer paper.

2 Place the cut interfacing shape, shiny side down, on the wrong side of the fabric, aligning the grain. Press with a steam iron set to the appropriate heat setting for the fabric, as shown above.

3 Cut out the shape with a 3/16-in. (4-mm) seam allowance. Fold and baste the seam allowance over the fusible interfacing, and finish as for basic needle-turn appliqué.

Dealing with Curves, Corners, and Points

To retain the original shape and form of the design, careful manipulation of the seam allowances of appliqué shapes is essential. Straight edges present few problems, but curves, inner and outer points, and inner and outer corners need special care.

Curves

1 For inner (concave) curves, clip the seam allowance to within ⅛ in. (3 mm) of the stitching line, freezer paper, or interfacing, making cuts at regular intervals, as shown below, so that they fan out when folded over. Press or baste the seam allowance in place, if necessary, and stitch to the background using the blind stitch.

2 For outer (convex) curves, you can clip the seam allowance as for inner curves, if desired, but remove small notches of fabric, as shown above, to reduce the excess bulk when the seam allowance is turned over. Stitch with the blind stitch.

Corners and Points

1 On inner points, clip the seam allowance to within a tiny amount of the stitching line, as shown at immediate right. Fold back the two adjacent seam allowances and complete stitching.

2 On outer points and acute angles, trim the point to reduce bulk. Fold down the remaining fabric at the point and then on the two adjacent sides, as shown at far right. Stitch.

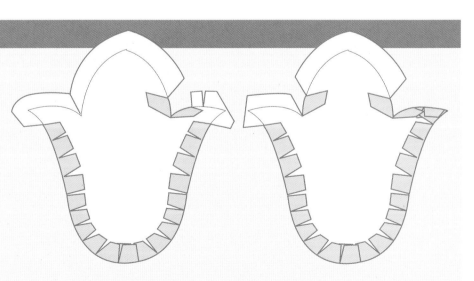

Stitches for Appliqué

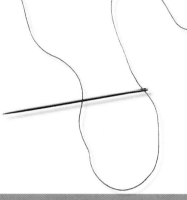

Depending on the effect you wish to create, a variety of stitches can be used to secure appliqué shapes in place. For an unobtrusive look, the blind stitch is the most successful for needle-turn appliqué, while the backstitch or stab stitch (*see pages 134–135*) gives more definition. To cover the edge of the appliqué shape (particularly for raw-edge appliqué), you could also use a decorative stitch, such as the buttonhole stitch, though this should be worked as small and neatly as possible, unless a primitive effect is desired.

◆ Blind Stitch

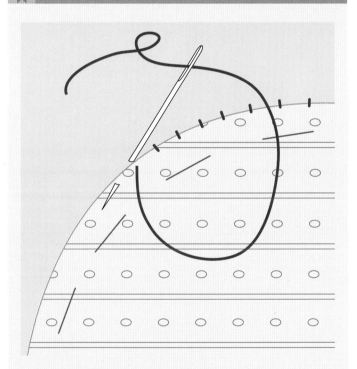

1 Bring the needle up through the background fabric, close to the edge of the appliqué shape, as shown above.

2 Make a tiny straight stitch next to the turned edge and repeat at regular ⅛-in. (3-mm) intervals, as shown above.

◆ Buttonhole Stitch

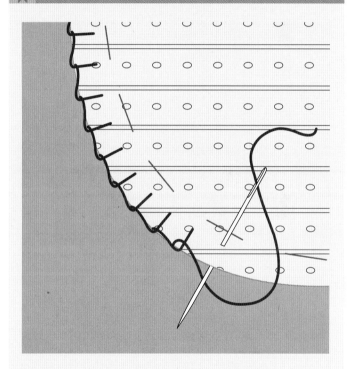

1 Bring the needle up through the background fabric, close to the edge of the appliqué shape.

2 Insert it below and to the right inside the appliqué shape and bring it out again through the loop immediately to the left. Continue making similar stitches, as shown above.

3 To finish, secure with a small stitch on the front to hold the final loop, and finish off at the back with a backstitch.

Folk-Art Appliqué Table Center

This attractive table center can be an eye-catching and colorful addition to your decor. Inspired by folk art designs, a simple heart and a stylized tulip motif are combined and repeated around a central star, quilted in a contrasting thread. The first method, with its bound, scalloped edge, uses appliqué shapes prepared with freezer-paper templates in advance of sewing. For the alternative template-free version, with a decorative prairie-point edging, the design is reversed, and the appliqué shapes are stitched directly onto the background fabric. Choose good-quality, lightweight cotton fabrics for both versions.

Template Method

Transferring the Design

Prepare a master pattern by transferring the design (*see page 241*), repeating it eight times to form a complete circle. This can be used in the template method for positioning the prepared freezer-paper shapes and for transferring the design onto the background fabric in the template-free method. Place the background fabric, centrally, on top of the master pattern and transfer the shapes with an erasable fabric marker. Mark the quilting lines of the central star and those that radiate from it.

Dimensions

Finished table center is approximately 19½ in. (49 cm) in diameter.

Equipment and Materials

- Dark green cotton fabric for background: 22 in. (56 cm) square
- Dark green fabric for bias binding: 1¼ x 74 in. (3 cm x 188 cm)
- Red cotton fabric for hearts: 7- x 18-in. (18- x 46-cm) piece
- Terra-cotta cotton fabric for tulip petals: 6- x 11-in. (15- x 28-cm) piece
- Gold cotton fabric for tulip centers: 6 in. (15 cm) square
- Green cotton fabric for leaves: 13 in. (33 cm) square
- Batting: 23 in. (59 cm) square
- Backing fabric: 23 in. (59 cm) square
- Threads to match the appliqué fabrics
- Embroidery threads in gold and terra-cotta
- Quilting thread to match the background fabric
- Fabric marker that is easy to remove
- Tracing paper to prepare the pattern: 20 in. (50 cm) square
- Basic sewing equipment and iron

Preparing the Appliqué Shapes

1 Trace each of the pattern shapes eight times onto the paper side of the freezer paper, as shown at right, and cut each one out along the marked line.

Stitching the Shapes

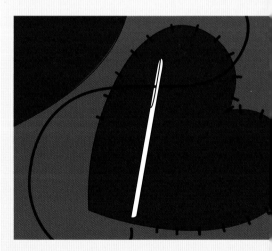

1 Blind stitch (*see page 159*) the prepared appliqué shapes in place, using a matching thread, and press from the wrong side.

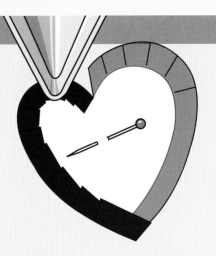

2 Iron the shapes onto the right side of the selected fabrics, as shown above, and cut them out with a ³/₈-in. (1-cm) seam allowance, as show at left. This can be reduced when the stitching is complete.

3 Working with one shape at a time, peel the freezer paper off the right side and pin it centrally onto the wrong side, with the shiny side up, as shown above. Snip the curves and inner corners (*see page 158*). Use the tip of the iron to ease the seam allowance over onto the freezer paper so that it adheres. A small area of freezer paper is still visible. Use it to press the shapes to the background fabric, ready for sewing.

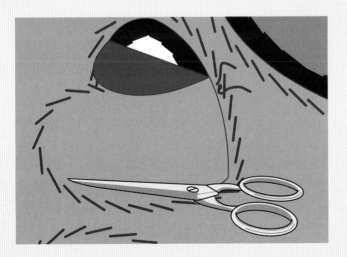

2 Using small, sharp scissors, cut away the background fabric from behind the appliqué, leaving a ¹/₄-in. (6-mm) seam allowance. Remove the freezer paper. Repeat for each appliqué shape.

Quilting

Place the appliquéd quilt top on top of the batting and backing squares, and pin or thread-baste them together. Using the gold and terra-cotta quilting threads, quilt the central star pattern with large, even stitches. With a thread that matches the background fabric, quilt around each heart and tulip appliqué shape—right up to the edge of the shape, and along the radiating lines (*see* Transferring the Design, *page 160*).

Finishing

In preparation for binding, trim the edge of the table center to make it scalloped, as shown on page 164. Stitch the prepared bias binding in place with a ¹/₄-in. (6-mm) seam allowance. Fold and stitch the binding to the back of the table center to complete (*see page 230*).

Template-Free Method

⬦ Transferring the Design

Transfer the design, using a light box, to the wrong side of the background fabric. Be aware that the pattern will be reversed on the right side.

Equipment and Materials

- Neutral cotton fabric for background: 22 in. (56 cm) square
- Red cotton fabric for hearts: 11½ in. (29 cm) square
- Blue cotton fabric for tulip petals: eight 2¾-in. (7-cm) squares
- Green cotton fabric for leaves: eight 7- x 3½-in. (18- x 8-cm) strips
- Terra-cotta cotton fabric for prairie points: ¼ yd. (23 cm)
- Neutral bias binding: 1¼ x 74 in. (3 x 188 cm)
- Batting: 23 in. (59 cm) square
- Backing fabric: 23 in. (59 cm) square
- Threads to match and contrast with the appliqué fabrics
- Quilting thread to match the background fabric
- Light box for transferring the design
- Tracing paper
- Fabric marker
- Basic sewing equipment and iron

Dimensions

Finished table center is approximately 19½ in. (49 cm) in diameter.

⬦ Stitching the Shapes

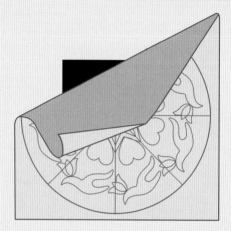

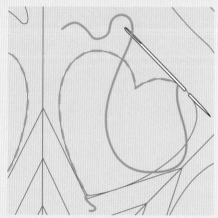

1 Starting with the circle of hearts, place the square of red fabric right side down on a flat surface. Place the background fabric on top, with the marked side uppermost, as shown above, so that the marked hearts lie on the red fabric and the grain lines coincide.

2 Working from the wrong side, stitch the two fabrics together with small basting stitches along the marked lines, around each heart shape, using a thread that contrasts with the appliqué fabric.

3 Turn the work to the right side and cut away the excess fabric from around each heart, leaving a ³⁄₁₆-in. (4-mm) seam allowance. Clip three quarters of the way into the curves and up to the line at the V (*see page 158*).

4 Working from right side, with a fine needle and a thread that closely matches the appliqué fabric, remove one or two basting stitches and start stitching, using the point of the needle to fold the seam allowances under to the basting line. Continue around the edge until the shape is complete. Complete the other appliqué shapes in the same way.

Continuous Prairie Points

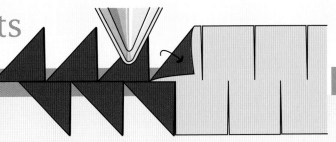

Preparation

Follow these steps to make a continuous line of prairie points, in the easiest way imaginable.

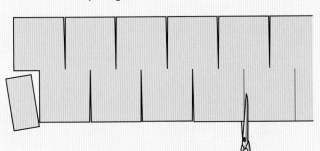

1 Cut and join several 4-in. (10-cm)-wide lengths of fabric to make a strip measuring 64 in. (162 cm) long. Press it in half lengthwise with wrong sides together. Open it again and lay it on a flat surface, wrong side up, for marking and cutting. Mark the center line along the fold so you can make accurate cuts. Measure and mark either side of the center fold line at 2-in. (5-cm) staggered intervals, as shown above. Trim the unwanted half square, 2 x 1 in. (5 x 2.5 cm) at the beginning and end of the length. Cut along these marked lines from the raw edge to the fold, along the entire length of the strip, as shown above.

2 Press each square in half on the diagonal to form triangles on both sides of the center fold, as shown above.

3 Fold each triangle in half again to make a smaller triangle so that the raw edges meet along the center fold, as shown above.

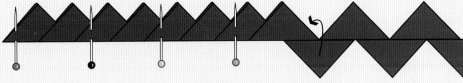

4 Fold the strip of folded triangles in half again lengthwise, tucking each prairie point into the previous one. Pin, press, and baste to hold them in place, as shown above, ready for attaching to the table center.

Finishing

1 Appliqué and quilt the table center as for the template version on pages 160–161. This sample shows alternative quilting lines: Here they appear as an echo of the shapes, ¼ in. (6 mm) away from the sewn edges. There are no radiating lines.

2 Trim away the excess fabric from around the outer edge to make a circular-shaped mat.

3 Pin the prepared prairie points around the edge with the points facing inward. Trim the length to fit the circle, tucking the first prairie point into the last to complete the circle.

4 Prepare a 1¼-in. (3-cm) bias binding to fit around the edge (*see page 233*) and stitch in place, securing the prairie points at the same time, as shown at right.

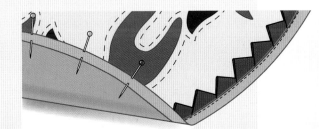

164

This design is just as effective with either gently scalloped edges,
as shown here, or with a circular edge complemented by a
prairie point border, as shown opposite.

A light background gives the same design as shown on
page 164 a completely different look while retaining
the folk-art quality of the appliqués.

Machine Appliqué

ALTHOUGH SPEED IS ITS OBVIOUS ADVANTAGE, MACHINE APPLIQUÉ HAS OTHER BENEFITS, TOO, SUCH AS THE ABILITY TO STAND UP TO HARD WEAR AND REPEATED LAUNDERING. ALL OF THESE THINGS MAKE MACHINE APPLIQUÉ SUITABLE FOR CHILDREN'S AND ADULTS' CLOTHING, AS WELL AS DURABLE TABLE LINENS AND QUILTS OF ALL SIZES AND SHAPES FOR ANY ROOM IN THE HOME.

Machine-appliqué shapes are prepared without seam allowances and stitched onto a background fabric with satin, zigzag, or decorative stitching. The two most popular techniques are the stitch-and-cut method and the fusible-web method. For either, you need to be able to alter the stitch length and width on your sewing machine, and if your machine has a transparent appliqué foot, it will allow you to see exactly where the needle pierces the edge of the appliqué shapes.

Any young child will love cuddling up under this fanciful Noah's Ark quilt, with pairs of animals surrounding the ark at the center.

Stitch-and-Cut Method

This technique is suitable for appliqué shapes that are cut from closely woven fabrics. With care, however, even fabrics that tend to fray can be stitched in this manner.

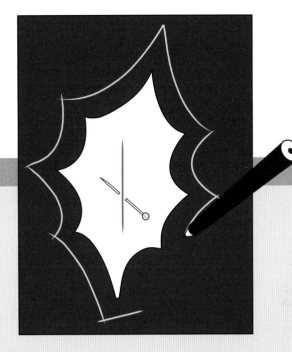

❖ Stitch and Cut

1 Trace each appliqué shape in your project onto freezer paper and cut it out on the marked lines. Press the freezer-paper templates on the right side of the fabric with the marked side up and mark around the edges. Mark and cut the shapes out with a margin of $1/2$ in. to $3/4$ in. (12–18 mm) all the way around, as shown at right.

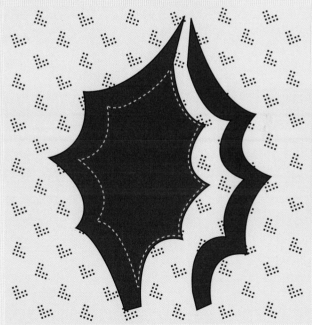

2 Position and pin each appliqué shape to the background fabric, making sure that both layers are smooth, as shown above.

3 Do straight machine stitching around the marked outline. Using sharp embroidery scissors, cut away the excess fabric close to your stitched line, as shown at right. You can leave the raw edges of the shapes as they are, or do zigzag or satin stitching over the straight stitching, if desired.

Fusible-Web Method

Fusible web is a paper-backed, double-sided bonding product that will secure even the most intricate, raw-edged appliqué shapes to background fabric.

◈ Fusible Web

1 Trace each appliqué shape in your project onto the nonshiny side of freezer paper or onto template plastic and cut it out on the marked lines. Place the templates wrong side up on the smooth side of the fusible web and mark around them, creating a mirror image of the original shapes. Cut out the fusible-web shapes with a 1/2–3/4-in. (12–18-mm) margin around them. With the rough side down, press the fusible-web shapes onto the wrong side of the fabric, as shown below.

2 When the fabric is cool, cut out the appliqué shapes along the marked lines and peel off the backing paper, as shown at right.

3 Position the appliqué shapes on the background fabric and press firmly in place, as shown below. Do straight, zigzag, or satin stitching around the edges of the shapes, as desired.

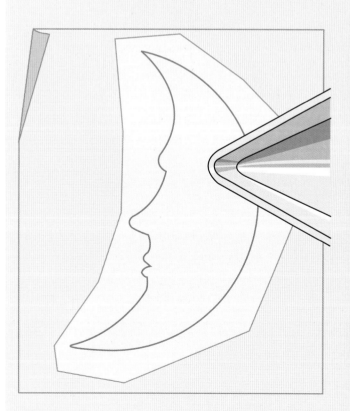

Zigzag and Satin Stitching

For zigzag stitching, it is helpful to refer to the owner's manual for your sewing machine and experiment by stitching on scrap fabrics until you find the stitch lengths and widths that please you. For satin stitching, make sure to shorten the stitch length on your machine until your stitches lie right next to one another. For both zigzag and satin stitching, follow these steps.

◇ Zigzag- and Satin-Stitch Edging

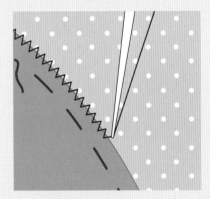

1 To zigzag along a straight edge or along shallow inner or outer curves, follow the edge of the appliqué shape, making sure that the needle pierces both the appliqué shape and the background fabric with each stitch you take, as shown above.

2 To stitch around an outer corner, stitch to the corner, stopping the machine with the needle to the right of the appliqué shape, as shown above. Keeping the needle in the background fabric, pivot your work and continue stitching along the next side.

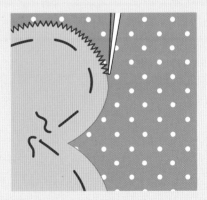

3 To stitch around a tight outer curve, pivot your work every few stitches, stopping the machine with the needle on the outside of the curve before you rotate the fabric. (For a tight inner curve, stop with the needle on the inside of the curve before rotating the fabric.)

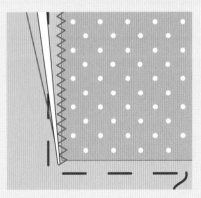

4 To stitch around an inner corner, work to the corner, stopping with the needle to the left, in the appliqué shape, as shown above. Pivot your work as for outer corners, and continue stitching along the next side. For all zigzag and satin stitching, end by leaving long thread tails, threading a needle with each one, and taking it to the wrong side of your work. Finish by taking two or three backstitches and clip the thread.

Noah's Ark Crib Quilt

This crib quilt is fun to make and provides colorful interest for a baby or small child. It can also be used as a wall hanging or as a play mat for a nursery. All the motifs are appliquéd to the background fabric sections, using machine satin stitch, and the sections are then machine-stitched together. The only hand stitching required is the light quilting along the strap sections and the finishing of the binding.

Dimensions

Finished blocks are approx. 6 in. (15 cm) square.

Finished quilt is approx. 42 in. (107 cm) square.

Changing Colors

If you are using a selection of your own scraps, refer to the photo of the quilt on page 177 for an idea of colors, then substitute your own fabrics as desired. You could also use just two or three colors, or coordinate the quilt with a nursery color scheme.

Equipment and Materials

- Patchwork backing: 28- x 39-in. (71- x 99-cm) rectangle of white muslin
- Quilt backing and binding: 1¼ yd. (114 cm) green fabric
- Batting: 28- x 39-in. (71- x 99-cm) rectangle
- Strips between panels: ½ yd. (45 cm) dark red fabric

For the central appliqué panel:
- Sky and grass: ½ yd. (45 cm) pale blue and dark green fabric
- Sea: 4-in. (10-cm) strip of dark blue fabric
- Ark: scraps of beige and brown print fabrics
- Dove: scrap of white fabric

For the animal and people patches:
- Animal background patches: ¾ yd. (68.5 cm) white fabric

Note: Each animal motif requires only small scraps or 6 in. (15 cm) of the following colors:
- Lizard: yellow abstract scraps
- Lion: small beige print, darker brown print scraps
- Lioness: beige scraps
- Dog: beige, black scraps
- People: beige, pink, red, brown scraps

- Chicken: orange print, red print scraps
- Elephant: mid-gray, black scraps
- Rabbit: light gray print scraps
- Cow: black, white scraps
- Horse: brown/orange mottled print, dark brown/black print scraps
- Duck: yellow print, orange print scraps
- Cat: orange, white scraps
- Giraffe: orange, brown small print scraps
- Donkey: mottled gray print, light gray scraps
- Snake: light gray scraps
- Monkey: light brown, dark brown scraps
- Panda: black, white scraps
- Fusible web: 1-yd. (91.5-cm) piece
- Basic sewing supplies
- Iron
- Hand-sewing needles
- White, black, brown, and green cotton embroidery floss
- Machine-sewing cotton thread to match various colored fabrics

Cutting

For the white animal patches, cut sixteen 6½-in. (16.5-cm) squares.

For the short red strips between patches, cut twelve 6½- x 1½-in. (16.5- x 4-cm) strips; also cut two 1½- x 13½-in. (4- x 34-cm) strips for the area between the central panel and the top and bottom animal patches.

For the two red strips between the patches and center panel, cut two 1½- x 41½-in. (4- x 105.4-cm) strips.

For the red outer strips, cut two 1½- x 27½-in. (4- x 70-cm) strips, and two 40½- x 1½-in. (103- x 4-cm) strips.

For the green binding, cut two 1½- x 29½-in. (4- x 75-cm) strips, and two 1½- x 42½-in. (4- x 108-cm) strips.

For the backing, cut one 31- x 45-in. (79- x 114.3-cm) rectangle of green fabric.

Using Fusible Web

Fusible web is an adhesive web that is used to fuse two fabrics together. It seals raw edges, preventing fraying, and is ideal for machine appliqué.

1 Trace each separate appliqué shape onto the paper side of the fusible web, as shown at right and cut roughly ½ in. (12 mm) outside the drawn lines. Press the fusible side of the web onto the wrong side of the fabric, as shown on page 168, and cut out each appliqué shape, as shown at right.

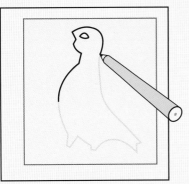

Fusible web

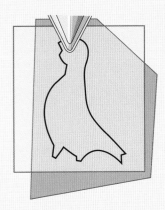

Appliqué shape

2 Peel off the paper backing to reveal the slightly shiny adhesive layer, as shown at right. Prepare all of the remaining appliqué shapes in this way.

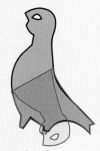

Wrong side of appliqué shape

3 Place the shape, adhesive side down, in the correct position on the right side of the background fabric. Then press it with a medium-hot iron to fuse the two fabrics together, as shown at right.

Machine Appliqué

Templates for all motifs are provided on pages 242–246. Note that some animal motifs share a body shape but have several head options. As you stitch the animals using the following directions, finish all ends of sewing thread securely on the wrong side with a few backstitches to prevent raveling.

4 Machine-satin-stitch the raw edges of the appliqué shapes, in order, to the correct background fabric, as shown at right. Repeat for the remaining appliqué shapes, referring to the photo on page 177.

171

Stitching the Central Panel

1 Lay the cut sky piece on a flat surface and add all the prepared ark pieces in order, as shown below. Press to fuse the pieces to the sky and satin-stitch over the raw edges.

2 Apply the sea and grass layers, as shown below, and baste them in place by hand. Machine-satin-stitch over the raw edges.

3 Machine-appliqué Mr. and Mrs. Noah, the heart, and the dove in the correct positions on the background panel in the same way.

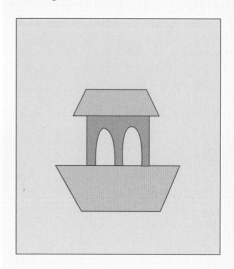

The Animal Patches

Prepare all appliqué pieces with fusible web, as described on page 171, then fuse each piece in the correct position on a 6½-in. (16.5-cm) white background square, following the numbered sequences. Machine-satin-stitch over the raw edges of each piece. Embroider tiny features with embroidery floss, referring to the quilt photo on page 177.

◆ Assembling the Quilt Top

1 Using ¹/4-in. (6-mm) seam allowances, join the two top animal patches together with a 1¹/2- x 6¹/2-in. (4- x 16.5-cm) red strip between, as shown below. Stitch another 1¹/2- x 6¹/2-in. (4- x16.5-cm) red strip between the bottom two animal patches. Press the seam allowances toward the red strips. Stitch a 1¹/2- x 13¹/2-in. (4- x 34-cm) red strip to the upper and lower edges of the central panel, then to the previously joined patches, as shown below.

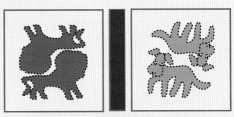

2 Assemble two side sections consisting of six animal patches each, with short red strips in between each square. Sew a 1¹/2- x 41¹/2-in.- (4- x 105.4-cm)-long red strip to each side of the central panel, as shown above. Stitch these strips to each side section. Press the seam allowances toward the red strips. (Continued overleaf.)

Assembling the Quilt Top (continued)

3 To complete the quilt top, stitch a 1¹/₂- x 27¹/₂- in. (4- x 70-cm) red-strip section to the upper and lower edges of the central panel. Press, as before. Sew a 1¹/₂- x 43¹/₂-in. (4- x 110.5-cm) strip along each side in the same way. Press the completed quilt top.

174

❖ Quilting

1 Lay the backing fabric on a flat work surface. Place the rectangle of batting on top, then place the quilted top over it. The batting and muslin edges are 2 in. (5 cm) wider on each side than the quilt top all around, and they will be trimmed to fit after the quilting is completed.

2 Baste through all three layers so that they will not shift while you quilt. Then, using red quilting thread and very small running stitches, quilt around the edge of the central panel, then around each of the animal patches in turn. Make sure you finish off all the threads securely by weaving the thread through three or four stitches inside the batting layer only. Then bring the thread to the surface and clip. Trim the edges of the batting and backing even with the quilt top.

❖ Finishing

1 Pin and baste the two 2- x 43$\frac{1}{2}$-in. (5- x 110.5-cm) green binding strips to the sides of the quilt, with right sides together, and matching the raw outer edges. Machine-stitch in place, taking a $\frac{1}{2}$-in. (12-mm) seam allowance, as shown above.

2 Apply the two 2- x 31$\frac{1}{2}$-in. (5- x 80-cm) binding strips along the top and bottom edges of the quilt in the same way, including stitching across the side binding strips, as shown above. (Continued overleaf.)

◆ Finishing (continued)

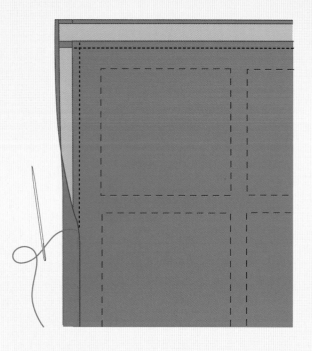

3 Turn the quilt over and lay it wrong side up. Fold a ¹/₂-in. (12-mm) hem along each raw edge of the side binding strips, and press them flat. Wrap the bindings over the edges of the quilt along both sides. Bring the fold to meet the previous stitching line. Baste along the fold, then slipstitch neatly in place and remove the basting stitches.

Appliqué

For the binding, you can use the same blind stitch as for needle-turn appliqué, taking care to stitch only through the binding and backing layer.

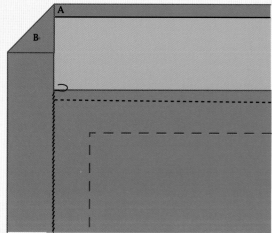

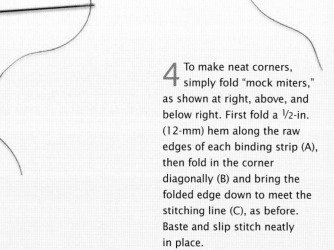

4 To make neat corners, simply fold "mock miters," as shown at right, above, and below right. First fold a ¹/₂-in. (12-mm) hem along the raw edges of each binding strip (A), then fold in the corner diagonally (B) and bring the folded edge down to meet the stitching line (C), as before. Baste and slip stitch neatly in place.

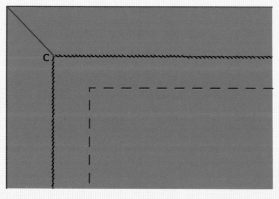

The eye-catching fabrics in this baby quilt are a delight
to behold, and the simple frolicking animals create a
joyful design around the classic Noah's Ark.

Other Appliqué Techniques

ALTHOUGH MOST HAND AND MACHINE APPLIQUÉ INVOLVES STITCHING COLORFUL SHAPES TO A LOWER PIECE OF BACKGROUND FABRIC, REVERSE APPLIQUÉ AND SHADOW APPLIQUÉ OFFER OTHER INTERESTING OPTIONS. AFTER YOU'VE BECOME FAMILIAR WITH REGULAR APPLIQUÉ METHODS, MOVE ON TO THESE TECHNIQUES AND ENJOY THE SPECIAL EFFECTS YOU CAN CREATE WITH THEM.

Reverse Appliqué

In reverse appliqué, a seam allowance is cut inside an appliqué shape that is marked on a top layer of fabric. The seam allowance is turned under and stitched to a layer of fabric below, creating a recessed look in the appliqué. One of the best-known forms of this technique is mola work, which is done by the Cuna Indians of the San Blas Islands, off the coast of Panama. Their designs depict animals, birds, and flowers, as well as legends and scenes from their daily lives. Originally, they reverse-appliquéd brightly colored rectangles and joined them to sleeves made from other fabric to create simple blouses. The Hmong people of the hill tribes in Northern Thailand also use reverse appliqué for garments and wearable accessories like collars, and their work has an incomparable delicacy and refinement.

For your first experience, use finely woven cotton fabrics so that the edges are easy to turn under without fraying. Solid-colored fabrics in contrasting shades work well, and you can often create interesting effects with small prints. As a rule, it is better to place dark fabrics on top of light ones to avoid seam allowances that show through the top layer. Choose a design that has simple lines without sharp angles, points, or narrow shapes, and work with only three layers of fabric. You can progress to adding more layers of fabric as your skills increase.

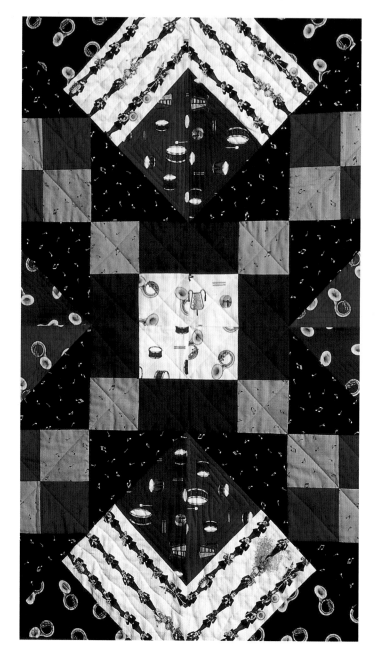

OPPOSITE **The scalloped border adds a cadence of curves that completes this design to perfection.**

RIGHT **The musical motifs in this quilt enhance the structure of the patchwork blocks that "march" alongside them.**

Stitching by Hand

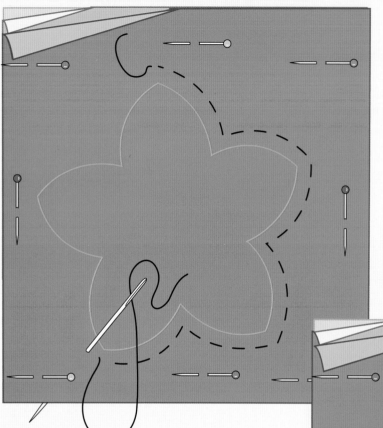

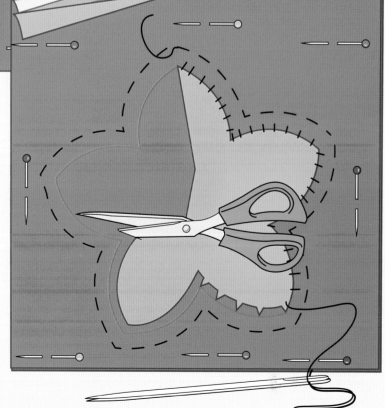

2 Using a small, sharp pair of scissors, cut away a short portion of the top fabric ¼ in. (6 mm) inside the marked lines of the design, as shown below. Along the inner curves, clip the seam allowance almost up to the line at close intervals, as shown below. Turn under the seam allowance and slip stitch it in place through all layers. At the inner corners, clip the seam allowance up to the marked point, as for hand appliqué (*see page 158*). At the outer corners, trim the seam allowance before turning it under.

1 Trace the flower design from page 246 onto the dull side of the freezer paper and cut it out. Cut three layers of fabric the same size, all on the straight grain. Mark the design on the top layer of fabric, using a quilter's pencil or water-erasable pen (*see page 16*). Pin the three fabric layers together, with the right sides facing up. Baste the layers together ½ in. (12 mm) outside the marked design, as shown above.

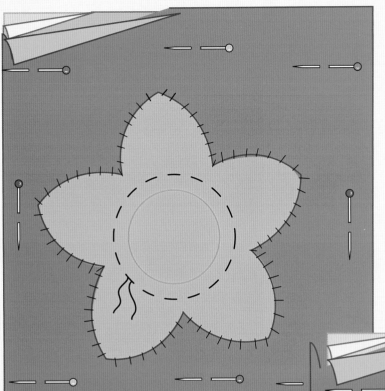

That Extra Touch

Add regular appliqué to reverse appliqué to add sparkle or shine, using specialty fabrics like lamé or sparkly, sequined fabrics. Cut small circles for flower centers and stitch them at the center of a reverse-appliquéd blossom.

4 Cut a seam allowance inside the circle and clip it at close intervals as before. Turn under the seam allowance and stitch it to the third layer of fabric. Remove the basting stitches. On the wrong side of your work, trim the third layer of fabric to 1/4 in. (6 mm) from the stitched line. Press the completed design.

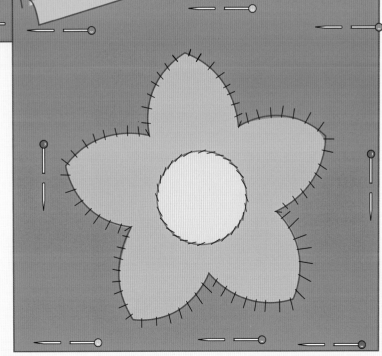

3 Continue cutting and stitching just an inch or two (2.5–5 cm) at a time until you complete the flower design, exposing the second layer of fabric. Remove the basting stitches. Trace a circle design onto freezer paper and cut it out. Mark around the circle template at the center of the flower shape, as shown above. Baste around the circle shape, as shown.

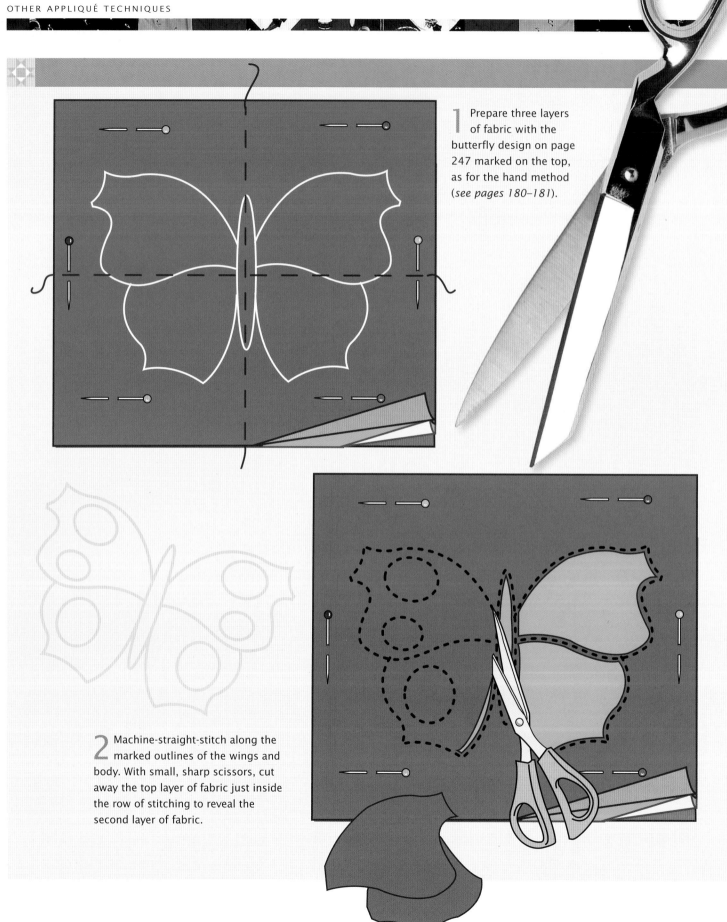

1 Prepare three layers of fabric with the butterfly design on page 247 marked on the top, as for the hand method (*see pages 180–181*).

2 Machine-straight-stitch along the marked outlines of the wings and body. With small, sharp scissors, cut away the top layer of fabric just inside the row of stitching to reveal the second layer of fabric.

3 Adjust the stitch width and length of the zigzag (or satin) stitch on your sewing machine to the scale of the design by experimenting on a fabric scrap. When you are pleased with the look of your satin stitch, satin stitch over the first row of straight stitching. On the wrong side of your work, trim the second layer of fabric to ¼ in. (6 mm) from the stitched lines. Mark the circle and oval shapes from page 247 onto the wings, as shown at right, using the direct tracing method (*see page 124*) or freezer-paper templates.

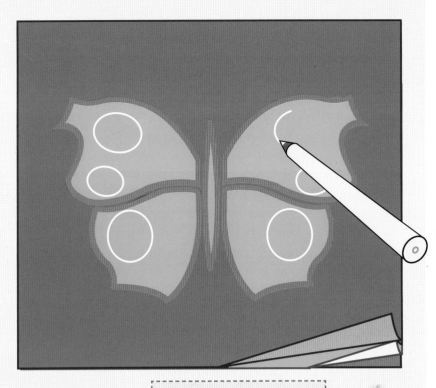

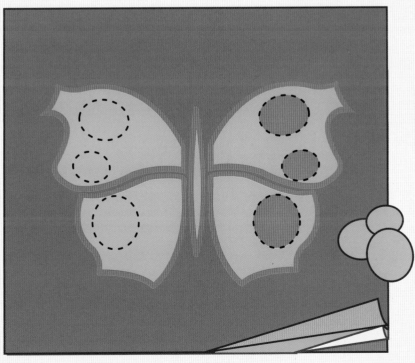

When to Add More Basting

You can increase the stability of a large-scale project that features several reverse appliqué shapes and multiple fabric layers by basting horizontally and vertically by hand through the center of the fabrics.

4 Repeat Steps 2 and 3 to reverse appliqué the circles and ovals on the wings, revealing the third layer of fabric. On the wrong side of your work, trim the third layer of fabric to ¼ in. (6 mm) from the stitched lines. Press the completed design.

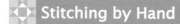

Shadow Appliqué

Transparent fabrics, such as organdy, voile, organza, nylon, or net give shadow appliqué a delicate appearance that, in addition to quilts, makes it suitable for lingerie, evening wear, scarves, or wedding veils. For your first experience, these fabrics will be fairly easy to handle because of their stiffness. You can move on to using softer fabrics, like chiffon or georgette, as you gain more experience.

In shadow appliqué, a top layer of transparent fabric is marked with the appliqué shape and stitched to a lower layer of fabric with the buttonhole stitch. The lower layer of fabric is then trimmed away just outside the embroidery stitches. Traditionally, two white fabrics were favored for the top and bottom layers, but you can also achieve interesting effects by using different colors for either the top or the bottom fabric.

Experiment with scraps, taking into account both the color, or colors, you choose and their intensity. For example, a yellow fabric placed beneath a blue voile will look green, while a bright red will become a paler pink beneath white organdy. After you have done shadow appliqué by hand, experiment with including colored appliqué shapes; then move on to machine techniques.

184

Accent Your Home Décor

Consider incorporating shadow appliqué into decorative items, such as lamp shades, pillows, or lacy curtains, to make the most of its see-through quality.

Stitching by Hand

Follow these steps to do shadow appliqué by hand.

1 Cut two pieces of transparent fabric, the same size, but in different colors. Trace the fish design from page 247 onto freezer paper and cut it out. Using a water-soluble fabric marker, mark very lightly around the freezer-paper template on the top fabric. Baste the two fabrics together, and mount them in an embroidery hoop, as shown below, aligning the straight grains.

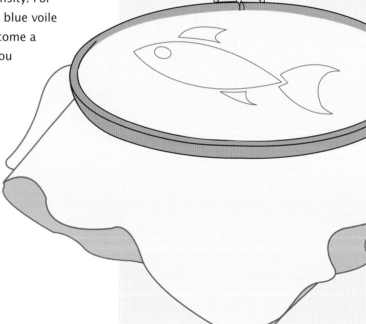

2 Using fine embroidery thread or floss, do small pin stitches by hand along the marked lines of the design through both layers of fabric. Start by bringing a knotted thread up on the marked line, and do a short backstitch, as shown at right.

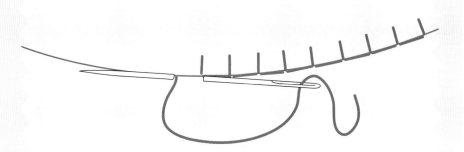

3 Do a second backstitch over the first one, this time bringing the needle out to the left and diagonally above the marked line. Insert the needle at your starting point again and bring it out to the left along the stitching line. Repeat Steps 2 and 3 to continue. End by taking the thread to the wrong side of your work and doing a few backstitches. Knot and clip the thread.

4 Remove your work from the hoop. On the wrong side of your work, trim the excess lower fabric just outside the embroidery stitches.

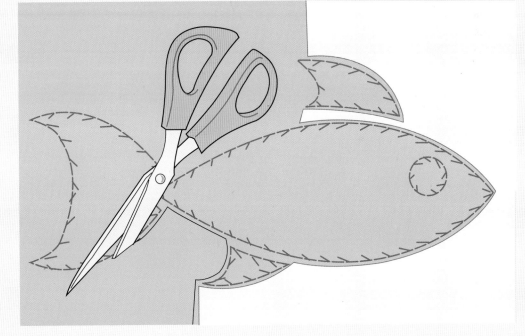

◆ Stitching by Machine

Trace the design from page 247 onto tracing paper. Prepare two transparent fabrics as for the hand method (*see pages 184–185*), with the traced design pinned and basted to the top layer. Do a row of straight machine stitching through the tracing paper and both fabrics. Tear the paper away. On the wrong side of your work, trim the excess fabric as for the hand method. Finish by doing a line of narrow satin stitching directly over the straight stitching, as shown below.

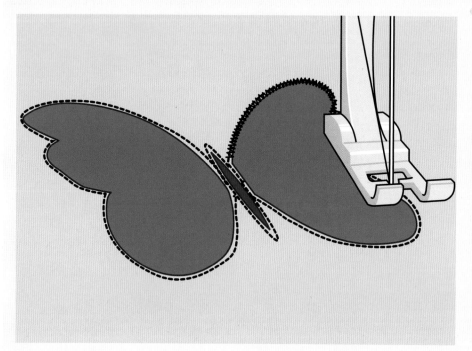

Trimming Tool

For trimming away seam allowances on delicate or cotton fabrics, use a sharp, small pair of embroidery scissors with a serrated blade.

◆ Carrickmacross Lace—British Methods

1 Although known as a lace, this textile from the Irish town of Carrickmacross is actually a net appliqué worked in a similar way to shadow appliqué, except that in this case, the appliqué fabric is placed on top instead of beneath the net background.

2 For this method, a layer of fine lawn or muslin is laid on top of cotton or nylon net. The outline is stitched by hand with the running stitch and the excess trimmed away around the appliqué shape. To prevent fraying, the running stitch is then overcast, and further decorative elements are embroidered to link the appliqué motifs.

Shadow Appliqué with Colored Shapes

This technique usually combines an opaque background fabric with a transparent top fabric and colorful appliqué shapes. For a padded effect, use felt or wool fabric for the appliqués.

1 Transfer the outline of your chosen appliqué design to a foundation fabric (*see pages 60–61*) and mount it in an embroidery hoop, as shown below. Cut out colorful appliqué shapes with no seam allowances. Position and baste the shapes onto the background fabric, knotting the thread on the underside, or use fabric glue to position them securely.

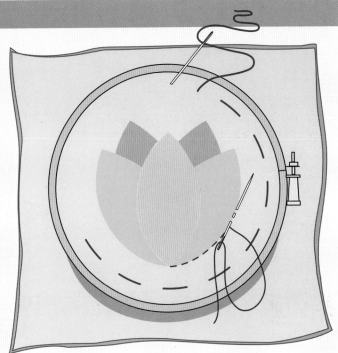

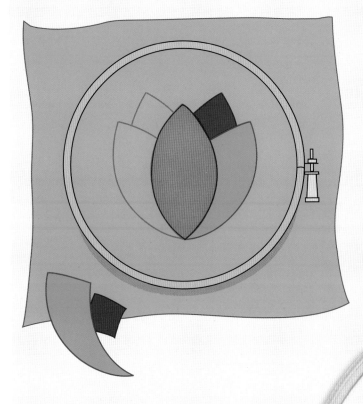

2 Cut a layer of transparent top fabric the same size as the background fabric. Pin and baste it in place over the background fabric, matching the grain lines. Using embroidery thread or floss that blends with the colors of the appliqué shapes, do running stitches, as shown above, backstitches, or decorative stitches around each shape.

March to the Music! Quilt

Bold colors strike just the right note in this dramatic quilt featuring musical fabrics by Gail Kessler of Andover-Makower Fabrics. The curved swags in the outer border are printed right on the fabric (*see page 193*), but they can also be appliquéd by hand or machine, using the templates on page 248.

Materials

- Gold notes fabric: 3/8 yd. (34.5 cm)
- Blue notes fabric: 3/8 yd. (34.5 cm)
- Black notes fabric: 5/8 yd. (58 cm)
- Red notes fabric: 5/8 yd. (58 cm)
- Cream Sousa fabric: 1/4 yd. (23 cm)
- Cream drums fabric: 1/4 yd. (23 cm)
- Blue drums fabric: 3/8 yd. (34.5 cm)
- Red drums fabric: 3/8 yd. (34.5 cm)
- Blue Sousa fabric: 3/8 yd. (34.5 cm)
- Red Sousa fabric: 3/8 yd. (34.5 cm)
- Black Sousa fabric: 1/2 yd. (46 cm)
- Marching Stripe fabric: 3/4 yd. (68.5 cm)
- Swag border fabric: 2 1/2 yd. (229 cm)
- Backing fabric: 4 1/2 yd. (411 cm)
- Batting: 72 in. (183 cm) square
- Binding fabric: 5/8 yd. (58 cm)

Four-Patch Blocks

The four-patch blocks form the diagonal design in each quadrant of this quilt. Follow these steps to cut and piece them.

Cutting for the Four-Patch Blocks

1 From the gold notes fabric, cut twenty 4 1/2-in. (11.5-cm) squares.

2 From the red notes fabric, cut eight 4 1/2-in. (11.5-cm) squares.

3 From the cream drums fabric, cut two 4 1/2-in. (11.5-cm) squares.

4 From the cream Sousa fabric, cut two 4 1/2-in. (11.5-cm) squares.

5 From the blue notes fabric, cut sixteen 4 1/2-in. (11.5-cm) squares.

Dimensions

Finished quilt is approximately 68 in. (173 cm) square.

Piecing the Four-Patch Blocks

1 Referring to the diagrams below and the quilt photo on page 193, lay out the following four-patch blocks in the order indicated.

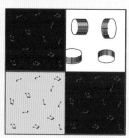
gold notes, red notes, red notes, cream Sousa

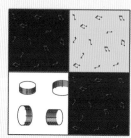
red notes, gold notes, cream drums, red notes

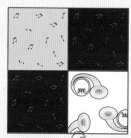
red notes, cream drums gold notes, red notes

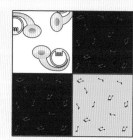
cream Sousa, red notes red notes, gold notes

2 Sew each of the four-patch blocks from Step 1 together in two horizontal rows. Press the seam allowances toward the red fabric. Sew the two horizontal rows together, as shown at left. Press the completed four-patch blocks. Do not sew the four four-patch blocks together at this time.

3 Sew a 4 1/2-in. (11.5-cm) gold square to a 4 1/2-in. (11.5-cm) blue square. Press. Repeat to make a second row. Reverse the position of one row and sew the two rows together, creating a four-patch block, as shown below. Press. Repeat to make a total of eight blue-and-gold four-patch blocks.

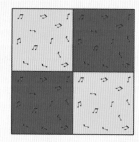
Make 8

Diagonal Rows

Follow these steps to make the diagonal rows for each quadrant of the quilt.

From the black notes fabric, cut eight 8⅞-in. (22.5-cm) squares. Cut these squares apart diagonally from corner to corner, to create 16 setting triangles.

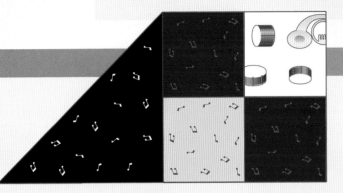

Piecing the Diagonal Rows

1 Lay out two blue-and-gold four-patch blocks with four black setting triangles between them, as shown at right. Sew the top setting triangle to the left edge of a red-cream-and-gold four-patch block to form the top row. Press.

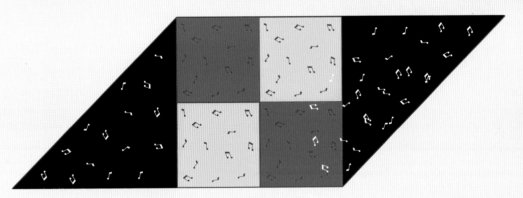

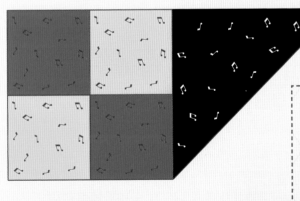

2 Referring to the Step 1 diagram above and left, sew two black setting triangles to opposite sides of a blue-and-gold four-patch block to form the middle row. Press.

3 Referring to the Step 1 diagram, sew a black setting triangle to the right edge of a blue-and-gold four-patch block to form the bottom row. Press.

Chain Piecing

To make it faster to piece the remaining diagonal rows of this quilt, lay out stacks of each piece in the proper assembly order and chain piece the units together, referring to page 33.

4 Referring to the Step 1 diagram, sew the three rows together to form one diagonal row. Press. Referring to the quilt diagram on page 191, and the quilt photo on page 193, make three more diagonal rows, taking care to position the four-patch blocks, as shown in the photo on page 193.

Setting Triangles

Follow these steps to piece the four striped setting triangles for the quilt.

Cutting the Sousa and Drums Setting Triangles

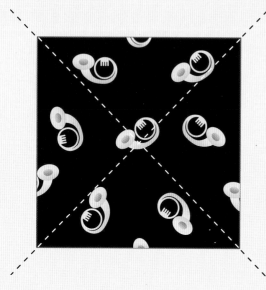

1 From the black Sousa fabric, cut two 13¼-in. (34-cm) squares. Cut these squares in half diagonally twice, to create a total of eight triangles.

2 From the red drums fabric, the blue drums fabric, the red Sousa fabric, and the blue Sousa fabric, cut one 8½-in. (22-cm) square each. Cut these squares in the same manner as explained in Step 1.

3 From the marching band striped fabric, cut eight 6½- x 13-in. (16.5- x 33-cm) rectangles, centering the marching band stripe within each rectangle, as shown in the diagram below for Piecing the Setting Triangles.

Piecing the Sousa and Drums Setting Triangles

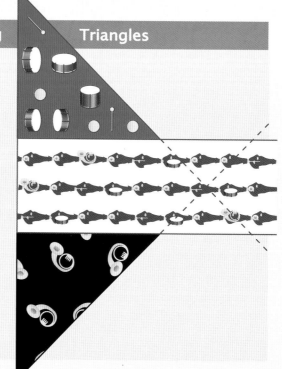

1 Lay out a 6½- x 13-in. (16.5- x 33-cm) marching band striped rectangle with a black Sousa triangle on one side and a blue drum fabric on the other side, and sew them together, as shown at right. You will be sewing the short side of each triangle to the marching band striped rectangle. Trim, as indicated by the dashed lines. Press.

2 Referring to the quilt photo on page 193, sew seven more setting triangles, taking care to place the triangle fabrics as shown. Press.

190

Putting It All Together

Follow these steps in order to assemble the four quadrants of the March to the Music! quilt.

◇ Adding the First Border

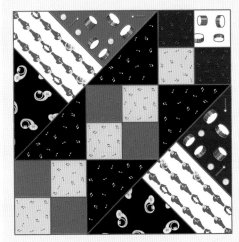

1 For the lower-left quadrant of the quilt, sew together one diagonal row and two Sousa and Drums setting triangles, as shown above. Press. Refer to the quilt photo on page 193 for the correct positions of the fabrics.

2 Referring to the quilt photo on page 193, sew the remaining three quadrants together. Press.

3 Referring to the quilt diagram above and the quilt photo on page 193, sew the top two quadrants together and press. Repeat for the bottom two quadrants.

4 Referring to the quilt diagram and the quilt photo on page 193, sew the pairs of quadrants together to complete the quilt center. Press.

Borders

Follow these steps to add the first and second borders to the quilt center.

 Cutting for the First Border

From the red notes fabric, cut six 2½- x 44-in. (6- x 112-cm) s

 Adding the First Border

1 Sew the short ends of the strips together with diagonal seams. From the long strip, cut four 2½- x 56-in. (6- x 142-cm) strips. Find the midpoint of each strip, and the midpoint on each side of the quilt center. Matching the midpoints, pin and sew a red border strip to each side of the quilt, starting and stopping each seam ¼ in. (6 mm) from the edge of the quilt center. There will be extra fabric at each end of each border strip to allow for mitering the corner seams.

2 Referring to page 231, miter the corner seams of the first border. Trim the corner seam allowances to ¼ in. (6 mm) and press them open.

 Cutting and Preparing Backing and Binding

1 From the backing fabric, cut two strips, each 36½ x 72 in. (96 x 183 cm). Sew the two strips of fabric together along the long edges, using a ¼-in. (6-mm) seam allowance. Press the seam allowance open.

2 From the binding fabric, cut eight 2½- x 44-in. (6- x 112-cm) strips. Sew the short ends of the binding strips together with diagonal seams. Trim the seam allowances to ¼ in. (6 mm) and press them open. Fold the binding in half lengthwise and press.

Cutting for the Second Border

From the entire length of marching band printed swag fabric, cut four border strips by cutting each strip ½ in. (12 mm) from the top of the heads on each side of the printed swags. There should be five swags on each second border strip, plus a partial swag at each end.

Adding the Second Border

1 Centering the middle swag of each second border strip on each side of the quilt, sew the second border strips to the quilt center, starting and ending each seam ¼ in. (6 mm) from the edge of the quilt. Press the seam allowances toward the second border strips.

2 Referring to page 231, miter the corner seams of the second border. Trim the corner seams to ¼ in. (6 mm) and press them open.

Finishing

1 Lay the quilt backing on a flat surface, with the wrong side facing up.

2 Place the 72-in. (183-cm) batting square on top of the quilt backing, smoothing out any wrinkles.

3 Position the quilt top over the batting, smoothing out any wrinkles. Baste the three layers of the quilt sandwich together by hand, using a sewing needle and the white cotton thread.

4 Quilt by hand or machine, as desired.

5 Sew the prepared binding to the edges of the quilt, mitering the corners (referring to page 231).

6 Add a label and display sleeve to the back of the quilt, if desired.

This graphic quilt would be equally as effective as a wall hanging, table topper, or lap throw. Use the pre-printed swag border fabric by Gail Kessler of Andover-Makower, or appliqué your own swags in any color you like, using the templates on page 248.

Hawaiian Appliqué

HAWAIIAN APPLIQUÉ DESIGNS ARE CREATED BY FOLDING PAPER INTO QUARTERS OR EIGHTHS AND CUTTING ALONG THE FOLDS TO PRODUCE SYMMETRICAL MOTIFS THAT RADIATE OUTWARD FROM THE CENTER. TRADITIONALLY, HAWAIIAN APPLIQUÉ FEATURED FRUITS AND FLOWERS OF THE ISLANDS, SUCH AS BREADFRUIT, PINEAPPLES, SUNFLOWERS, OR PRICKLY PEARS. YOU CAN USE THESE MOTIFS SINGLY, FOR SMALL ITEMS LIKE PILLOWS, OR REPEAT THEM IN A LARGE QUILT.

For your first experience, use a simple design with gentle curves, rather than one that features steep curves, acute angles, or sharp corners. Choose finely woven cotton for both the top and the background fabric; avoid springy, synthetic fabrics that are difficult to handle. Hawaiian appliqué is usually done with two solid, strongly contrasting colors, but as your experience grows, you can introduce a third or fourth color, or even prints, if desired.

Needle-turn hand appliqué is the method of choice for stitching Hawaiian designs. Echo quilting (*see page 137*), which is said to resemble ocean waves, is the traditional way of quilting the background fabric. Follow these steps to learn this time-honored form of appliqué.

LEFT Viewed at certain angles, the secondary shapes created by the light background fabric can often be as interesting to look at as the symmetrical Hawaiian motifs they surround.

RIGHT Lines of the quilting can be stitched in as few as two rows that follow the Hawaiian motifs (as shown at right), or they can be repeated to fill in entire background areas densely, if desired.

Needle-Turn Hand Appliqué

Staples for Security

Before you cut the paper pattern for a Hawaiian appliqué design, staple the layers of the paper together inside the lines of your design.
That way, you can cut the pattern accurately, without the shifting that can cause distortions or irregularities.

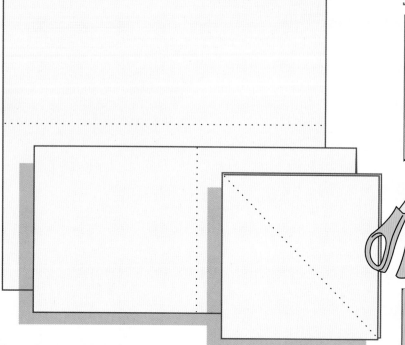

2 Bring the folded edges of the freezer-paper square together to form a triangle that divides the original square into eight sections. Draw a continuous line along the folded edges of the freezer-paper triangle. Keep in mind that the pattern you create will include the seam allowances for the appliqué. Cut the pattern out through all layers of the folded paper, as shown at left.

1 Cut a square of freezer paper to the exact dimensions of the finished background area for your Hawaiian appliqué motif. Fold the paper in half; then in half again, forming a smaller square, as shown above. Make sure that all of your folds are accurate.

Continuous Border Designs

You can create complementary border designs for Hawaiian appliqué motifs. For a rectangular quilt, cut a piece of paper in the finished width and length of the top border, and another in the finished width and length of the side border. Fold each piece of paper into the desired number of segments. Mark the design on the top segment, and staple the layers of paper together. Cut out the design. For a square quilt, cut only one length of paper for the border design. You may need to press multiple lengths of freezer paper together to achieve the total border length on a large quilt. You can overlap two freezer-paper edges and press them easily to achieve long lengths.

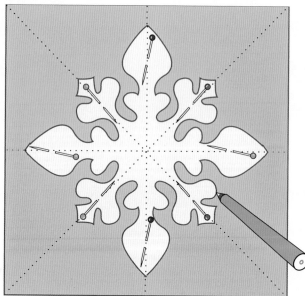

3 Cut a square of appliqué fabric ½ in. (12 mm) larger all the way around than your paper pattern. Fold and press the fabric into the same number of sections as the freezer-paper pattern. Repeat for your background fabric. Press the freezer-paper pattern to the appliqué motif fabric, matching the fold lines. Mark around the design, as shown above. Remove the freezer-paper pattern.

4 Carefully cut along the marked lines of the appliqué motif. Pin the cut motif to the background fabric, matching the grain lines and folds. Baste the motif to the background fabric along the fold lines, as shown at right. Also baste about 3/16 in. (4 mm) in from the edges of the motif, as shown.

Hawaiian Appliqué by Machine

To do Hawaiian appliqué by machine, start by bonding the appliqué fabric with fusible web (*see page 168*). Mark and cut out the motif with no seam allowances and bond, then stitch it to the background fabric with narrow satin stitching, covering the raw edges.

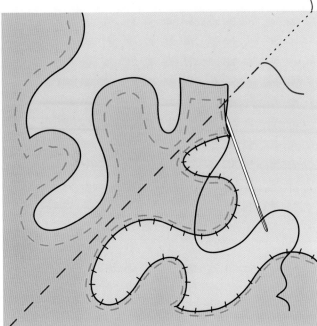

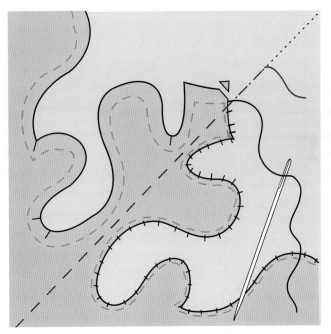

5 Starting near the center of the motif, smooth out the appliqué and background fabrics so that both lie flat. Thread a sharps needle (*see page 14*) with thread that matches the appliqué fabric. Turn under a 1/8-in. (3-mm) seam allowance with the point of the needle, and stitch the appliqué motif to the background fabric as shown above, holding the edge of the motif in place with the thumb of your nonstitching hand. Work with the fold facing you or facing away from you, as desired.

6 To stitch an outer point, stitch up to the tip and trim the excess fabric at the seam allowance, as shown above. Using the needle tip, turn under the seam allowance on the other side of the point and continue stitching. To stitch an inner point, clip the seam allowance to the point. Stitch to the point, and take one or two stitches there to prevent fraying. Continue stitching the adjacent side.

Hawaiian Floor Pillow

This unusual style of appliqué originated in Hawaii in the early 1800s, when seven missionaries formed a sewing circle, together with four native women, to teach them the art of patchwork. They did not have access to the quantity of scrap fabrics that North American needlewomen had, and Hawaiian women were reluctant to cut up large pieces of fabric, only to sew them together again. A compromise was reached, and the result was this unique form of appliqué and quilting.

Dimensions

Finished motif is 13½ in. (34 cm) square.

Finished pillow is approximately 29 in. (73 cm) square.

Cutting

For the pillow front: rotary-cut one 29-in. (73-cm) square of white fabric.

For the pillow backs: cut two 29-in. (74-cm) x 22-in. (56-cm) rectangles of white fabric.

For the Hawaiian motifs: cut four 13½-in. (38-cm) squares of red fabric.

Equipment and Materials

- Solid white fabric: 1½ yd. (137 cm)
- Red print fabric: 1 yd. (91.5 cm)
- Backing fabric: 33 in. (84 cm) square
- Batting: 33 in. (81 cm) square
- ³⁄₁₆-in. (4-mm)-thick piping cord: 3½ yd. (320 cm)
- Freezer paper: 15 in. (38 cm) square
- Pencil
- Quilter's chalk pencil
- Red cotton sewing thread
- White sewing thread
- Quilter's ruler and rotary cutter
- Cutting mat
- Basic sewing supplies and iron
- Pillow form: 28 in. (71 cm) square
- White cotton quilting thread

Note

Reserve remaining red fabric for piping.

Reducing the Pattern

You can make a smaller pillow simply by reducing the size of the motif on a photocopy machine.

Cutting the template

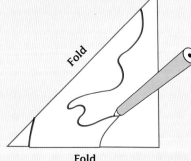

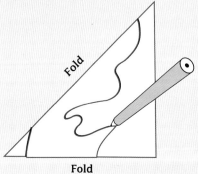

1 Trace the full-size template shown on page 248 onto freezer paper. Cut the template out.

2 Fold a 15-in. (38-cm)-square sheet of freezer paper into quarters, then diagonally, as shown above. Press the waxy side of the cut template onto the folded freezer-paper triangle and trace around the edges with a pencil, as shown at left. Label the folds. The template includes an ⅛-in. (3-mm) seam allowance except at the folded areas.

3 Remove the freezer paper pattern. Using sharp scissors, cut along the marked lines carefully, and open out the paper template as shown at right.

◈ Cutting Out the Hawaiian Motifs

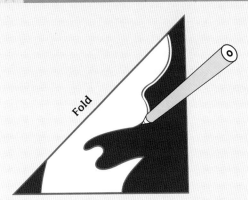

Fold

1 Fold the red appliqué motif fabric into eighths, as for the freezer paper on page 198. Press the freezer-paper template onto the folded fabric, as shown above, matching the straight and bias edges with the folds of the template. Carefully mark around the edge using a sharp chalk pencil—hold the template in place with one hand while you mark with the other. You can use pins to hold it in place, but this tends to wrinkle the paper and alter the accuracy of the cutting line.

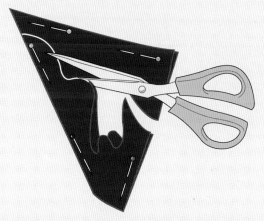

2 Remove the template and use pins to hold all the layers of fabric in place. If the fabric shifts slightly during the cutting process, the finished design will not be completely symmetrical. Cut along the chalk lines carefully and accurately using sharp scissors. Repeat Steps 1 and 2 with the other three red fabric squares.

◈ Preparing the Appliqué Motifs

1 Open out each motif and press to remove the fold lines. Fold the 29-in. (73-cm) white pillow front into quarters and press each fold. This creates guidelines for positioning the motifs. Lay the pillow front on a flat work surface, and position and pin each red motif in each quarter of the white square. Each motif has an 1/8-in. (3-mm) seam allowance. When the edges are turned in, there will be a small gap between each piece.

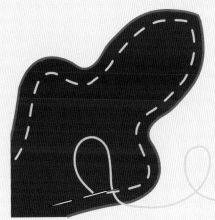

2 Pin and baste all the motifs 1/4 in. (6 mm) from the edge on the pillow front, as shown at left. Your basting stitches should follow the outline of each motif, as shown.

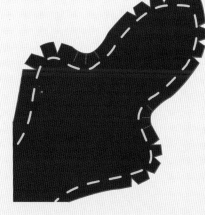

3 Use small sharp scissors to snip into the raw edges around all inner curves to facilitate turning the fabric under. Each snip should be a little less than 1/8 in. (3 mm). It is best to snip the edges of one motif at a time because this lessens the danger of fraying at the point of the snip.

Stitching the Pieces in Place

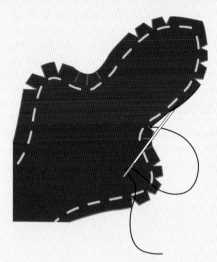

1 Using matching red thread, hand-appliqué the motifs in place. Secure the sewing thread to the back of the work with backstiches and bring the needle to the right side. Use the point of your needle to turn in the raw edge, taking no more than an $1/8$-in. (3-mm) allowance. Press lightly with your finger to flatten the fold a little as you go.

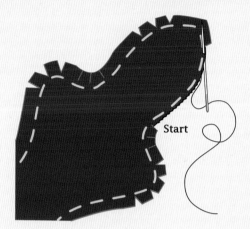

2 Stitch the fold to the pillow front, using very small slip stitches. Begin at a part of the design that is long and smooth, so you will be familiar with the technique when it is time to negotiate a corner or point. Tight inner and outer curves and corners are characteristic of Hawaiian appliqué, so it pays to take your time over these areas. Run the tip of your needle several times around the curve before you stitch so that the fabric is smoothly turned. Press again with your finger before slip stitching the curved edge securely in place.

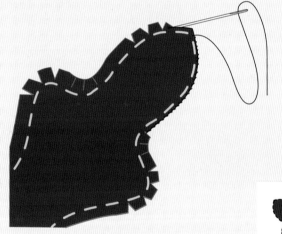

3 Sharp points take a little time to master, but it is well worth the effort. Slip stitch in the usual way to the marked point. Use the point of the needle to tuck the raw seam allowance well under, pushing toward the line of stitches just completed, as shown above. Press firmly in place with your finger, then continue to slip stitch the next side, as before.

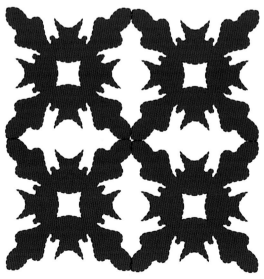

4 Repeat Steps 1 through 3 for the remaining three red motifs. Press the completed pillow front.

Quilting the Pillow Front

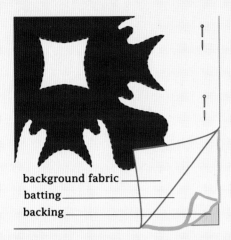

background fabric
batting
backing

1 Place the backing fabric on a flat work surface with the batting on top. Place the appliquéd pillow front on top of the two layers and pin in place. Baste in vertical and horizontal rows about 3 in. (7.5 cm) apart to secure all three layers together.

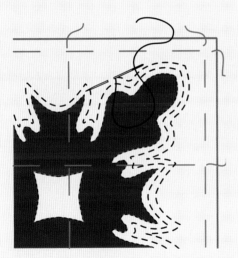

2 Begin echo quilting, using white cotton quilting thread. Quilt lines of short running stitches about $1/8$ in. (3 mm) apart, beginning at the edge of each motif, then radiating outward, following the outline of each shape. You may also quilt the red motifs in this way, but quilting only in the background color adds to the three-dimensional appearance. Remove all basting threads upon completion. Trim any excess batting or backing fabric to match the edge of the pillow front.

Adding the Piping

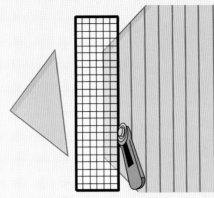

Rotary-cut $1\,1/2$-in. (4-cm) bias strips.

1 You will need to mark and cut approximately $3\,1/2$ yd. (320 cm) of $1/2$-in. (12-mm) bias fabric strips to make the piping. You will need to join several strips together to make the required length of 124 in. (314 cm). Open out the remaining red fabric on a flat work surface. Rotary-cut a line at an angle of 45 degrees to the selvage. Continue to rotary-cut several more strips $1\,1/2$ in. (4 cm) apart. Cut carefully along the chalk lines.

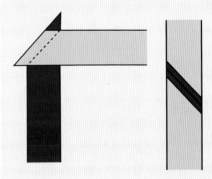

2 To join the piping strips, place two together with right sides facing and at right angles to each other, as shown at left. Machine-stitch diagonally across. Join all the strips in this way and press the seams open, taking care not to stretch the fabric. Trim all the extending points even with the piping strip.

3 Wrap the wrong side of the fabric strip around the piping cord and, keeping the raw edges together, baste close to the cord, using a piping foot on your sewing machine, as shown at left. (Continued overleaf.)

201

Adding the Piping (continued)

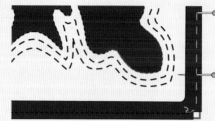

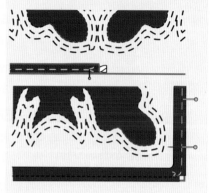

4 Place the piping on the right side of the quilted pillow front, matching the raw edges, and baste in place. Using a piping foot on your sewing machine, stitch as close to the piping as you can. It is best to begin about halfway across one side of the pillow and leave 1 in. (2.5 cm) of fabric and cord unstitched, as shown above.

5 When you reach the first corner, snip into the seam allowance of the piping. Machine-stitch up to the base of the snip. Reverse stitch for three stitches, then continue stitching forward and stitch the next side. This strengthens the corner. Turn the remaining three corners in the same way.

1 For the pillow backs, fold and stitch a ¼-in. (6-mm) double hem along one long raw edge of each piece and press. Place the pillow backs onto the pillow front with right sides together, matching the raw edges around the outside and overlapping the hemmed edges at the center. Pin and baste around the outer edge, keeping the stitches close to the piping cord. Machine-stitch close to the piping cord using a piping foot on your machine, as before.

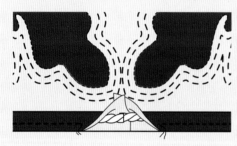

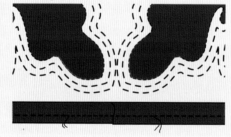

6 To join the ends of the piping, snip the excess cord, so that the ends overlap slightly. Trim the binding, so the end overlaps the beginning by approximately ¾ in. (2 cm). Unpick a few stitches at the beginning of the stitching, then fold back ⅜ in. (1 cm) along the raw edge at the end of the binding. Tuck the raw end under the folded end and twist the ends of the cord together, as shown above.

7 Machine-stitch the join close to the cord as before to finish.

2 Trim diagonally across the seam allowance at each corner of the pillow, then turn it through to the right side. Finally, insert the pillow form.

Bold two-color quilts are traditional in Hawaiian
appliqué. Use red and white, as shown here, or choose
any two highly contrasting colors that please you.

Celtic and Stained-Glass Appliqué

BOTH CELTIC AND STAINED-GLASS APPLIQUÉ FEATURE DESIGNS THAT ARE OUTLINED BY NARROW BIAS STRIPS. WHILE THE TECHNIQUES ARE SIMILAR, CELTIC AND STAINED-GLASS DESIGNS ARE VERY DIFFERENT IN CHARACTER. EXPLORE BOTH TYPES OF APPLIQUÉ, AND ENJOY USING THEM TO GIVE YOUR PROJECTS A DISTINCTIVE FLAIR.

204 ⟩ Celtic Appliqué

The intricate spirals and circular designs of Celtic appliqué take their inspiration from traditional Celtic motifs on ancient stone crosses and illuminated manuscripts with sinuous, interlaced symbols and imagery. Celtic motifs are often featured on bags, pillows, or small wall quilts. For larger projects, such as lap throws or bed-size quilts, Celtic motifs can be repeated, mirrored, or reversed, and continuous, interlaced Celtic designs are great for borders.

In Celtic appliqué, bias strips are stitched by hand or machine to a foundation fabric to form the design. For your first experience, choose a finely woven, solid-colored cotton fabric for the bias strips and a solid-colored cotton fabric in a contrasting color for the foundation. A bias press bar in the desired finished width for your bias strips is helpful for pressing turning lines.

You can leave Celtic appliqué unquilted or quilt the background areas to throw the design into relief. As your skills increase, you can experiment with adding contrasting fabric inserts to portions of the design. Whether you use commercial patterns or design your own from original Celtic sources, a protractor or circle-slice ruler, available from quilt shops, will be useful for marking the lines of the design.

Angela Madden's Celtic pieces are works of art. Enjoy learning these techniques, so you can make your own Celtic quilts.

◆ Stitching by Hand

1 Using a quilter's pencil or water-erasable fabric marker, trace the lines of the design from page 249 onto the background fabric as many times as desired. To calculate the length of the bias strip you will need, lay a piece of yarn along the lines of your marked design, as shown at right. Cut a bias strip (or strips) 2–3 in. (5–7.5 cm) longer than this length and twice the desired finished width plus ½ in. (12 mm) for seam allowances.

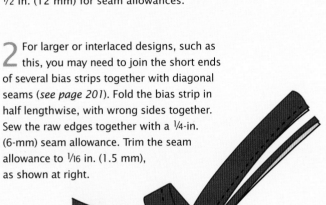

2 For larger or interlaced designs, such as this, you may need to join the short ends of several bias strips together with diagonal seams (*see page 201*). Fold the bias strip in half lengthwise, with wrong sides together. Sew the raw edges together with a ¼-in. (6-mm) seam allowance. Trim the seam allowance to ¹⁄₁₆ in. (1.5 mm), as shown at right.

3 Insert a bias press bar into the bias strip and press, centering the seam allowances on one side, as shown at right.

4 Start stitching the bias strip to the foundation fabric at a point where the bias strip will eventually be overlapped, as shown at right. Pin a short section of the bias strip over the marked line, with the seam allowances centered underneath. Slip stitch first along the inner curve of the bias strip; then along the outer curve, stretching the bias strip so it lies smoothly. Continue pinning and stitching in this manner. When you approach the next intersection of marked lines, stop approximately ½ in. (12 mm) before the lines cross.

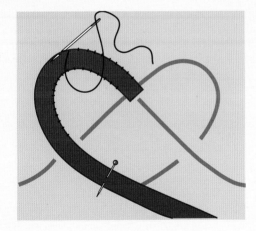

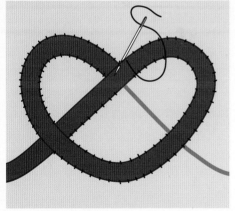

5 Begin stitching approximately ½ in. (12 mm) beyond the intersection and continue stitching the remainder of the design. To finish areas like these, tuck the end of the bias strip underneath the gap in your stitching at each intersection; then stitch the edges of the overlapped bias strips in place, as shown above.

◇ Stitching by Hand: Adding Fabric Inserts

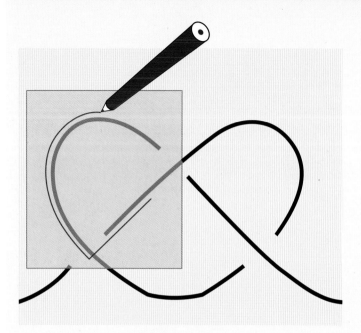

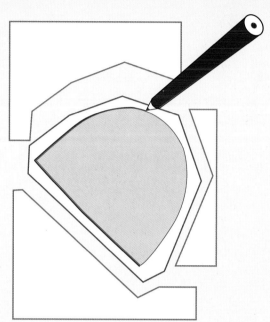

1 Trace the portion of the motif you wish to fill with a fabric insert onto freezer paper, adding ⅛-in. (3-mm) seam allowances, as shown above. Cut this shape out to use as a template for fusible web (*see page 168*).

2 Place the freezer-paper template wrong side up on the smooth side of a piece of fusible web. Trace around the template, as shown above, creating a mirror image of the original shape. Cut out the fusible-web shape with a rough ¼-in. (6-mm) margin around it, as shown.

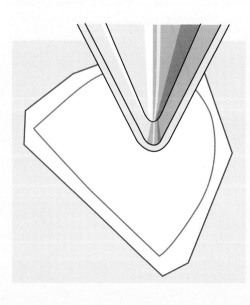

3 Press the rough side of the fusible web onto the wrong side of the insert fabric, as shown at left. Cut along the marked lines of the insert shape and peel off the paper backing.

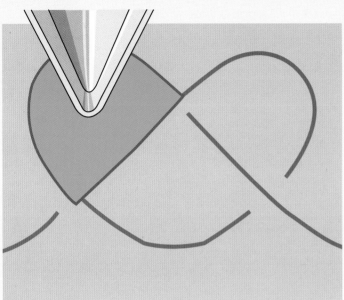

4 Position the fabric insert right side up in the appropriate area on the background fabric and press it firmly in place.

5 Stitch bias strips by hand along the marked lines of the motif (*see page 205*), covering the raw edges of the fabric inserts.

Stitching by Machine

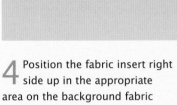

1 To do Celtic appliqué by machine, mark the design onto the background fabric and prepare the bias strips as for the hand method (*see page 205*).

2 Thread your sewing machine with invisible thread on top and thread that matches the background fabric in the bobbin. If desired, you can pin or baste the bias strips in place along the marked lines of the design, although this is not necessary. Stitch the bias strip over the marked lines, using a narrow zigzag stitch, as shown at right, and take care to ease around curves and pivot and fold the strip accurately at points.

3 Leave gaps in your stitching for overlapping bias strips at intersections, allowing long-enough thread tails for finishing on the wrong side after you complete the design.

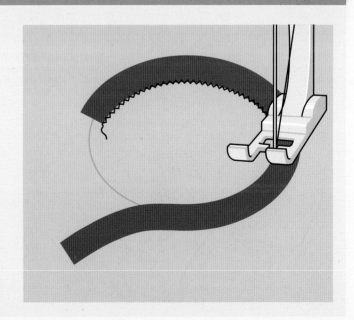

Stained-Glass Appliqué

As in Celtic appliqué, bias strips also define the lines of Stained-Glass designs. Bright, jewel-tone fabrics and contrasting bias strips emulate the look of leaded divisions in a church window. Stained Glass appliqué is often used for decorative items, such as pictures, wall hangings, or soft furnishing items.

For your first experience, choose a bold, simple design that has no steep angles. Avoid isolated motifs that do not connect with other shapes; all of the lines of a Stained-Glass appliqué design should interconnect and lead to the edges of the finished piece, as in real stained glass.

Alternatives to Bias Strips

For designs made up entirely of straight-sided geometric shapes, such as squares and rectangles, narrow ribbon can replace the bias strip. An even quicker alternative is to cover the joins with wide, machined satin stitch.

208 ◇ **Making the Design**

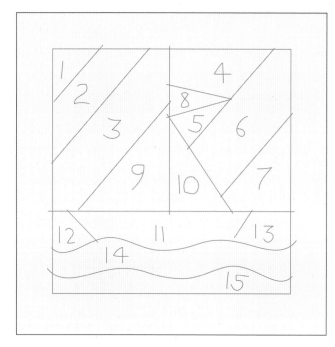

1 Trace the design of your choice onto a neutral-colored, cotton foundation fabric (*see pages 124–127*) and number each section, as shown above. Estimate the lengths of the bias strips you will need by laying string or yarn along the marked lines. Prepare bias strips as for Celtic appliqué (*see page 205*).

2 Trace each section of the design onto the nonshiny side of freezer paper, marking fabric grain lines, and cut them out. Number the sections to correspond with the numbers on the foundation fabric. Press the templates onto the right side of your chosen fabrics, matching grain lines. Mark around the templates and cut out the fabric shapes on the marked lines. Remove the freezer paper, as shown above.

Fusible Web

An alternate method for basting fabrics in Stained-Glass appliqué is to bond the fabric shapes onto the foundation fabric with fusible web, as for Celtic appliqué (*see pages 206–207*).

209

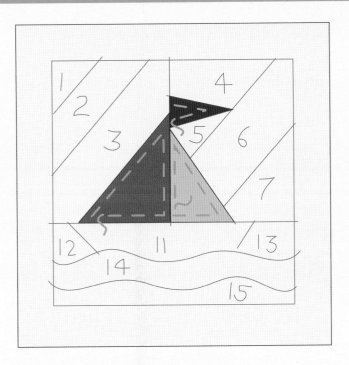

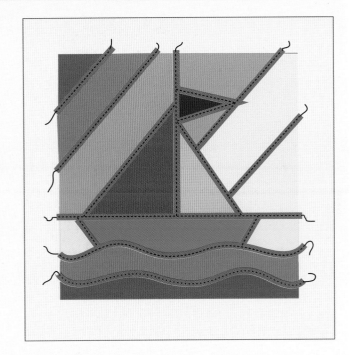

3 Baste the fabric shapes in place on the foundation fabric, as shown above, matching the numbers.

4 Prepare bias strips as for Celtic appliqué (*see page 205*), cutting them to lengths that match the outlines of the design. Stitch the bias strips onto the foundation fabric by hand (*see page 205*) or machine (*see page 207*), covering the joins between the fabric shapes, as shown above.

Celtic Batik Quilt

Celtic designs are usually associated with the prehistoric Celtic peoples of the British Isles, but this intriguing art style can be found in many other cultures throughout the world, as well. The patterns appear to be constructed from intertwined "cords" that pass alternately under and over each other and have neither beginning nor end, traditionally representing "eternity, infinity, or continuity." More correctly called "interlace" or "knotwork," many experts believe the origins of these patterns are to be found in eastern Indian art. In our project, the Celtic cords are created with batik fabrics entwined around a tropical flower. The added gold inserts bring light and warmth to this colorful modern variation on an ancient theme.

Tips on Celtic Cord Design

- The Celtic cord design is completed by a new raw-edged appliqué method that is fast and easy.
- Any worries about the raw edges can be dispensed with because the bias cords cannot fray. The use of fusible web also strengthens the fabric edges.
- Since fusible web is used behind the cords and nowhere else, no stiffness will occur. The piece will remain soft to the touch and quilt beautifully.
- This design may appear complicated at first glance, but the use of fusible web makes the cord application speedy and efficient, and the sewing is a basic zigzag throughout. The project is easy enough for a beginner to complete.
- The quilting (which can be done by either machine or hand) and colored inserts fill the spaces between and around the cords. Both provide opportunities for using alternatives from the options used here—for example, you could choose to put inserts in areas other than the ones suggested and thereby add an original touch to your finished project.

Dimensions

Finished quilt is approximately 26 x 29 in. (66 x 73 cm) square.

Materials and Equipment

- Tracing paper: 20 in. (50 cm) square
- Heat transfer pencil
- $1/2$ yd. (45 cm) paper-backed fusible web called "Wonder Under," (or "Vliesofix" or "Bondaweb" in England). Please note that substituting other fusible brands is not recommended. Once applied, many do not allow the fabric to stretch, a vital requirement for successful Celtic appliqué.
- Background fabric: 21 x 24 in. (54 x 61 cm) wide
- Backing fabric: 26 x 29 in. (66 x 73 cm) wide
- Hanging sleeve fabric: 9 x 24 in. (23 x 61 cm), to be folded in half lengthwise
- Bias cord fabric color 1: 12-in. (30-cm) square, cut on the straight fabric grain
- Bias cord fabric color 2: 12-in. (30-cm) square, cut on the straight fabric grain
- 4 border strips: two 28 x 3 in. (71 x 7.5 cm) and two 31 x 3 in. (79 x 7.5 cm), and one strip binding fabric: 3 yd. x $2^{1}/2$ in. (270 x 6 cm) can be joined
- Flower center fabric: 14 in. (35 cm) square
- Gold fabric insert: 20 in. (50 cm) square
- Cotton batting: $26^{1}/2$ x $29^{1}/2$ in. (67 x 75 cm) piece
- Thread to match backing fabric
- Nylon monofilament (invisible thread): a fine, soft variety for stitching the bias cords
- Sewing machine for the appliqué technique, (hand quilting is optional)
- Size 60/8 machine needle for use with the invisible thread, because it makes smaller holes
- An "open toe" embroidery presser foot (this gives clear view right up to needle)
- Iron and board (mini-iron optional)
- A nonstick ironing sheet
- Chalk pencil
- Sharp scissors and pins
- Circle stencil

❖ Preparing the Flower Center

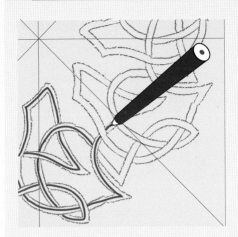

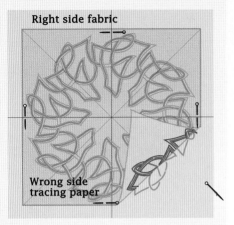

Right side fabric

Wrong side
tracing paper

Right side fabric

Wrong side
tracing paper

1 Fold the 20-in. (50-cm) tracing paper square into quarters. Fold it again, this time diagonally into eighths. Make sure all folds are aligned exactly on top of each other. Lay the paper out flat. Using the folds as a guide, trace the design on page 249 in each eighth section, linking them together as a continuous rotated design, as shown above. Draw a single red heavy line in the center of each cord section, using the heat transfer pencil, as shown above. This will be the center of, and covered by, the applied bias.

2 Fold the background fabric into quarters, finger-pressing the folds. Place a pin at the center of the paper and fabric, and pin the traced design on top of the fabric, pencil side down, with folds matched. Pin at the paper's edge, on the folds and corners. Remove the center pin.

3 Press with a medium-hot dry iron to transfer the design to the fabric. Check the transfer one corner at a time by removing the pin and lifting the tracing paper. Always replace the pin before going onto the next corner. Once the transfer is complete, the interlacing of the design can be easily understood. All cords passing under are shown as broken lines, and those passing over are continuous lines.

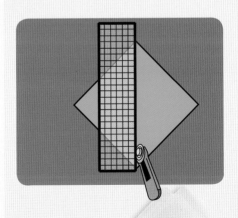

4 Iron the fusible web to the wrong side of both fabric squares intended for the bias cords. Rotary-cut diagonally across each square to establish the true bias. Start cutting strips at the point of the square, as shown at left. Cut ¼-in. (6-mm)-wide strips from one half of the square. Cut ½-in. (12-mm) strips from the other half. Separate the fusible's backing paper from the fabric strips by holding each end and giving it a sharp tug. The paper will separate as the fabric stretches. Do not throw the backing paper away.

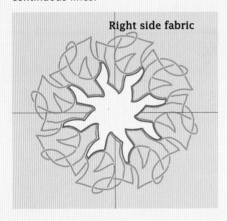

Right side fabric

5 Cut out and remove the "flower" center from the backing fabric, leaving an ⅛-in. (3-mm) approx. margin of fabric inside the line. Use the flower fabric cutout as a template to cut a new color flower insert. Cut it about ½ in. (12 mm) larger all around—check that the right side of both fabrics are facing the same direction before cutting. (Continued overleaf.)

211

◈ Adding the Inserts

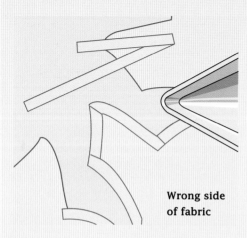

Wrong side of fabric

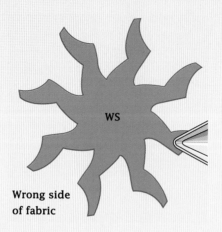

WS

Wrong side of fabric

6 Rotary-cut as many ¼-in. (6-mm) strips of fusible web as you can from the leftover piece. Lay the backing fabric wrong side up. Iron the ¼-in. (6-mm) strips of fusible web all around the edge of the flower-center hole, as shown above. (It does not matter if it folds or requires joining.) Turn the fabric right side up and trim away any fusible web visible in the hole. Peel off the paper backing from the fusible web.

7 Working from the wrong side of the background fabric, correctly position the new color flower fabric over the hole, as shown above. Make sure both fabrics overlap by the allowed ½ in. (12 mm) all around. Iron in place to bond. Repeat with all other gold-colored inserts (shown in yellow in the Step 13 diagram), completing each one before cutting another.

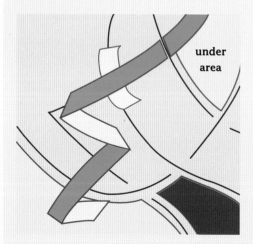

under area

8 Using a bias strip in color 1, begin to apply the bias cord starting from an "under" area (i.e., a broken line). This ensures that the end will be hidden beneath an "over." Iron the bias in place centrally over the heavy cord line you drew in Step 1. It does not matter which cord line is chosen. Each time you reach a crossing where the cord you are applying is an "over" (i.e., is a continuous line), insert a small temporary tab of the backing paper from the fusible web, as shown at left, so that your cord will not stick to the backing fabric, preventing the other cord from passing "under." Place each tab at right angles beneath the cord, as shown at left. (It is safest to use the widest width paper if you are unsure which width the "under" cord will be.)

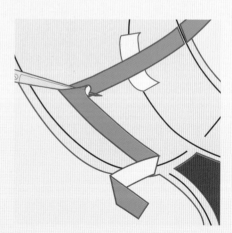

9 Use the closed point of a pair of scissors to help fold a small miter everywhere the cord direction changes with a point, as shown above. All folded miters cannot lie centrally at 45 degrees. The position of the fold will depend on the angle of the direction change. These variations will not be noticeable when they are stitched.

◆ Fusing the Cords

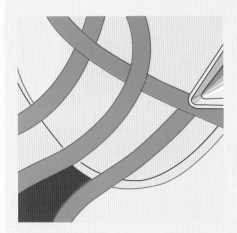

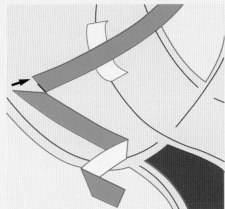

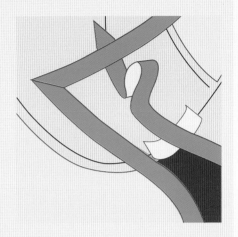

10 Cords pass straight through any crossing where they are the "under" cord. The "over" cord just gets bonded on top. (Mini-irons are ideal for applying bias cords.) Cord lengths should end on an "under." The start of the new one should butt up to the end of the ended one. That way, both ends will be hidden by the "over." If a cord is not long enough to reach the next "under," it should be cut off at the last "under" (or see Step 11 as an alternative).

11 You can also end on a point. The end is cut off along the marked line, as shown above. The new cord has the start trimmed to a point, so that it will look like a miter when it is bonded in place. Both cut and folded miters need to be completely stitched down when you sew the cords in place.

12 Passing one cord under another is not difficult as long as the backing-paper slip has been put in place. It helps if the tip of the "under" cord has a short tab of backing paper attached to the fusible side of the cord and is trimmed to a sharp point, as shown above. This acts as a "needle" to thread the tip under the "over" cord once the paper slip has been removed with a sharp tug. Untwist the "under" cord as necessary, so that it does not get damaged and lies flat.

13 Apply one complete first-color cord to the design, as shown at left, starting and stopping the bias cords at "under" areas before beginning to apply the second-color cord in the same way. (Continued overleaf.)

Stitching the Cords

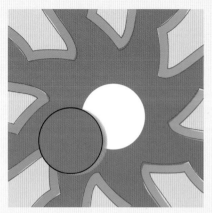

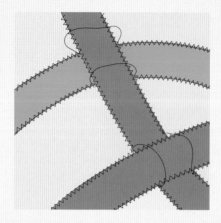

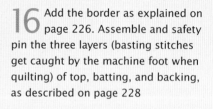

16 Add the border as explained on page 226. Assemble and safety pin the three layers (basting stitches get caught by the machine foot when quilting) of top, batting, and backing, as described on page 228

14 Using a chalk pencil and circle stencil, draw around a center circle to create a flower-center circle of a size to suit you. Make sure that it is a uniform distance from all the cord points before cutting out and removing the center, as previously described for adding colored inserts. Add a gold insert. (In the example shown, no bias cord has been applied around the circle. It has simply been zigzagged in place as follows.)

15 Stitch along both edges of both color 1 and color 2 bias cords with a size 60 machine needle, using invisible thread on the top of the machine and any preferred thread in the bobbin. Use a machine setting of 1.5 zigzag width and 1.0 stitch length. All stitching falls on the bias cords. The outside swing of the needle should just encase the bias edge to seal it. Use "clear" or "smoke" invisible thread to suit light- or dark-colored fabric. When stitching "under" cords, do not stitch across "overs." Do a few tiny straight stitches as an anchor before "jumping" across the "over" and doing a few more "anchor" stitches before starting to zigzag again. This will leave a loop of thread that can be cut away later.

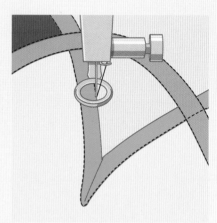

17 Machine-quilt or hand-quilt in the ditch on both sides of each bias strip. "Jump" across "overs," leaving loops, as before. Be creative with quilting patterns in other places on the quilt. The examples shown are only one alternative. Quilting can be done with the "open toe" embroidery foot and the machine feed dogs in the up position (as for machine-guided stitching). It is, however, faster and more efficient to drop the feed dogs and use either a darning foot or a quilting foot on your machine. Both of these feet need practice to use, but they do not require the work to be turned when stitching around corners and are well worth the effort.

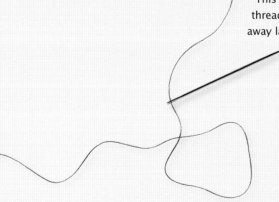

214

Angela Madden's beautiful Celtic designs are known throughout England and America. Based on equal divisions of a circle, these interlaced bias strips and colorful fabric inserts create a true work of art. Radiating designs like this create a feeling of joy in bright, saturated colors and gold.

Embellishments

PATCHWORK PROJECTS ARE DECORATIVE ENOUGH IN THEIR OWN RIGHT, BUT SOME QUILTS LEND THEMSELVES TO FURTHER ORNAMENTATION WITH EMBELLISHMENTS, SUCH AS YO-YOS, PRAIRIE POINTS, COVERED CORDING, OR GATHERED LACE. TRY THE FOLLOWING TECHNIQUES WITH SCRAP FABRICS, RIBBONS, AND LACE, AND EXPLORE THEIR POTENTIAL FOR ADDING GRACEFUL ACCENTS TO YOUR QUILTS.

216

Piping provides a neat embellishment to the trapunto pillow (above). Prairie points embellish this folk-art table center, as well as the red contrast thread color in the central star of this quilt (left).

Yo-Yos

These circular motifs are usually stitched by hand, but it is also possible to make them by machine. Yo-yos are often stitched together to form openwork throws or quilts, but they also make lovely appliqué motifs for garments or home decorations. Follow these steps to make yo-yos by hand.

Yo-Yos Unlimited!

You can attach yo-yos to a project with a few slip stitches, or sew several of them together before attaching them. You can also add beads or inserts of contrasting fabric to embellish them. Consider decorating vests, blouses, sweaters, jackets, skirts, bags, and totes with yo-yos in different colors and sizes. You can also include yo-yos in table runners, door banners, place mats, or other home decorating accents—the possibilities are never-ending!

The Basics

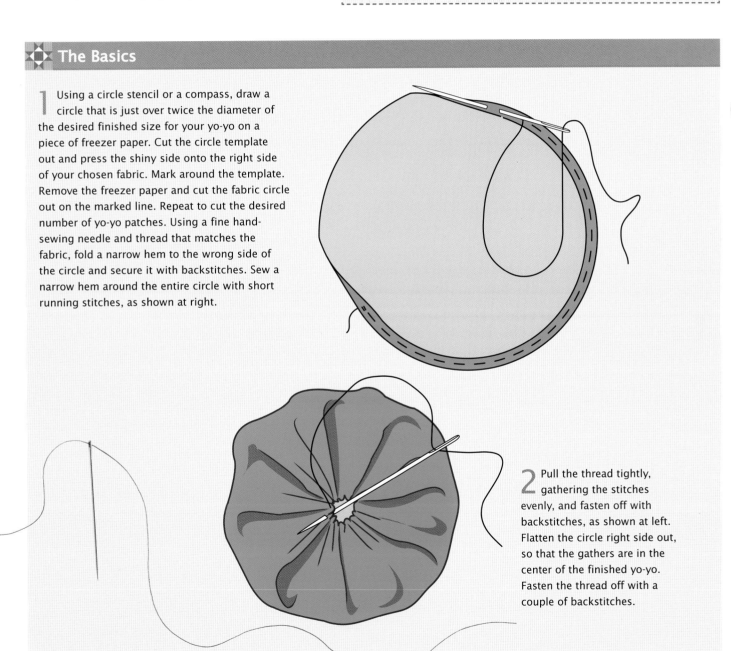

1 Using a circle stencil or a compass, draw a circle that is just over twice the diameter of the desired finished size for your yo-yo on a piece of freezer paper. Cut the circle template out and press the shiny side onto the right side of your chosen fabric. Mark around the template. Remove the freezer paper and cut the fabric circle out on the marked line. Repeat to cut the desired number of yo-yo patches. Using a fine hand-sewing needle and thread that matches the fabric, fold a narrow hem to the wrong side of the circle and secure it with backstitches. Sew a narrow hem around the entire circle with short running stitches, as shown at right.

2 Pull the thread tightly, gathering the stitches evenly, and fasten off with backstitches, as shown at left. Flatten the circle right side out, so that the gathers are in the center of the finished yo-yo. Fasten the thread off with a couple of backstitches.

Traditional Prairie Points

These triangular trimmings are usually inserted into a seam or added to the edge of a quilt. Follow these steps to make prairie points in two different ways. Choose a fabric, such as fine cotton, that can be crisply pressed. The colors can be arranged to your liking, and the size can be varied by first experimenting with folded paper squares.

◇ Single-Fold Prairie Points

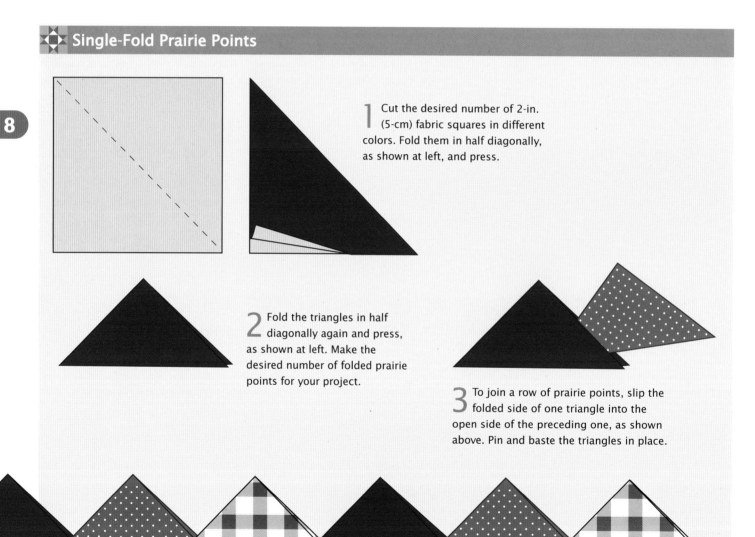

1 Cut the desired number of 2-in. (5-cm) fabric squares in different colors. Fold them in half diagonally, as shown at left, and press.

2 Fold the triangles in half diagonally again and press, as shown at left. Make the desired number of folded prairie points for your project.

3 To join a row of prairie points, slip the folded side of one triangle into the open side of the preceding one, as shown above. Pin and baste the triangles in place.

4 Repeat Step 3 to join as many triangles as required for your project. Adjust the positions of the prairie points as needed.

Baste First, Then Sew

After you have pinned your prairie points together into a length suitable for your project, baste the lower edges together by hand or machine and remove the pins before applying them to your quilt.

Continuous Prairie Points

For still a third way to make prairie points that is especially good for round quilts, see page 163 for continuous prairie points.

Double-Fold Prairie Points

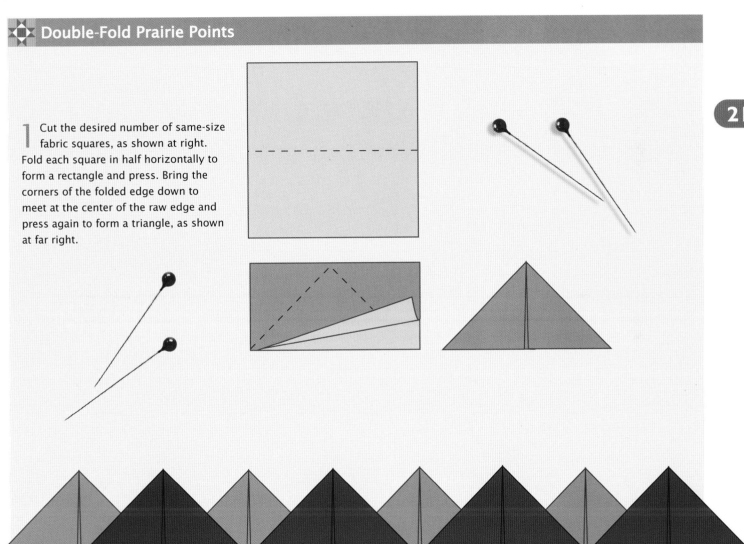

1 Cut the desired number of same-size fabric squares, as shown at right. Fold each square in half horizontally to form a rectangle and press. Bring the corners of the folded edge down to meet at the center of the raw edge and press again to form a triangle, as shown at far right.

2 Overlap and pin the prairie points together, so they are ready to insert into a seam. The lower points of each triangle should touch the center folds of the adjacent triangles, as shown above.

Covered Cording

Fabric-covered cording is often used for making button loops, but it can also be formed into spirals and knots, and stitched into the seams of a pieced quilt. For an appliqué project, covered cording would also make nice flower stems. Choose a fine, soft fabric, such as silk or poplin, so it will be easy to turn the fabric tubes right side out.

◆◇◆ Preparing Covered Cording

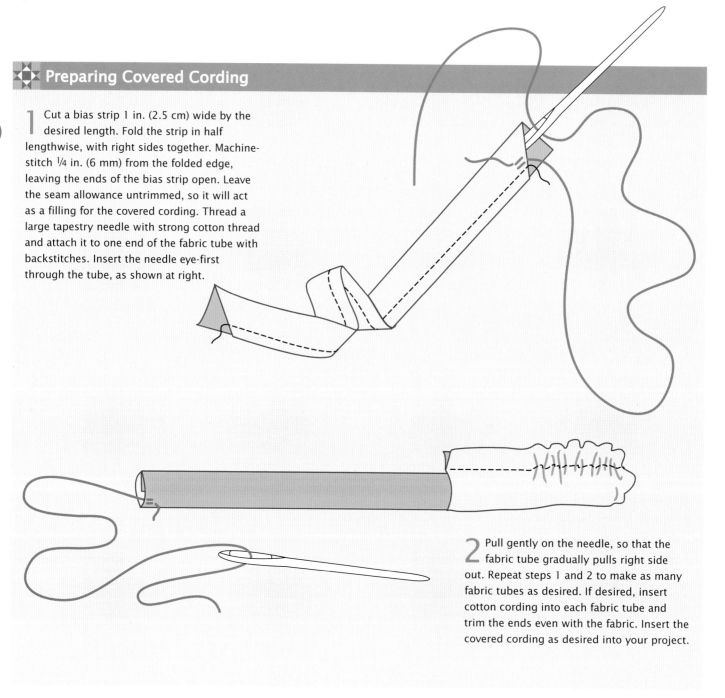

1 Cut a bias strip 1 in. (2.5 cm) wide by the desired length. Fold the strip in half lengthwise, with right sides together. Machine-stitch ¼ in. (6 mm) from the folded edge, leaving the ends of the bias strip open. Leave the seam allowance untrimmed, so it will act as a filling for the covered cording. Thread a large tapestry needle with strong cotton thread and attach it to one end of the fabric tube with backstitches. Insert the needle eye-first through the tube, as shown at right.

2 Pull gently on the needle, so that the fabric tube gradually pulls right side out. Repeat steps 1 and 2 to make as many fabric tubes as desired. If desired, insert cotton cording into each fabric tube and trim the ends even with the fabric. Insert the covered cording as desired into your project.

Inserting Embellishments into a Seam

Follow these steps to insert prairie points, covered cording, or gathered lace into a seam of a quilt or other project.

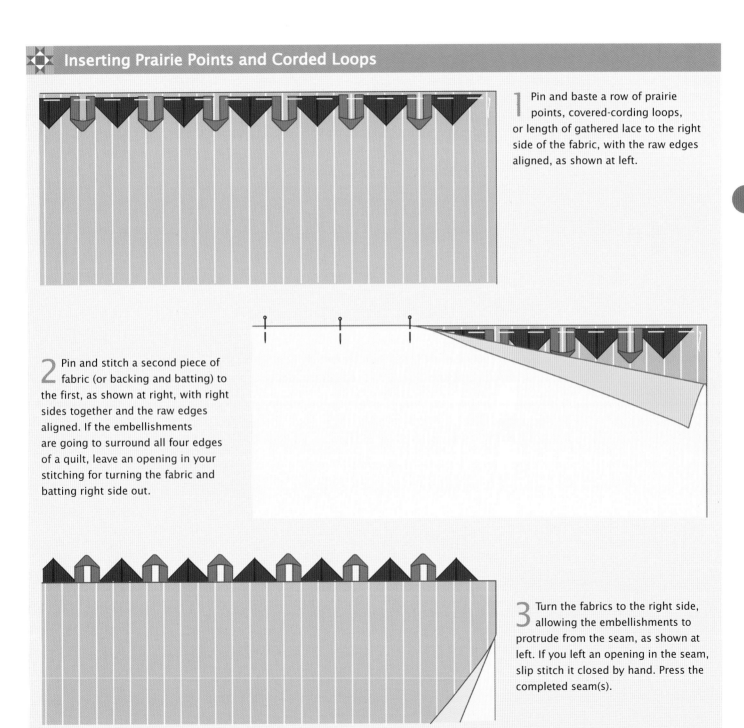

◆ Inserting Prairie Points and Corded Loops

1 Pin and baste a row of prairie points, covered-cording loops, or length of gathered lace to the right side of the fabric, with the raw edges aligned, as shown at left.

2 Pin and stitch a second piece of fabric (or backing and batting) to the first, as shown at right, with right sides together and the raw edges aligned. If the embellishments are going to surround all four edges of a quilt, leave an opening in your stitching for turning the fabric and batting right side out.

3 Turn the fabrics to the right side, allowing the embellishments to protrude from the seam, as shown at left. If you left an opening in the seam, slip stitch it closed by hand. Press the completed seam(s).

221

Creative Ways with Ribbon and Lace

Ribbon and lace can add interesting decorative elements to a patchwork or appliqué quilt. You can attach ribbons in straight lines by machine, but avoid inserting straight pins through satin ribbon, which can leave unsightly holes. Another option for attaching ribbons to fabric is fusible web, which is available in narrow widths. Tape laces can be treated in a similar fashion as ribbons, and lace edgings with one scalloped edge can be gathered and inserted into a seam (*see page 221*). Besides simply stitching ribbons and laces in straight lines, explore the following imaginative treatments, including pleating, folding, twisting, and looping, and think about where you can introduce them into your quilts.

◈ Three-Dimensional Shell Edging

1 Machine-stitch a zigzag line of very long stitches along the length of a soft, medium-width satin ribbon, as shown at right.

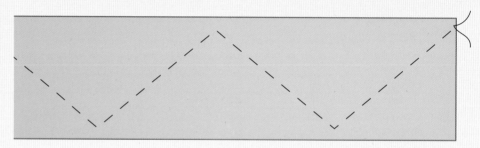

2 Pull up the stitches to form a series of gathered scallops, as shown at left. Fasten off with backstitches and stitch the shell edging on your project, as desired.

◈ Rosettes

To make a ribbon rosette, machine-stitch a row of tiny gathering stitches along one edge of a length of 1-in. (2.5-cm)-wide ribbon. Pull up the stitching and fasten off with backstitches. Sew the two edges together by hand and stitch the finished rosette on your project, as desired.

Ribbon edge

Seam

Rosebuds

1 To make a ribbon rosebud, fold a 2-in. (5-cm) square of ribbon in half diagonally, as shown at right.

2 Bring the top and bottom corners together at the lower corner, folding one over the other, as shown below.

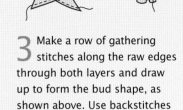

3 Make a row of gathering stitches along the raw edges through both layers and draw up to form the bud shape, as shown above. Use backstitches to secure the edges together.

223

Full Ribbon Roses

1 Fold one end of a 20-in. (50-cm) length of 1-in. (2.5-cm)-wide ribbon into a small, tight roll, working clockwise. Secure the rolled edges together at the bottom with a few backstitches, forming the center of the rose, as shown at right.

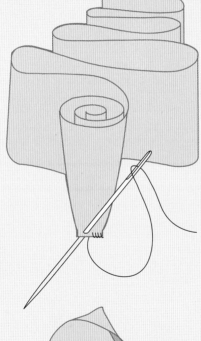

2 Fold the ribbon down at an angle and away from you, keeping the folded edge slightly above the center roll, as shown at right.

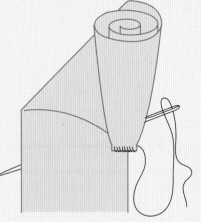

3 Turn the center roll toward the fold and take a few stitches at the bottom edge to form the first petal.

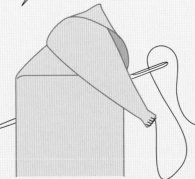

4 Continue by folding the ribbon diagonally and away from you and turning the center roll, shaping and stitching the petals in place until the rose is the desired size. Finish with a few backstitches and stitch the rose, as desired, on your project.

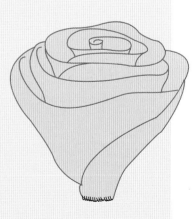

Setting and Finishing a Quilt

THE SETTING AND EDGE FINISH FOR A PATCHWORK OR APPLIQUÉ QUILT ARE TWO OF THE MOST IMPORTANT DECISIONS QUILTMAKERS FACE. IN ORDER TO ACHIEVE A PROFESSIONAL LOOK IN YOUR FINISHED WORK, THE SASHING, BORDERS, BINDING, AND EMBELLISHMENTS SHOULD ALL BE PLANNED FROM THE OUTSET. EXPLORE THE FOLLOWING IDEAS AND TECHNIQUES AND CHOOSE THE ONES YOU LIKE BEST TO ENHANCE YOUR QUILTS.

Sashing

Sometimes also called lattice, sashing is used to separate and frame the blocks of a quilt, as shown in the photo at left. The proportion and scale of the sashing strips should enhance and unify the quilt design, rather than dominate it. Explore the following sashing methods to determine which will best suit your quilts.

Sashing with Corner Squares

Follow these steps to set quilt blocks with sashing strips and corner squares.

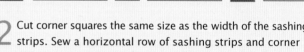

1 After determining the desired width for your sashing strips, cut them the same length as the side of the unfinished quilt blocks. To start setting the quilt blocks together, sew the vertical sashing strips alternating with blocks, beginning and ending with a sashing strip, as shown above. Press the seam allowances toward the sashing strips.

2 Cut corner squares the same size as the width of the sashing strips. Sew a horizontal row of sashing strips and corner squares, as shown above, starting and ending with a corner square. Press the seam allowances toward the sashing strips.

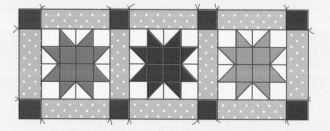

3 Stitch the horizontal row of sashing strips and corner squares from Step 1 to the blocks with the vertical sashing strips from Step 2, matching the seams carefully. Press. Repeat with additional rows as required for your quilt.

Sashing Without Corner Squares

1 Determine the width of your sashing strips and cut them the same length as the side of the unfinished quilt blocks. With right sides together, sew a horizontal sashing strip between each block, and at the top and bottom, forming a vertical row, as shown below left. Press each seam allowance toward the sashing strips. Repeat for the remaining rows of blocks on your quilt.

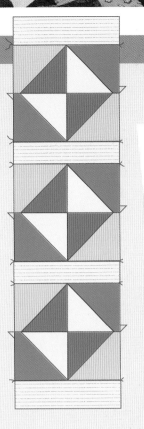

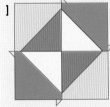

]

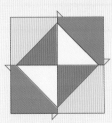

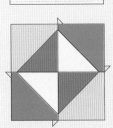

2 Cut long vertical sashing strips along the lengthwise grain of the fabric to fit the entire length of the stitched vertical row of blocks and sashing strips from Step 1. Place a pin at the center of the long sashing strip and another pin at the center of the vertical row. With right sides together, pin and sew a long sashing strip to the first vertical row. Press.

3 Repeat Step 2 to join additional vertical rows of blocks and sashing strips and long sashing strips together. Press.

Borders

A well-designed border can greatly enhance a quilt or wall hanging. Whether you decide on pieced, appliquéd, or plain border(s), use the following techniques for attaching them to your quilts with precision.

Mitered Corner Seams

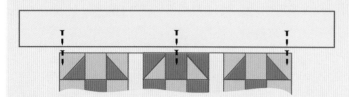

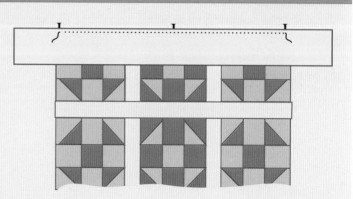

1 Cut the border strips required for your quilt on the lengthwise fabric grain, adding two border widths plus 2 in. (5 cm) to the length of each strip. Place a pin at the center on each side of your quilt. Also place a pin ¼ in. (6 mm) in from each corner of the quilt. Place a pin at the center of each border strip and place pins at the same distance from the center point as on the quilt top, as shown above.

2 Matching the placement of the center and corner pins, sew the first border strip to the quilt top, starting and stopping at the marked corner points. Repeat on the other three sides of the quilt. Do not sew over pins; remove them as you reach them.

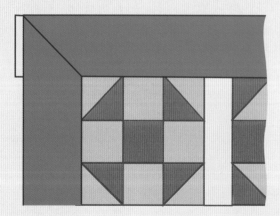

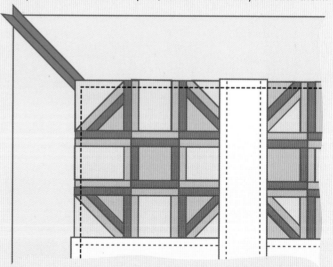

3 Lay the quilt top right side up on a flat surface. Fold one of the border strips under at a 45-degree angle and fold the adjacent border strip under to meet it, as shown above. Press the folds.

4 With right sides together, fold the quilt diagonally from the corner and align the edges of the two adjacent border strips. Pin, baste, and sew the diagonal seam along the pressed lines, stitching outward from the corner of the quilt top. Trim the excess fabric from the border strips to ¼ in. (6 mm) and press the mitered seam allowances open, as shown above. Trim the excess fabric at the corner. Repeat for the remaining three border corner seams.

Straight Corner Seams

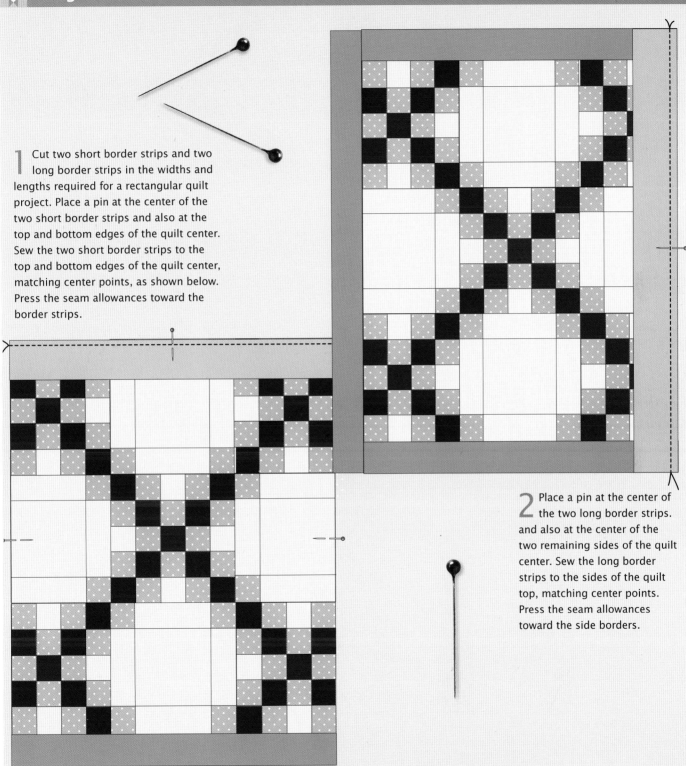

1 Cut two short border strips and two long border strips in the widths and lengths required for a rectangular quilt project. Place a pin at the center of the two short border strips and also at the top and bottom edges of the quilt center. Sew the two short border strips to the top and bottom edges of the quilt center, matching center points, as shown below. Press the seam allowances toward the border strips.

2 Place a pin at the center of the two long border strips. and also at the center of the two remaining sides of the quilt center. Sew the long border strips to the sides of the quilt top, matching center points. Press the seam allowances toward the side borders.

Backing and Layering

Your choice of backing fabric for a quilt or wall hanging should be compatible with the color and texture of the quilt top. Try both of the following methods of preparing a quilt sandwich for quilting and see which you prefer.

Traditional Method

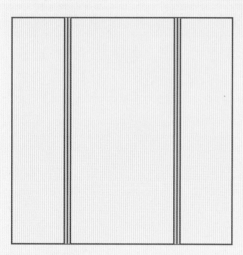

1 The backing should be 2 in. (5 cm) to 4 in. (10 cm) larger all around than the quilt top. If you need to join fabrics together for the backing, place a full fabric width down the center of the backing and add two narrower lengths on either side, as shown above. Press the seam allowances open.

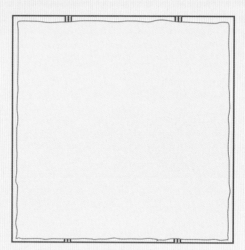

2 Lay the backing wrong side up on a flat surface. Lay the batting on top of the backing, smoothing out any wrinkles, as shown at left.

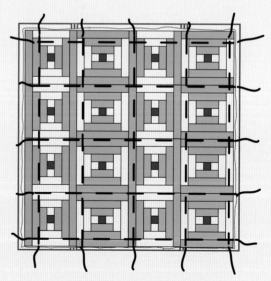

3 Center the quilt top right side up on top of the batting. Thread-baste the three layers of the quilt sandwich together in a grid, as shown above.

◈ Envelope Method

1 Place the quilt top right side down on a flat surface. Lay the batting on top and smooth out any wrinkles. Baste the two layers together in a grid, as shown at right.

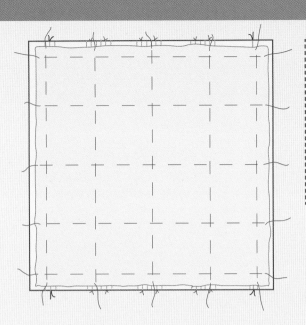

229

2 Cut the backing to the same size as the batting. Place the backing on top of the quilt top with right sides together, as shown at right. Pin or baste around the edges. Sew the three layers together around the perimeter by machine, leaving a large opening (up to 10 in./25 cm) in your stitching. Trim the excess batting from the seam and trim the corners diagonally.

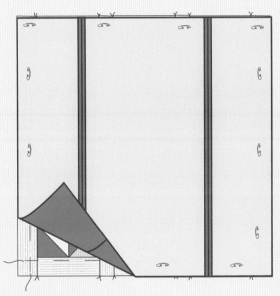

3 Turn the quilt to the right side through the opening. Turn the raw edges of the fabric to the inside at the open area. Finger-press and slip stitch the edges of the open area together, as shown at right. Baste the three layers together to prepare the quilt sandwich for quilting.

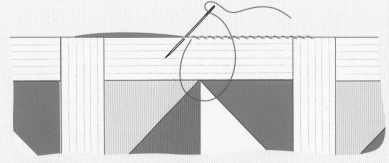

Edge Finishes

Both single-fold binding with butted corners and double-fold binding with mitered corners are good options for straight-edged quilts. For quilts with curved edges, bias binding is best. For other projects, such as bags, totes, or pillows, corded piping makes a neat and effective finishing touch. You can also decorate the edges of a quilt or pillow with gathered or pleated ruffles. Try all of these techniques for beautiful edge finishes and see which are your favorites.

Binding

Try the following binding methods and choose the ones that are most suited to your quilts. To determine the binding length, measure around the edges of the finished quilt and then add a little extra for the seam allowances and going around corners.

Single-Fold Binding

Follow these steps to bind a straight-edged quilt with single-fold, straight-grain binding.

1 To work out the width for the binding strips, double the measurement of the desired finished binding width, and add ½ in. (12 mm) for seam allowances, as shown at right. Cut the number of binding strips needed for your project for this width. If necessary, sew the short ends of the strips together on the straight fabric grain.

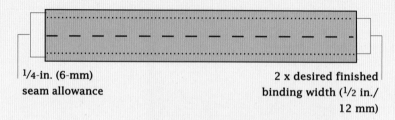

¼-in. (6-mm) seam allowance

2 x desired finished binding width (½ in./ 12 mm)

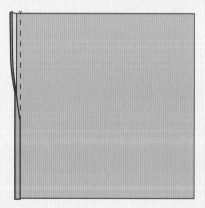

2 With right sides together, align the raw edges of the binding and an edge of the quilt. Pin and sew the layers together by hand or machine. Fold the binding in half lengthwise, turn under the raw edge, and slip stitch the fold (*see page 231*) to the back of the quilt, as shown above. Trim the short ends of the binding even with the edges of the quilt.

3 Repeat Step 2 to bind the opposite edge of the quilt. Bind the remaining two sides of the quilt in the same manner, folding the excess fabric in to form neat corners. Slip stitch the folded edges in place along the corners.

Double-Fold Binding

Follow these steps to bind a quilt with double-fold straight-grain binding.

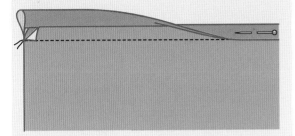

1 Cut the number of binding strips required for your quilt on either the crosswise or the lengthwise fabric grain. Calculate the width for the binding strips by multiplying the desired finished binding width by 4 and adding 1/2 in. (12 mm) for seam allowances. If necessary, you can sew the short ends of the strips together diagonally or on the straight fabric grain. Fold the binding in half lengthwise, with wrong sides together, and press. Align the raw edges of the binding with an edge of the quilt and sew the layers together as for single-fold binding (*see page 230*).

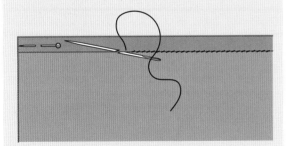

2 Fold the binding over to the back of the quilt and slip stitch the fold to the backing fabric just below the stitched line, as shown above. Attach the binding to the opposite edge of the quilt in the same manner. Trim the ends of the binding strips even with the edges of the quilt. Bind the remaining two edges of the quilt in the same manner, folding the excess fabric in to form neat corners. Slip stitch the folded edges in place.

Mitering Corners

Follow these steps to miter the corner seams of double-fold binding.

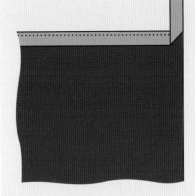 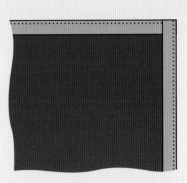

1 Sew the binding strip to the quilt as for double-fold binding, stopping 1/4 in. (6 mm) from the first corner of the quilt, as shown above. Clip the threads. Fold the binding up, creating a 45-degree-angle fold, as shown.

2 Fold the binding back down on itself, so that the fold aligns with the top edge of the quilt, as shown above. Starting where the previous seam ended, sew the binding to the next side of the quilt, as shown above. Repeat at each of the remaining corners of the quilt.

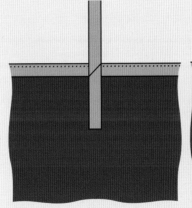 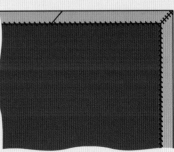

3 Fold the end of the binding and the beginning of the binding so they meet at a 45-degree angle, as shown above. Open and stitch the binding strips together along the fold lines. Trim the excess fabric to 1/4 in. (6 mm) from the stitched line. Finger-press the seam allowance open. Refold the binding and finish stitching it to the quilt.

4 Fold the binding to the back of the quilt and slip stitch it in place as for double-fold binding. Slip stitch the folded miter in place at each corner, as shown above.

231

Fold-Over Binding

Follow these steps to bind a quilt with fold-over binding.

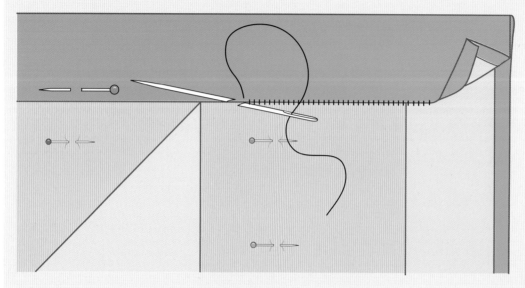

1 Cut the backing fabric at least 3–4 in. (7.5–10 cm) larger all around than the quilt top. Place the backing wrong side up on a flat surface, and position the batting and the quilt top right side up on top. Turn under and press a ¼-in. (6-mm) hem along all edges of the backing. Fold it over to the front of the quilt top and slip stitch it in place, as shown above. Attach the binding to the opposite side of the quilt in the same manner.

2 Fold the backing fabric to the front of the quilt along both remaining edges, and slip stitch it to the front of the quilt top, including the corner areas, as shown below.

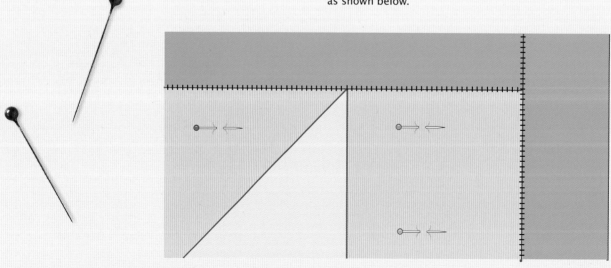

Bias Binding

Follow these steps to bind a quilt with curved edges, using bias binding strips.

1 Determine the width and length of the bias strips in the same manner as for single- or double-fold bindings (*see pages 230–231*), adding 10 in. (25 cm) extra for inverted corners. Cut as many bias strips at a 45-degree angle to the selvage as required for your project. You can use the diagonal line on your quilter's ruler as a guide, or fold the fabric at a 45-degree angle, as shown at right, to establish the first bias edge.

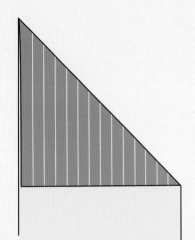

2 With right sides together, sew the short ends of the bias binding strips together at right angles. Press the seam allowance open. Repeat for the remaining bias strips.

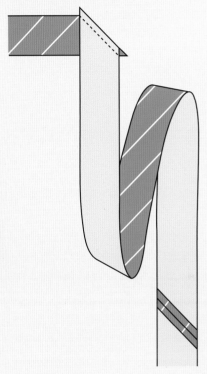

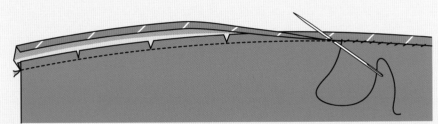

3 Fold the binding in half lengthwise with wrong sides together and sew it to the quilt as for double-fold binding (*see page 231*), as shown above.

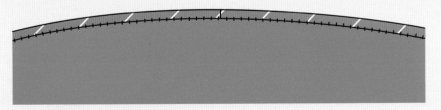

4 To finish, turn under a ¼-in. (6-mm) hem along the adjacent edge of the binding strip. Fold the binding in half again and stitch it in place, overlapping the beginning of the binding, as shown at left.

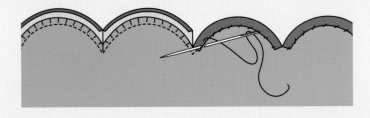

5 For a scalloped edge, snip the curves of the edge of the quilt, and into the corner between each scallop. Fold the binding as for the straight edge, mitering the fullness at the inner corners. Make sure that the short ends are folded under.

233

◈ Piping

Piping is a raised, fabric-covered cord. Inserted into seams, it makes a lovely finish for pillows, bags, and garments. Follow these steps to make corded piping.

1 If the piping cord has not been preshrunk, wash it in boiling water and dry it before using it. Cut a bias strip of fabric twice the width of the piping cord, plus ½ in. (12 mm) for seam allowances. With the right side out, fold the bias strip over the cord, bringing the raw edges together. Baste the cord inside the bias strip, as shown at right, leaving the ends open.

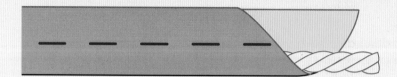

234

2 With the raw edges aligned, baste the piping to the desired seam of your project, clipping the seam allowance along the curves and around any corners, as necessary. Using a zipper foot or piping foot on your sewing machine, sew the piping in place, as shown at right.

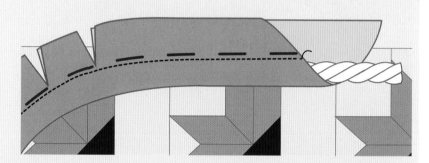

3 To join the end of the piping to the beginning, sew the ends of the bias strips together with a ¼-in. (6-mm) seam allowance, as shown at right. Finger-press the seam allowance open. Butt the ends of the cord and baste them together. Fold the bias strip over the joined cord and sew through the layers, enclosing the cord.

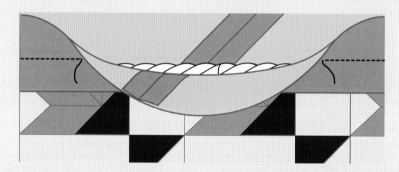

4 Position the layer of fabric for your quilt on top of the corded piping and stitch through all layers, enclosing the piping in the seam. Turn the seam right side out, exposing the corded piping, as shown at right.

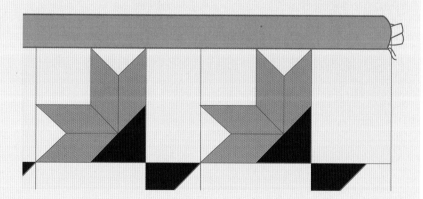

Ruffles

Gathered or pleated ruffles can add a delicate finish to baby quilts or small items, like pillows. Choose a soft, fine fabric or lace for gathered ruffles, and a crisp fabric for pleated ruffles. The depth of the finished ruffle should be in proportion to the scale of the project.

Gathered Ruffles

Follow these steps to add gathered ruffles to the seams of a quilted project.

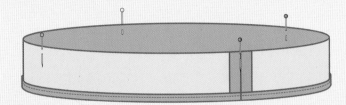

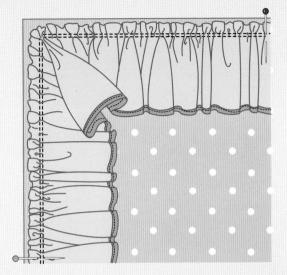

1 For a single ruffle, determine the desired finished width and add 1/2 in. (12 mm) for seam allowances, plus 1/2 in. (12 mm) for a hem. Cut a strip of fabric this width and approximately twice the length of the edge to be trimmed. If necessary, join the short ends of two or more strips of fabric. Turn under and machine-stitch a 1/4-in. (6-mm) hem twice along one long edge of the ruffle. Divide and mark the length of the ruffle at four equidistant points along the raw edge, as shown above.

2 Do two parallel rows of gathering stitches 1/4 in. (6 mm) and 3/8 in. (1 cm) from the raw edge of the ruffle. Mark the edge of the item to be trimmed at four equidistant points. Pull up the gathering threads evenly along the ruffle, so that each quarter coincides with the marks on the item to be trimmed. With right sides together, pin and baste the ruffle in place, distributing the gathers evenly and allowing a bit of extra fullness at the corners, as shown above.

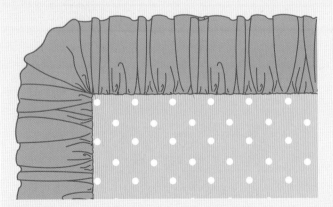

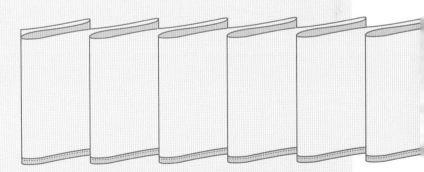

3 Sew the second layer of fabric to the first, with the ruffle sandwiched between them, leaving an opening in your stitching for turning. Turn the fabrics right side out, allowing the ruffle to extend from the seam, as shown above. Slip stitch the opening closed.

Pleated Ruffles

Cut and prepare the ruffle, as shown above, making it three times the length of the item to be trimmed. Pin pleats in the ruffle at the desired intervals and depths. Baste the pleats in place and press accurately to make sure that each finished pleat will be identical. Do two rows of machine-gathering stitches along the raw edge of the ruffle to hold it in place before attaching it to your project, as for a single ruffle.

235

Templates

USE THE FOLLOWING TEMPLATES AS REQUIRED FOR THE PROJECTS IN THIS BOOK, ENLARGING THEM TO THE SIZES INDICATED.

DASH OF PROVENCE PAGES 52–59

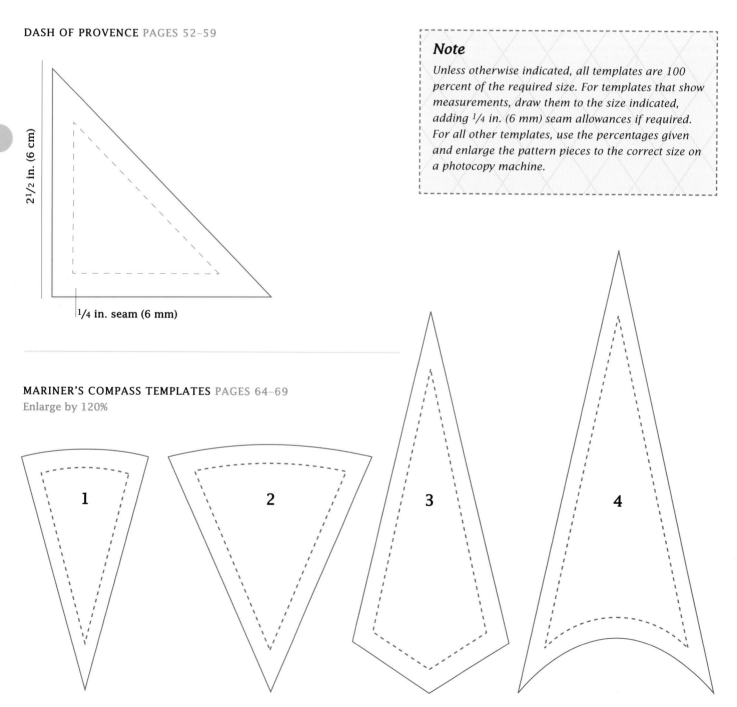

2¹/₂ in. (6 cm)

¹/₄ in. seam (6 mm)

> ### Note
> *Unless otherwise indicated, all templates are 100 percent of the required size. For templates that show measurements, draw them to the size indicated, adding ¹/₄ in. (6 mm) seam allowances if required. For all other templates, use the percentages given and enlarge the pattern pieces to the correct size on a photocopy machine.*

MARINER'S COMPASS TEMPLATES PAGES 64–69
Enlarge by 120%

1

2

3

4

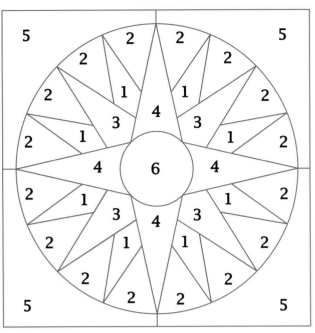

Foundation Piecing Diagram

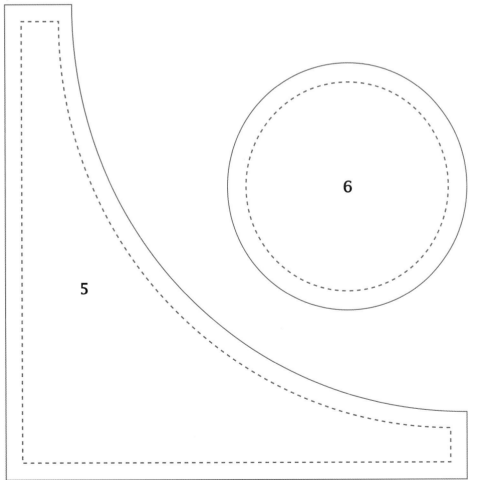

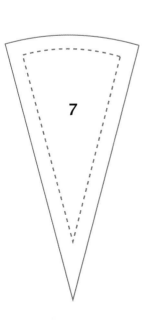

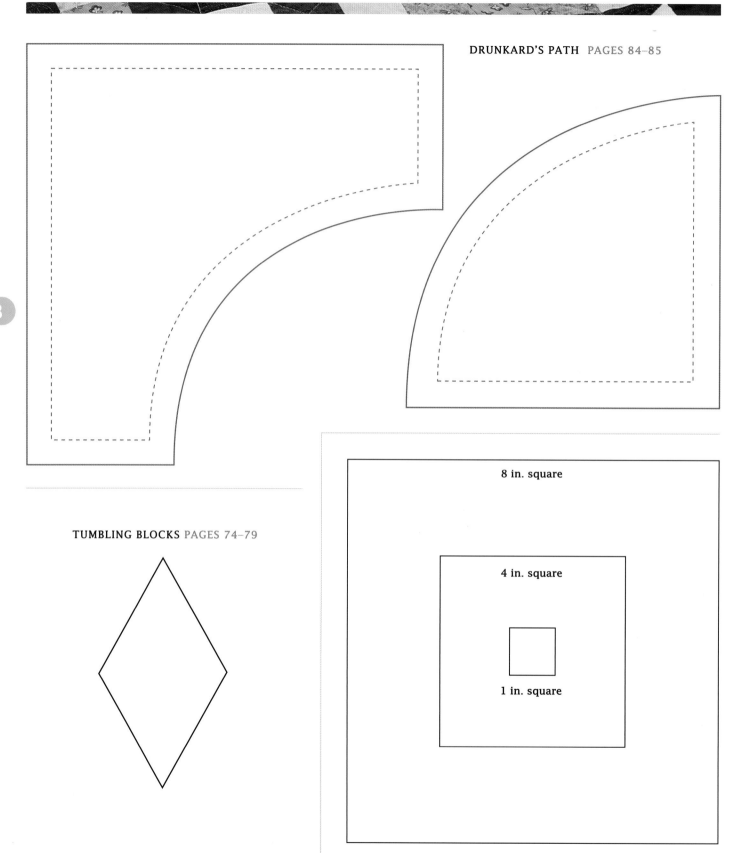

DRUNKARD'S PATH PAGES 84–85

TUMBLING BLOCKS PAGES 74–79

8 in. square

4 in. square

1 in. square

SECRET GARDEN GLEN PAGES 94–97 enlarge by 200%

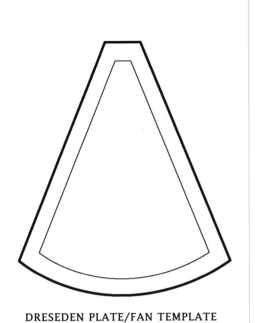

DRESEDEN PLATE/FAN TEMPLATE
PAGE 102

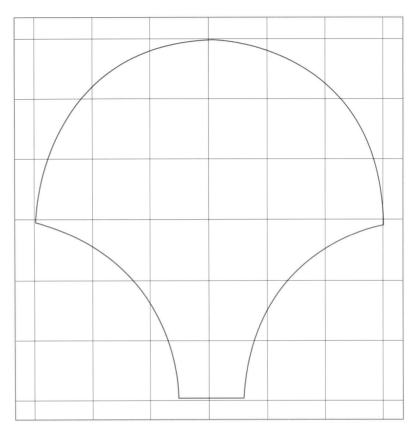

CLAMSHELLS PAGE 100

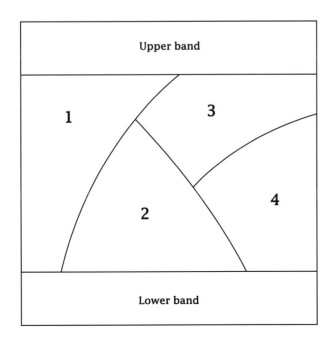

CRAZY PATCHWORK PILLOW
PIECING GUIDE PAGES 106–109

TRAPUNTO PAGES 148–153

Enlarge by 200%

FOLK-ART TABLE CENTER PAGES 160–165

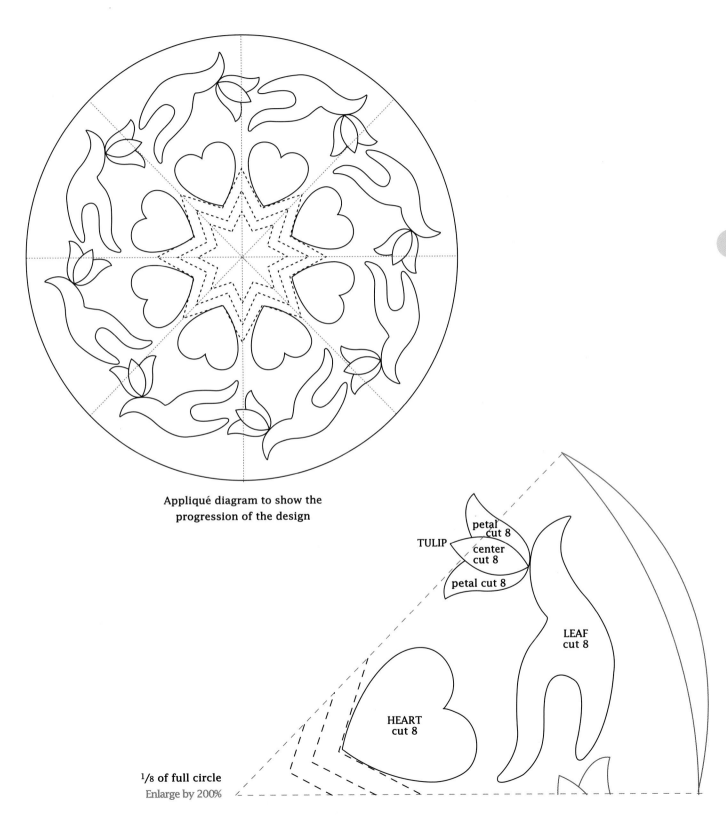

Appliqué diagram to show the
progression of the design

TULIP

petal
cut 8

center
cut 8

petal cut 8

LEAF
cut 8

HEART
cut 8

¹/₈ of full circle

Enlarge by 200%

NOAH'S ARK ANIMAL TEMPLATES PAGES 170–177
enlarge by 200%

Cat

Chicken

Cow

Duck

Rabbit

Dog

Horse

Panda

Donkey

Lizard

Snake

NOAH'S ARK ANIMAL TEMPLATES PAGES 170–177
enlarge by 200%

Elephant

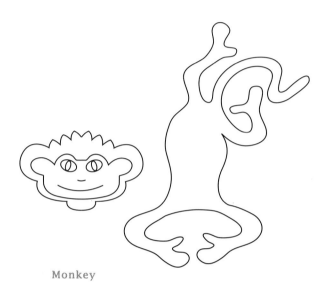

Monkey

244

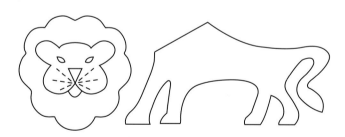

Lion

Lionness

NOAH'S ARK TEMPLATES PAGES 170–177

enlarge by 133%

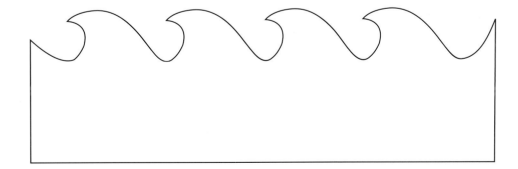

NOAH'S ARK TEMPLATES PAGES 170–177
enlarge by 133%

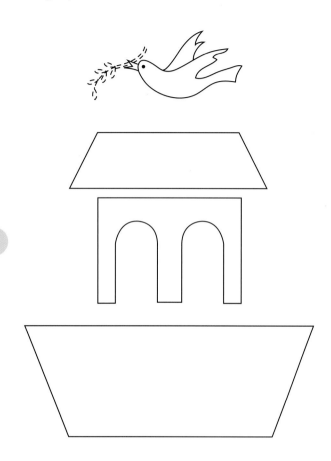

REVERSE APPLIQUÉ PAGES 180–181
Enlarge or reduce to desired size

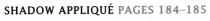

SHADOW APPLIQUÉ PAGES 184–185
Enlarge or reduce to desired size

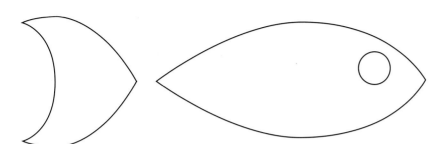

SHADOW APPLIQUÉ PAGES 182–183
Enlarge or reduce to desired size

MARCH TO THE MUSIC! PAGES 189–193
Enlarge by 400%

HAWAIIAN FLOOR PILLOW
PAGE 198–203 Enlarge by 120%

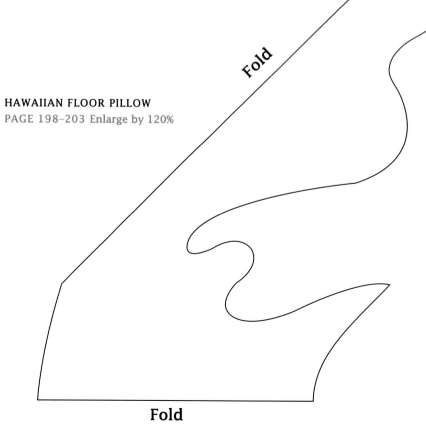

Fold

Fold

CELTIC MOTIF PAGES 205–207

Bias strip goes underneath

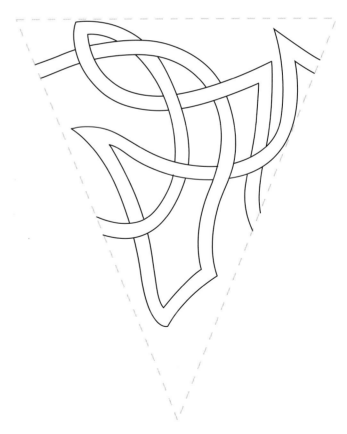

CELTIC BATIK QUILT PAGES 210–215

Glossary

APPLIQUÉ—the stitching of fabric shapes to a background fabric.

BACKGROUND FABRIC—the visible fabric on which appliqué motifs are stitched.

BACKING FABRIC—the fabric used for the underside of a quilt or pillow or the back of a hanging.

BIAS—the grain of fabric at an angle of 45 degrees to the selvage.

BLOCK—a design of geometric fabric patches or appliqué shapes stitched together, usually in the shape of a square.

CHAIN PIECING—a quick method of piecing several patches or blocks assembly-line fashion.

FABRIC GRAIN—the direction in which the warp and weft threads of the fabric are aligned.

FOUNDATION FABRIC—a fabric acting as a support, and completely covered by onlaid fabric patches.

FOUNDATION PIECING—a type of patchwork worked on a foundation fabric.

ITALIAN QUILTING—a type of quilting with raised linear designs against a flat background.

LOFT—the thickness of batting.

ON-POINT—the direction when a square block is turned to form a diamond.

PATCH—a single geometric fabric shape, often part of a block.

PIECING—the stitching of geometric patchwork shapes together by hand or machine.

REVERSE APPLIQUÉ—an appliqué technique consisting of several layers of fabric that are cut away to reveal the fabric below.

SASHING—the strips of fabric that separate patchwork or appliqué blocks within a quilt.

SEAM ALLOWANCE—the extra fabric allowed beyond the stitching line for piecing.

SELVAGE—the tightly woven outer edges of a woven fabric.

SETTING—the way that patchwork or appliqué blocks are arranged within a quilt top.

SLEEVE—a channel of fabric stitched to the back of a quilt for hanging purposes.

STRIP PIECING—a patchwork made up of strips of fabric, which can, if desired, be cut up and rearranged to form different patchwork designs.

TRAPUNTO—a type of quilting in which focal points are padded and appear in relief against a flat background.

WHOLECLOTH QUILT—a quilt made entirely by hand-quilting one fabric, without a patchwork or appliqué design.

Resources

IN THE UK

Cotton Patch
1283-1285 Stratford Road
Hall Green
Birmingham
B28 9AJ
0121 702 2840
www.cottonpatch.co.uk

The Fat Quarters
5 Chopwell Road
Blackhall Mill
Newcastle upon Tyne
NE17 7TN
01207 565728
www.thefatquarters.co.uk

Quilt Pieces
16 Trinity Road
Wimbledon
SW19 8QX
0208 286 7292
www.quiltpieces.co.uk

Quilters Domain
www.quiltersdomain.co.uk

The Quilters Guild of The British Isles
Room E113
Dean Clough
Halifax
West Yorkshire
HX3 5AX
01422 347669
www.quiltersguild.org.uk

Quilters Haven
68 High Street
Wickham Market
Suffolk
IP13 OQU
01728 746275
www.quilters-haven.co.uk

IN THE USA

Andover Fabrics
462 7th Avenue
New York, NY 10018
(212) 760-0300
(800) 223-5678
www.andoverfabrics.com

Fabrics for many of the projects in this book were supplied by Andover Fabrics and are available at independent retail fabric stores and quilt shops worldwide. The swag border print in the "March to the Music!" quilt on pages 188–193 is entitled "Marching Band," by Gail Kessler for Andover Fabrics, #2923. It is available in two colors: M and K, from Andover Fabrics (see above). We used color M in the quilt border on page 193.

Ethan Allen Home Interiors
5064 Hamilton Boulevard
Allentown, PA 18106
(610) 395-4944
e-mail: info@allentown.ethanallen.com

J. P. Hamel Photography
www.jphamelphotography.com

Ladyfingers Sewing Studio
Owner: Gail Kessler
75 Oley Turnpike Road
Oley, PA 19547
(610) 689-0068
www.ladyfingerssewing.com

Andover Fabrics, threads, and sewing supplies are available at this quilt shop. Mail-order service is available.

IN CANADA

Bernice's Fabric Gallery
111 4th Street
Reston, Manitoba ROM 1X0
(204) 877-3955

Freckles Quilt Shop
13A-728 Northmount Drive NW
Calgary, AB T2K 3K2
(403) 270-2104 or 1-888-644-6699
www.frecklesquiltshop,com

Hamels Fabrics & Quilting
B-45923 Airport Road
Chilliwack, B.C V2P 1A3
(604) 792-3231 or 1-877-774-2635
www.hamelsfabrics.com

La Maison de Calico
324 Lakeshore Road
Pointe-Claire, QC H9S 4L7
(514) 695-0728
www.economusees.com/la_maison_de
_calico_en.cfm

The Quilter's Palette
4947 Dundas St. West
Etobicoke, ON M9A 1B6
(416) 916-0398 or 1-800-455-4372
www.quilterspalette.ca

Tiger Lily Quilts
1228-4th Street
Estevan, SK, S4A 0V5
1-306-634-2900
www.tigerlilyquilts.com

Trudy's Sewing Room
Bayers Road Shopping Centre
Halifax, NS B3L 2C1
(902) 445-1725 or 1-877-888-7839
www.trudyssewingroom.ca

251

Index

Acknowledgments

QUILT PROJECTS

Thanks to the following people for the quilt projects featured in this book:

PAULA DIGGLE A Dash of Provence Quilt. DYLIS FRONKS Folk-Art Table Centers.
ALISON JENKINS Rail Fence Pillow, Mariner's Compass Wall Hanging, Drunkard's Path Pillow, Tumbling Stars Pillow, Crazy Patchwork Pillow, Hawaiian Floor Pillow. CATHY KUCENSKI Two Choices Quilt, Oh, My Stars! Quilt, March to the Music! Quilt.
ANGELA MADDEN Celtic Batik Quilt. FRIEDA OXENHAM Secret Garden Glen Quilt.

SPECIAL THANKS TO...

256

ANDOVER FABRICS, for donating the beautiful fabrics featured in the quilts throughout this book. For more information on Andover, see Resources, page 251.

DIANE BIERI and ANDREA MATHIAS, of Ethan Allen Home Interiors in Allentown, PA, for their generosity in allowing us to photograph three quilts in such beautifully furnished settings. Your creative input, unfailing help, enthusiasm, and generosity of spirit enabled the creation of the most beautifully coordinated setting imaginable. To contact this store, see Resources, page 251.

J. P. HAMEL, for his artistic eye, ongoing patience, and incomparable photographic talent, which resulted, as always, in magnificent photos of three lovely quilts. To contact J. P. Hamel Photography, see Resources, page 251.

GAIL KESSLER, for her creative genius in designing extraordinarily beautiful fabrics for Andover Fabrics, and for allowing your talents to be displayed in the fabrics in many of the quilts throughout this book. To contact Gail Kessler's quilt shop, Ladyfingers Sewing Studio, see Resources, page 251.

CATHY KUCENSKI, for allowing her quilts, "March to the Music!," "Two Choices," and "Oh, My Stars!" to be featured in this book. Your incredible workmanship enhances your gorgeous designs.